Understanding the Media

Understanding the Media

A practical guide

Andrew Hart

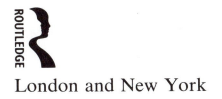

London and New York

First published 1991
by Routledge
11 New Fetter Lane, London EC4P 4EE

Simultaneously published in the USA and Canada
by Routledge
a division of Routledge, Chapman and Hall Inc.
29 West 35th Street, New York, NY 10001

© 1991 Andrew Hart
Set in 10/12pt Times by
J&L Composition Ltd, Filey, North Yorkshire
Printed and bound in Great Britain by
T J Press (Padstow) Ltd, Padstow, Cornwall

British Library Cataloguing-in-Publication Data
Hart, Andrew
  Understanding the media: a practical guide.
  1. Secondary schools. Curriculums. Media
  I. Title
  302.23071041

Library of Congress Cataloging-in-Publication Data
Hart, Andrew.
    Understanding the media: a practical guide/Andrew
    Hart.
    p.   cm.
    Includes bibliographical references and index.
    1. Mass media.   I. Title.
  P90.H3346   1991
  302.23—dc20   91–9514

ISBN 0–415–05712–4
ISBN 0–415–05713–2 pbk

Contents

List of figures

List of tables

Preface

Many existing books on Media Education and Media Studies are either too inaccessible for teachers or too detached from any coherent concepts and theories about both the media and about teaching. At the same time, they are often poorly designed and presented. By drawing selectively on previous work, this book provides both a grasp of the issues and practical guidance in a way which is easy for teachers to select from and follow. It contains a continuous and coherent argument about media teaching and breaks it down into manageable chunks which are clearly signposted and subheaded.

This book does not simply move from 'theory' to 'practice' with teaching ideas tagged on at the end. Rather, as in good Media Education, theory and practice constantly interact. The ideas for teaching suggested in each chapter extend and re-examine the theory upon which they are based. They are also constantly related to the requirements of the National Curriculum and Examining Boards and presented in a form which is easily adaptable for classroom use.

In order to make it more visually attractive and helpful, the text is constantly reinforced by illustrations. It is also presented in a 'layered' form so that readers can treat some material as optional without disturbing the flow of the argument. These optional elements are highlighted in the text. As a result, readers should be able to enjoy the local 'colour' without losing sight of the argument, as in a good documentary programme.

Since the first transmission of the BBC Radio 4 series upon which the book was originally based, the programmes have been used in conjunction with the Support Notes in a wide range of teacher-training contexts. The book is therefore able to build on this experience and to fill some of the gaps. It shares the same aim of providing a map of the media terrain which will help teachers to develop their confidence and competence in teaching about the media. It draws extensively on interviews from the radio programmes in order to enliven and authenticate difficult ideas. But it also allows for in-depth examination of major issues through extensive use of new documentary material (like audience data, accounts of production processes and 'insider' views from writers, editors and producers). In this way, the book manages to combine the vividness and authenticity of the 'insider' view mediated by teachers, researchers and media professionals with the depth and breadth of the 'outsider' view which is needed to enable a critical response to what they have to say.

In terms of content, the approach is more thematic than media-specific. The main focus is on the familiar media of television, the press, radio, comics, magazines and pop music, but we examine a range of forms which cross the boundaries between media, like news, chat-shows, drama, fiction, public relations and advertising. In this way, different media can be constantly seen in relation to each other and general questions about value, control, quality and ideology can remain central.

All of these major areas are examined in the context of rapidly changing technologies, patterns of ownership, production processes and audience responses (especially of young people). They are also related to the problems of how teachers can get started on teaching about the media, how they can organise practical work, and to policies for future development. As we look to that uncertain future, this book should provide some encouragement and inspiration for teachers themselves to be more confident and competent practitioners.

Andrew Hart
September 1991

Acknowledgements

So many people have contributed in different ways to this book that if the convention of acknowledgements did not exist, it would be necessary to invent it. I should like to thank the BBC (and, in particular, our producer Merilyn Harris) for giving Gordon Cooper and myself the opportunity to make the series *Understanding the Media* for Radio 4 in 1990 which was the first step on the road to writing the book. Her sympathetic understanding of what we were trying to do was a great encouragement during a lengthy and demanding production process.

I should also like to thank all those interviewed for the series whose contributions feature as extracts in the book. In particular, I owe a debt of gratitude to the members of Southampton Media Education Group who helped to provide concrete classroom examples of the teaching approaches featured here and who contributed to the general discussion of teaching problems and strategies. Exposing one's teaching to public view can be an intimidating process, so I hope that I have been true to their intentions and preserved their integrity. Many of them have also played an active role in trying out and evaluating a stream of teaching ideas which have been presented to them over the last few years. Their names appear against the extracts from their contributions throughout the book. If the book has any merits in helping readers with their work in future, it will be in large part due to long-standing members of SMEG, successive groups of PGCE students and the many experienced teachers with whom I have worked on Masters' courses. Their insistence on the need for practical ideas based on sound educational principles has been the driving force behind my own development as a teacher over the last decade.

Above all others, however, stands Gordon Cooper's contribution. Gordon became an active member of the group after making a short item about us for Radio 4's *Education Matters* in 1987. It was his sense of the importance of Media Education and potential public interest in it which set the two of us off on the process of making the series for the BBC. It was his experience as a broadcaster which saw it to fruition. His skills as an interviewer, his expertise as an editor and his clarity as a presenter are plainly evident in the finished programmes. His keen editorial ear and his constant commitment to making sense to listeners gave relevance and immediacy to the programmes. They also, through his comments on early drafts of the book, had a great impact on its general approach and tone. Gordon also contributed generously to the book, by researching and writing much of the sections on the press and public relations in Chapter 3, on comics and radio drama in Chapter 4 and on radio and pop music in Chapter 5. He also devised several of the teaching ideas. All writers would do well to have a collaborator like him at their side.

For permission to use material previously published elsewhere, I should like to thank Andrew Irving Associates, the BBC, BFI Publishing, BIFF Products, Keith Birch, *Broadcast*, the Broadcasters' Audience Research Board, Roger Bussell, Channel 4 Broadcasting Support Services, Comedia, the Department of Health, Epson UK, Mike Fann, Margaret Ferré, Roma Gibson, Brenda Gvozdanovic, HMSO, Martin Jackson, Derek Jones, Kimberley-Clark (Kleenex Tissues), Gerald Knight, Amelia Lakin, Manchester University Press, Caroline Marshall, Eamon McCabe, Nigel Newson-Smith, Pirelli, Pitman Publishing, Piers Plowright, Sonia Polan, Radio Merseyside, Byron Rogers, Anne Routledge, Posy Simmonds, Barbara Taylor, Gill Tester, the Electricity Association, the *Guardian*, Sarah Whale, Malcolm White, WMGO and Yellowhammer.

Finally, but not least, I am grateful for the patience, indulgence and encouragement of my wife Jean and for the forbearance of my daughter Zoe in listening to my silly questions.

Contributors to the radio programmes referred to in the text

Quotations followed simply by a name are all extracts from the original BBC Radio 4 series (also available from Routledge as a cassette package).

Martin Barker (Bristol Polytechnic)
Steven Barnett (Henley Centre)
Cary Bazalgette (Deputy Head of Education, British Film Institute)
Mike Benton (School of Education, University of Southampton)
Tony Bisson, Mark Prowse and students of Alderman Quilley School, Eastleigh, Hampshire
David Buckingham and Bob Ferguson (University of London Institute of Education)
Rita Clifton (Planning Director, Saatchi and Saatchi)
Anne Dawson (Calypso Voice-Over Agency)
Peter Estall (Series Producer, *Wogan*)
Lilie Ferrari (Co-editor, Wham Wrapping! BFI)
Sarah Hammett, Alec Lawrie, Andy Revill, Sue Thale, and students of Totton Sixth Form College, Hampshire
Mike Hapgood (Programme Organiser, BBC Radio Solent)
Roger Ingham (University of Southampton)
Len Masterman (School of Education, University of Nottingham)
Máire Messenger Davies (Researcher and writer)
Jane Mitchell (Taunton's Sixth Form College, Southampton)
Professor Graham Murdock (Loughborough University)
Beverley Naidoo (Writer)
Mike Poole (Writer and broadcaster)
Nick Prosser (TV director)
Michael Regester (PR Consultant, Charles Barker, Traverse-Healy)
Professor Laurie Taylor (University of York)
John Teasey and Frank Myzsor (Robert May's School, Odiham, Hampshire)
Tim Traverse-Healy (PR Consultant, Charles Barker, Traverse-Healy)
Jo Vale (Journalist and broadcaster)

Ian Wall (Film Education)
Andreas Whittam Smith (Editor, *The Independent*)

A NOTE ON REFERENCES

Throughout this book, the Harvard system of referencing is used: full bibliographical details therefore appear at the end.

Introduction

THE IMPORTANCE OF STUDYING THE MEDIA

Over a quarter of a century ago, Marshall McLuhan argued that education is ideally a defence against 'media fall-out' but that we have not yet created the means to 'meet the new media on their own terms' (McLuhan 1973: 208). The deregulation of broadcasting and the speed of development in new information technologies now make our need more urgent. Information management has become a large-scale industry which seems at times to threaten some of the basic rights of a democratic society. 'Information anxiety' is spreading and there is no obvious remedy. The mass media have become so widespread and so powerful in the 1980s and 1990s that there is general concern about their influence.

In consciously echoing the title of Marshall McLuhan's fullest account of the media, this book partly accepts his well-known idea that 'the medium is the message' but emphasises that it is far more than that. McLuhan's work is misguided and misleading as social theory. He does not recognise that media and messages are elements within complex institutions which are themselves created and sustained through social and cultural interactions. So the strategies for Media Education suggested here go far beyond his call for education as civil defence.

It is vital that we create an educational framework which encourages intelligent and active responses to the new media and enables us to grasp the nature of knowledge itself. We need both skills and understanding in visual and aural communication as well as in the traditional areas of speaking, reading and writing. When we are able to evaluate media messages with confidence and respond critically to them, we are much less likely to rely on the opinions of others and more likely to become autonomous rather than automatons. In learning how meaning is made in the media, we can gain more understanding of the world in which we live. We can be determined not to be determined.

|| If we're going to develop them in a cognitive sense, it's not enough to
|| just say everyone should be going around thinking all the time . . . it also

ought to be an area which encourages people and enables people to find a voice. Media Studies at its most successful is something where people have a voice that they will use outside school as well as inside school.

(Bob Ferguson)

McLUHAN, MEDIA AND LITERACY

What would a Media Educated Person be like? What would he or she know, understand, or be able to do? We all know something about the mass media. But most of what we know is as consumers rather than as users. We may be 'media-literate' in a crude sense, but how competent are we in using the media? We may be able to recognise television or radio genres, know which pages of particular newspapers or magazines carry the material we want, but what do we know about how we as audiences interact with media forms? How can we learn to interact with the new technologies of communication?

McLuhan says little about how education might actually deal with the new media. His advice is basically that we need do nothing except not look backwards. He sees the global village as a place of tribal harmony, a 'seemless web of interdependence and kinship'. We should therefore simply embrace it and look forward to 'a Pentecostal condition of universal understanding and unity' (McLuhan 1973: 59, 90).

We live today in the Age of Information and of Communication because electric media instantly and constantly create a total field of interacting events in which all men participate.

(McLuhan 1973: 264)

McLuhan's ideas were often greeted with euphoria in the flower-powered west of the late 1960s. The media welcomed him because he exonerated them from any responsibility for the content of their messages. He validated the abandonment of thinking.

Media 'hot' and 'cool'

He insisted that the forms of media mattered more than their content. He saw the effects of the media as implicit and subliminal. All media were either 'hot' or 'cool'. 'Hot' media, like print, radio and film, are high in definition and low in audience participation. 'Cool' media, like the telephone, writing and television, are low in definition and high in participation. He also claimed that the media actually shape our social institutions, rather than vice versa. He attacked print as restrictive in form and in effect. He blamed its linear regimentation for the growth of nationalism and imperialism. He held literacy responsible for social fragmentation, political division and cultural disintegration. But he claimed that the new media would restore the authenticity of a lost oral culture through 'instant electric technology'.

|| repeatable print intensity led to nationalism and the religious wars of the
|| sixteenth century.

(McLuhan 1973: 32)

His 'one-liners' and catch-phrases have often been invoked but rarely thought through. When his ideas are examined more carefully, serious flaws emerge. His binary system for classifying media actually raises more questions than it answers. Why, for example, should film be 'hot' while television is 'cool'? And what happens to a film when it is shown on television? Does it become 'warm'? He claims that the reason we 'doodle' on the telephone is because we resent its demand for the total participation of our senses, not because there happens to be a pencil and paper near by. More absurdly, he credits the telephone with the abolition of urban red-light districts and centralised political control (McLuhan 1973: 284–5).

The global village

In spite of recent revolutions in Eastern Europe, the global village has not materialised. Indeed, in many countries, global pillage and global bondage are more apparent. The flow of international communication has followed the contours of power created by western multinational corporations like IBM. Local cultures are threatened and distorted and ethnic identities are lost as a result of (mainly American) media colonisation. More and more people are being addressed with the same messages from the same centres of communicative power.

|| We are beginning to learn that de-colonization and the growth of
|| supranationalism were not the termination of imperial relationships but
|| merely the extending of the geo-political web which has been spinning
|| since the Renaissance.

(Smith 1980: 176)

As Jonathan Miller has pointed out, McLuhan's most impressive achievement is his reputation (Miller 1971: 7). Most of what he has to say is either unsound or untrue. History has failed to fulfil most of his predictions. Yet he was the first person to draw attention to the media as worth thinking about. He fired imaginations in a way that few writers on the media have ever done.

In *Understanding Media* McLuhan tried to create in print the cool mosaic of electronic forms, by writing in a fragmentary and repetitious way. But the tone of the writing is so strident and insistent (so 'hot', in McLuhan's terms) that it often degenerates into the super-heated patter of the salesperson. Yet, ironically, as we look back at it, the passage of time has cooled its prose. In the 1990s we are so much more aware of the way media operate that we are less susceptible to his rhetoric. Paradoxically, his ideas have begun to work in a 'cool' way because we have so much to say in response.

So, in spite of its limitations, McLuhan's work can still speak to us and at least provide a point of departure for understanding the media.

WHAT ARE 'THE MEDIA'?

Let us now consider more carefully what the media actually are. One standard definition sees media simply as ways of transforming a signal into a message, of making sense of raw data. Another sees them as devices for transmitting messages simultaneously to large numbers of people. Whatever definition we use, there are clearly many different kinds of media and these differences partly depend on the degree to which they rely on technical devices for transforming signals into messages. Looked at in this way, we can distinguish three main kinds of media: (1) **Presentational media**, (2) **Representational media**, (3) **Mechanical/electronic media**.

Presentational media require the presence of a face-to-face communicator (e.g. speech), while *representational* media enable messages to be stored, passed over a distance and reproduced in the absence of the participants. Telegrams, newspapers, comics and magazines are *representational* media because they use the symbolic codes of print, graphics and photography to communicate. They differ from *presentational* media because they rely on technical devices for producing their messages. *Mechanical/electronic* media are also representational because they use codes to carry messages. But they differ from simple representational ones because they depend on technical devices both for sending messages and for receiving them. Mechanical/electronic media rely on technical devices at the point of decoding as well as encoding. Telephone, radio and television signals require technical transmitting devices, but they differ from simple representational media because they also need receiving devices in order to be decoded.

So there are clear differences between these three different kinds of media, but there is also some overlap. Firsly, all media use codes, so even presentational media like speech and sign-language are to some extent representational. Secondly, different kinds of media are often used at the same time. For example, television uses speech, television codes and electronic transmission of messages through the air.

McLuhan was quite happy to include cars, clocks and clothing in his list of media. Indeed, since any substance can in principle be used as a means of passing messages, this is a defensible position. Yet some media have proved more flexible and adaptable than others for human communication. So when we speak of '*the* media' we are assuming a different focus from

Figure 0.1   Kinds of media

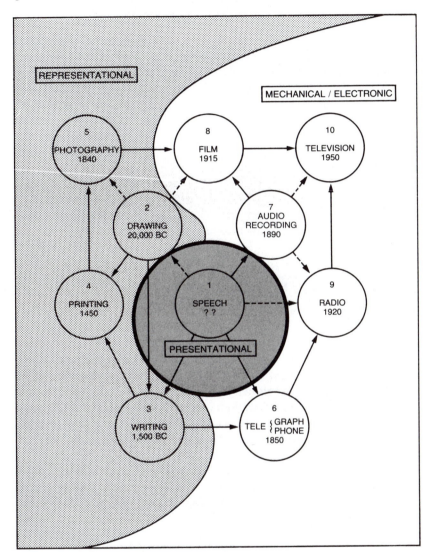

simply speaking of 'media'. 'The media' are usually taken to be the *mass media*, the relatively modern mechanical/electronic media which involve technical devices and which have been developed specifically for the purpose of communication.

The study of media in the twentieth century has arisen in response to the growth of mechanical/electronic media and the spread of literacy since the Industrial Revolution. The mass media are on the public agenda because they are capable of reaching large numbers of people at about the same time and therefore have a greater potential for influence and power than, say, one of King Alfred's pastoral letters or an illuminated manuscript.

Yet there are dangers in making such a crude distinction between modern and traditional media. Firstly, the process of a minority addressing a very large public is not exclusively modern. Secondly, the emphasis on modern technologies can mean that we suppress some of the actual differences between the way audiences attend cinemas (very large numbers seeing a single film but in groups of varying sizes, on different occasions and in public places) and the way audiences watch television (very large numbers watching the same programme but in small unconnected groups or individually at home).

> There is no simple history of continuity and expansion; within the systems and between the systems there are many kinds of unevenness, contradiction and mixtures of intended and unintended effect.

(Williams 1981: 15)

WHICH MEDIA SHOULD WE BE STUDYING?

This is not simply a technical question. To answer it, we would have to explain why books are not included in most current Media Studies syllabuses and we would have to consider the cultural and political assumptions behind our current concentration on media which are thought by some people to have particular dangers. Such assumptions are clearly implicit in the early interest shown by the DES in the role of television in relation to children. One of the recommendations of the 1983 report suggested that broadcasters and teachers should work together to under-stand better the impact of television on young people and to ensure that it is a positive and constructive influence.

Although we might all agree that we should work together and that we would like the influence of media to be positive and constructive, the reasoning behind this call is somewhat arbitrary. It is also rather defensive and slightly paternalistic. The potential of such an agenda for studying the media is limited. Why focus on television? Why be concerned only with 'impact'? Why not with understanding, with criticism or with self-determination?

> Media Education is often seen as a way of defending children from television. It ought to be seen as a way of giving them high expectations of television, and of all media.

(Bazalgette 1991)

Whatever the rationale, most Media Studies syllabuses include the modern mass media such as television, film, the press, radio and pop music. We shall be looking here at most of these and at some forms which appear in several media, like news, soap opera and advertising.

> It's important, I think, for them to recognise that the media [are] a dominant part of their lives. I think we ought to make them aware of what's happening in the media, how it affects them, and for them to make their own opinions, make their own decisions about those influences, and their own decisions about what they want to watch, listen to, read.

(Mark Prowse)

Watchdogs of the mind

The dominant sociological tradition in Britain and the USA has often been negative about the mass media. Audiences are envisaged as victims manipulated by hidden persuaders and subliminal seduction. McLuhan saw audiences as being passively 'massaged' by data which cross the sensory threshold unnoticed. One of his famous conceits likens the content of the media to a juicy piece of meat left by a burglar to distract the watchdog of the mind (McLuhan 1973: 26). McLuhan and his successors have seen audiences as mere extensions of communication technology; or worse, as actual elements within the technology. Such assumptions have set the agenda for most public discussion of the mass media and have dominated thinking about their effects. The result has often been a protective paternal concern exemplified in the Video Recordings Act and the Broadcasting Standards Council. At the same time, critiques of media distortion like the Glasgow University Media Group's have shown open hostility towards the media industries and received bellicose reactions from them.

Yet there have also been many positive moves. The media themselves have begun to examine and display their inner workings, not just in such explicit ways as the BBC's *See for Yourself*, but also in critical series like *Inside Television* (BBC) Thames's *Understanding Television* and Channel 4's *Television* or *Open the Box*. And the British Film Institute's *One Day in the Life of Television* project in 1988, with support from broadcasting, showed a new attention to the ways in which media audiences behave. The ghost of Glasgow has apparently been laid by the spirit of Glasnost.

Media in the National Curriculum

Becoming a Media Educated Person should begin in primary school. So what does the new National Curriculum offer? If understanding current technical and institutional changes in the media is important, Media

Education should figure prominantly. Cary Bazalgette (1991) has produced a very helpful outline scheme of what may happen at Key Stages 1 to 3. Media Education will also find space in secondary schools at Key Stage 4, especially within English. According to the Cox Report, students should be asking of every text 'who is communicating with whom and why; how has the text been produced and transmitted; how does it convey its meaning?' (DES 1989: 7.23) Many schools are already doing GCSEs in Media Studies, BTEC, TVEI and CPVE courses are being developed and many students are following A-level courses.

> Surely that's the nub of education isn't it, to get people to ask questions and not to accept things blindly? And young people especially don't realise that . . . all of the things that are put in front of them through the media, are constructed by somebody for somebody.
>
> (Frank Myzsor)

TEACHING ABOUT THE MEDIA

Teaching about the media involves new ways of looking at familiar things. It also means listening to what students tell us about their media habits. We now need teachers who are confident and competent to teach the new courses. But there is little initial training in Media Education on offer for would-be teachers, and in-service training and advanced courses are under threat from new financial arrangements for LEAs.

Five basic principles

Understanding the Media shows how a Media Educated Person would understand five basic principles about the media:

- The media do not simply reflect or replicate the world.
- Selection, compression and elaboration occur at every point in the complex process of editing and presenting messages.
- Audiences are not passive and predictable but active and variable in their responses.
- Messages are not solely determined by producers' and editors' decisions – nor by governments, advertisers and media moguls.
- The media contain a multiplicity of different forms shaped by different technologies, languages and capacities.

Media and messages

The media select and process facts for us. Because they do so systematically, they necessarily affect the way we interpret what they are saying. As well as informing us, the media also shape us. In order to understand more fully how the process works, we need to become literate in the various languages of the media. Media literacy means more than just responding to media messages. It also means understanding how they work, how they differ from personal experience and how they differ from each other. It means learning about their dominant styles and being able, when necessary, to use them.

Media audiences

To find out more about how young audiences use the media, we studied some Hampshire comprehensive students. On the surface, their involvement with media seemed passive: logs of their viewing, reading and listening initially suggested that they did little but watch television soaps and listen to pop music on commercial radio. The only thing which broke this continuous involvement was school, where, one student claimed: 'There's not much media.' But when we talked to them in more depth, we found evidence of more active motivation. Under the apparent indifference lay quite complex personal agenda. Most of their listening and viewing was done alone (except at the all-important Youth Centre, where they met to hear the same music and talk about the same television). Almost none of their viewing was in groups or with their families. The main motives for their habits were clearly credibility with their peers and differentiation from their families. When we asked them to track their families' habits, we found that strange dialogues began. One 14-year-old student had to enlist the help of her older sister in getting her father to take her survey questions seriously. Apparently some families don't talk to each other much, not even about television. Far from being a shared experience, television has become for this group a privatised medium which can be used like radio.

We also found that for these teenagers, reading was a very private activity which they were slow to talk about because much of it drew on sensitive issues. It was a process which, like music, closely involved their identities. One boy talked intelligently about how *Dennis the Menace* in *The Beano* deals symbolically with problems of relationships (Dennis the Hard Man v. Walter the Softie) and coping with parental authority (Dad's Slipper).

They are beginning to learn something of a critical idea. It's not so much a question of finding answers as asking the appropriate questions.

(Andy Revill)

Media determinants

Current patterns of ownership and control in the media, the growth of 'advertorials' 'infotainment', 'product placement', programme sponsorship and the blending of editorial and promotional material make an understanding of economic forces more urgent. The profit motive has traditionally been blamed for the worst excesses of the media. Yet learning about the media demands much more than a knee-jerk condemnation of advertising. There are many more interesting questions to ask at a time when government is using national advertising campaigns against AIDS, drink and drugs and when pop musicians are raising millions for the relief of famine. A Media Educated Person would know something about why some campaigns work and others fail and would be able to explore questions like why Britain can sustain such a successful advertising industry in such a fragile economy; or how advertising can claim that many products are environmentally friendly when the very process of advertising has traditionally been to promote consumption.

Critical media users

These are just some of the things a Media Educated Person would grasp. We shall be exploring them in depth in the chapters which follow. But Media Education is not just about understanding the media. It is also about enjoying them, valuing them and participating in them in a reflexive way.

> The aim of Media Education is not merely to enable children to 'read' – or make sense of – media texts, or to enable them to write their own: it must also enable them to reflect systematically on the processes of reading and writing themselves, to understand and to analyze their own activity as readers and writers.
>
> (Buckingham 1990: 219)

It will be helpful to keep at the front of our minds throughout this book a clear sense of the purpose of Media Education as expressed most comprehensively in the Cox Report:

> Media Education ... seeks to increase children's critical understanding of the media ... [It] aims to develop systematically children's critical and creative powers through analysis and production of media artefacts ... Media Education aims to create more active and critical media users who will demand and could contribute to, a greater range and diversity of media products.
>
> (DES 1989: 9.6)

Chapter 1

Getting started

If we are concerned with understanding the media, we need to get to grips with what we mean by Media Studies and by Media Education. We also need to make sense of such key concepts as genre, audiences, representation, institutions and ideology. We want to provide help in devising workable approaches to teaching about the media and suggest some practical ideas for the classroom. In this chapter, we therefore look at some of the everyday problems of teaching about the media, like:

- Where does media teaching fit into the existing curriculum?
- What are the main curricular problems in teaching about the media?
- What is the place of specialised concepts and language?
- What is the role of practical work and how does it relate to theory?
- How can we create appropriate forms of assessment?

We shall also be suggesting ways of dealing with these problems.

WHERE DOES MEDIA TEACHING FIT INTO THE CURRICULUM?

One obvious way of studying the media is as a specialised subject in its own right. Study of media has its own academic integrity as a timetabled subject outside the National Curriculum. But it also has a strategic place within one of the core subjects of the National Curriculum as a major area of study within English. Both of these possibilities for media teaching are welcomed by the Report of the Cox Committee for English 5–16 (DES 1989: 9.4). Media are constantly suggested as objects of study and most of the Attainment Targets demand media work. (Chapters 3, 4 and 5 of this book explore in detail the kind of work on 'fact', opinion, persuasion and presentation envisaged.) No less than six Statements of Attainment refer explicitly to media work. Media forms are also seen as useful vehicles for studying literature and for language work (e.g. story-boards, news items, audio-recordings and photographic work as approaches to the class novel (DES 1989: Appendix 6)). But Cox's most radical move is its recommendation of some of the theoretical approaches developed in media work as necessary parts of every English teacher's practice.

The distortion of society's information base offers a threat which is amply recognised by the Cox Report. Study of the media is seen as a crucial element in providing defences against it by 'enlarg(ing) pupils' critical understanding of how messages are generated, conveyed and interpreted in different media' (9.2). But, since it deals with 'fundamental aspects of language, interpretation and meaning' it is also seen in a more positive way as an aspect of personal and social development (9.9).

At several notable points, the Cox Report suggests that 'the kinds of question that are routinely applied in Media Education can fruitfully be applied to literature' (7.23) and that 'Media Education has often developed in a very explicit way concepts which are of general importance in English' (9.9). It recommends not only that the media should be studied within English but that students should understand how such key concepts as viewpoint, editing and audience apply to language and literature as well.

Key concepts

What are the key questions and concepts? The main ones are helpfully listed by Cox as 'selection (of information, viewpoint, etc.) editing, author, audience, medium, genre, stereotype, etc.' (9.9). The questions resolve themselves into 'who is communicating with whom and why; how has the text been produced and transmitted; how does it convey its meaning?' (7.23).

Teachers of Media Studies will be familiar with the questions and concepts listed in the Cox Report. The approaches which they suggest to the study of texts already figure strongly in the current GCSE and A-level Media Studies syllabuses. They also correlate easily with the 'sign-post' questions suggested by the BFI for primary (Bazalgette 1989) and secondary work on the media (Bowker 1991), and with the key concepts in *English in the National Curriculum: Non-Statutory Guidance* (DES 1990c). What is new is the expectation of their normality and that they should begin as early as primary schools.

Media Studies and Media Education

The Cox Report's early drafts spoke of Media Studies rather than Media Education. This suggests either that there is some confusion or that the two terms have much in common. Both of these suggestions probably contain some truth. The key concepts are the same in both approaches. Media Education can be seen as a watered-down version of Media Studies, but at the same time it can be seen as more powerful in its scope. In this light, Media Education is not just a politically useful label which discourages

Figure 1.1   Signpost questions

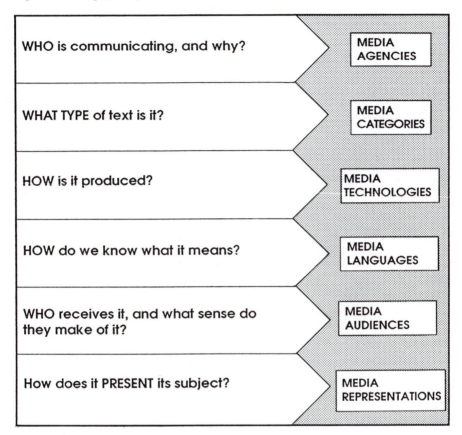

WHO is communicating, and why?	MEDIA AGENCIES
WHAT TYPE of text is it?	MEDIA CATEGORIES
HOW is it produced?	MEDIA TECHNOLOGIES
HOW do we know what it means?	MEDIA LANGUAGES
WHO receives it, and what sense do they make of it?	MEDIA AUDIENCES
How does it PRESENT its subject?	MEDIA REPRESENTATIONS

Source: Bazalgette 1989: 8

dissent from studying the media (who could object to 'Education'?) but also a powerful generic title which demands a comprehensive approach to the whole curriculum.

Media Studies already has a long history within the sociological tradition on both sides of the Atlantic. In Europe, there is also a tradition which combines aspects of literary and linguistic studies. Much has already been done by Social Studies, Humanities, General Studies, Art and Drama teachers, but English teachers have probably made the most active contributions to the development of Media Studies. For example, recent work in English has concentrated on how readers respond to texts and what differences their readings show. This has led to some useful links between the two areas. Media Studies has focused on the active role of mass media audiences in the process of creating meaning, both at the level of individual consciousness and at the socio-cultural level of ideological formations.

Table 1.1 NEA study areas: radio, popular music/pop videos

RADIO	
1 Media language	Music, speech, sound effects. Cue, clip, copy. Different musical genres. Accent, dialect, mode of address.
2 Media audiences	Who tunes in? When and Why? How channels create an audience through: What is broadcast (genres) Scheduling Celebrities and Stars Audience reception figures How radio advertises itself Phone-ins
3 Media industries and institutions	Commercial/community radio franchises and licenses. BBC and relationship to Government, pirate radio. Advertising and funding, 'needle time'. News (see newspapers). Local and national radio. World service. Organisation of radio stations and transmission areas.
4 Media representations	What view of the world is being offered to radio audiences? Male and female roles within broadcasting. What is reported and what is left out. Types of programmes (genres).
POPULAR MUSIC/POP VIDEOS	
1 Media language	Musical forms (genre), folk, rock, etc. Presentation of images (L.P. covers, pop press), technology (from garage bands to Michael Jackson).
2 Media audiences	Pop music and the youth market – changes in buying power of young people. Sub-cultures, gender differences. Fan clubs.
3 Media industries and institutions	Production and promotion of acts/records – advertising – structure of music industry. Independent record labels. Recording studios – costs and availability. Spin-offs. International marketing.
4 Media representations	Rebel images and commercial success. Concept of teenager – changes in star images – sexuality and stars.

Source: Northern Examining Association: GCSE Media Studies Syllabus, 1992–3: 15

Specialist courses in Media Studies are not enough: all teachers should be involved in examining and discussing television programmes with young people.

(DES 1983: 27)

We shall consider the practical implications of this demand more fully later in this chapter and again in the final chapter. For the moment, we can suggest that familiarity with Media Studies is a prerequisite for teaching

Media Education. But the more generalised, cross-curricular approach associated with Media Education is likely to precede specialised Media Studies work at Key Stage 4 (14+) in school and college curricula.

Yet there remain deep-seated anxieties about the media amongst the general public. So it is not surprising that teachers are also uncertain as to how to teach about the media. Many teachers are able to recognise their difficulties and are brave enough to acknowledge them.

> I wasn't sure about where I stood with this and I think that's been the main problem really; having to find my own position regarding Media Studies, at the same time as getting it together to go into teaching it.
>
> (Sue Thale)

But there are many different kinds of difficulty and it is worth looking at them separately. The main ones can be seen as:

- *curricular* (where does it fit?);
- *conceptual* (what is it all about?);
- *practical* (how do you do it?);
- *assessment* (how do you measure what has been learnt?).

CURRICULAR PROBLEMS

Most of the teachers we talked to had two main problems in getting started on teaching about the media. Introducing media into the curriculum demands expertise and time. How, for example, does an English teacher cope with the demands of media teaching? Can he or she expect to have or acquire all the necessary expertise? In many schools and colleges, there may well be a reservoir of untapped skills.

> I think our skills are limited and when I look at the colleagues at present in my own school, there are others with skills we don't have. I'm thinking of the already quite sophisticated use of the vido camera within the drama department. I'm thinking of the graphics teacher who came into the school from advertising, the Head of Science with considerable photographic skills – all of those areas seem to me to have eventually a contribution to Media Studies.
>
> (John Teasey)

Even if all of this expertise can be mobilised and used, there remains the problem for secondary schools of finding time for media on the timetable. But recent changes by the Northern Examining Association to its English GCSE syllabuses have made this much easier.

> The introduction . . . of dual certification in English and Literature . . . reduced the pressure on students by about 50 per cent in terms of course work . . . Had dual certification not been accepted we could not have

realistically introduced Media Studies without increasing the time available for English on the syllabus.

(John Teasey)

It is also possible to increase the actual amount of teaching time available for media by starting at an earlier age and easing the pressure of an overcrowded GCSE timetable.

The problems seem to be preparing pupils early enough. We feel that at least a year's preparation, that is preparing third years to start the course in the fourth year, [is] probably necessary. Things like looking at images for perhaps 5 weeks as an introduction to some kind of closer analysis of film. Or perhaps doing a news project . . . But we'd probably keep it very basic and perhaps introduce them to things that they can build on, basic concepts, and then perhaps to work backwards and start right back in the first year with first of all analysis of photograph and image study, before actually looking at moving images.

(Frank Myzsor)

CONCEPTUAL PROBLEMS

I felt absolute panic, because, although it's around you in the air you breathe and it's part of one's daily diet, it's really quite a complicated subject to get to grips with in order to teach it.

(Jane Mitchell)

I was floundering, I think. I very quickly realised that they weren't going to get anything out of it, and I hadn't really got anything else to do for 40 minutes or so.

(Sue Thale)

One of the factors that has often made life difficult for media teachers has been that they have had to dive in (or, in some cases, be thrown in) at the deep end. Media Studies has been dogged for many years by a multiplicity of different approaches, often taught in a haphazard or opportunist way as 'a bit of an extra'.

One of my colleagues left the school leaving a fifth year he'd taken in the fourth year for the old CSE film and television studies, and he needed someone to fill in during their fifth year, and somebody else refused to do it, so I was left with the film and television. He'd already ordered the films from BFI, so it meant watching them quickly after school the night before, having a quick chat with my colleague about what to look out for in *Psycho* and *Strangers on a Train* . . . it was really just close analysis of a film.

(Frank Myzsor)

It is actually very hard to know what to focus upon and exactly what structure to build your course round.

(Vicky Finney)

Our course was a disaster from the start. We were inadequately prepared . . . and had no philosophical background from which to start. We were both committed English teachers, utterly print-orientated, linear thinkers, unable to see any positive goals or benefits in studying the media.

(Potts 1987: 3)

Although most Media Studies syllabuses are now a lot more specific in suggesting what students should learn, there are still many problems in teaching in a more systematic and holistic way (Masterman 1985). The Northern Examining Association Syllabus, in addition to setting out its six 'study-areas', feels it necessary to provide a glossary of such technical terms as denotation, connotation, signification and positioning. These terms often cause problems for teachers as well as students, so we have to ask whether they are necessary.

It's a new subject and it needs to have its own terms . . . to define it as a new subject . . . I need to have specialist terms to make me feel that I can grasp a certain subject area. I feel that the pupils in turn ought to have that as well, so that they feel they've got hold of something.

(Frank Myzsor)

We might not all agree that students need to master these technical terms. But what is clear is that teachers need to get to grips with them in order to understand the key concepts. And that is no easy matter, since it involves starting with an evaluation of our own positions. This is especially so when we think about a key concept like *ideology*.

I don't think I knew where my own views were really when I started off. And I don't know that I do now . . . so that's one of the problems really – trying to really do a lot of background reading as well as actually teaching it in a classroom situation . . . I think because it's a very amorphous subject and it expands out into so many other areas . . . It's important to think about it and question it and question where you stand in relation to it. I think that's been the important thing for me really, it's made me . . . think about my own ideological position and you can't escape coming up against that in the end.

(Sue Thale)

But even when we have sorted out our own positions, we may still find that students think differently.

They thought people who watched *Coronation Street* or *Crossroads* must be dumb, and assumed that the ignorance of the masses is *proved*

> rather than perhaps *encouraged*, by their readership of the *Sun*, *Star*, and *Mirror* . . . Unless you can find any analagous situation in their own experience, and make it problematic for them – they will never grasp the ideological relation between 'text' and 'reader'.
>
> (Williamson 1982: 84)

> I put a lot of emphasis on *their* experience of the media. But I did find that one of the problems was that the media is just something that . . . you ignore. It's not something to be studied . . . it's just something you don't even think about.
>
> (Vicky Finney)

Students may see their teachers' ideologies as a threat to their own and be unwilling to ask the sort of questions that we are interested in.

> If they see you as questioning their values they tend to clam up or go 'Oh there she goes again on her feminist stance' . . . you happen to be looking at representation of women, and that's I think a teaching problem to try and overcome . . . how to tackle that subject without taking up a particular position.
>
> (Sue Thale)

But this is not a problem which can be overcome by adopting or pretending to adopt a neutral stance. Our own ideologies are the basis of what, how and why we teach, whether we are aware of it or not. Similarly, our students' ideologies are the basis of what, how and why they learn.

> I found that anything beyond advertising just drew a baffled response – why are we studying this?
>
> (Bob Hopkins)

We need to ask what our students already know about the media, and how they have come to this knowledge. We can then begin to think about what we hope they will learn so that they themselves can be clear about the purpose of their learning. We may then find teaching approaches which build on these understandings.

> Neutrality isn't possible, however much one tries. That does not mean, however, that one is constantly ranting and raving about one's own position. What it does mean is that over a period of teaching (and I don't mean 40 minutes, I mean a period of a year, two or three years) one's own position will be recognisable and shouldn't be hidden, nor should it be exclusive. Contradictions exist. They can be drawn upon, they are interesting and when one gets to the stage where the teacher and the class want to make judgements, they should make judgements. Those judgements cannot be seen as 'objective' in the sense that they are 'the truth', but they can be seen as approaching objectivity if what

one says is: 'I believe the conclusions I draw from my reading of that programme are ones I would like other people to agree with, and I'm going to argue for them.'

(Bob Ferguson)

PRACTICAL PROBLEMS

The problems teachers have are not just conceptual or curricular. We also have to cope with the practical problems of teaching media, like classroom management, using resources and organising appropriate practical work. Although practical work can include anything which happens in the classroom, many teachers think of it as to do with technology. But media technology needs approaching with care. Using video, for example, requires technical skills, is often time-consuming and frustrating. It may also lead to poor quality work and does not magically guarantee any increase in understanding the media. Using complex technology may actually mystify rather than clarify. The two main problems are using the technology effectively and ensuring that theoretical issues are raised in the process. Mastering the technology without understanding the issues is as inadequate as theoretical understanding without experience.

We're now in a situation with highly sophisticated technology which is likely to get even more sophisticated. It doesn't mean, however, that people are making better pieces of material ... It doesn't necessarily follow. The fact that you've got a fountain-pen instead of a quill doesn't make people better writers. The issue is whether it is being used to keep people occupied or whether there's some kind of feeling that there is some-thing to say, something to do, something to study ... and produce from.

(Bob Ferguson)

WHAT IS PRACTICAL WORK?

We define practical work as any activity which involves the process of constructing meanings using images, sound, film or video ... from brief exercises which act as agenda-setters or talking points with limited outcomes, through to fairly complex simulations or polished pieces of video: the end product will vary according to the context and objectives of the exercise.

But in all cases, we believe three factors to be crucial:

- the *process* of production is the key to learning, rather than the end product itself (if indeed there is one);
- theory, analysis and practical activity should be inter-related and complementary, so that practice is integrated throughout, rather than hived off as a separate specialised activity;

– practical work is about constructing and producing, but *not re-producing*. Students cannot and should not aspire to the standards of broadcasting and should work within the limitations of the technology at their disposal to construct alternatives rather than replications of existing material.

(Grahame and Mayman 1987: 9–10)

There is a basic distinction between doing practical work and doing production work. It is a similar distinction to that between production for dramatic performance (theatre) and participation in drama processes (drama in education). Both are important areas within Media Education but should not be confused. The essential focus of practical work is on having something to say. But it is not just a question of articulation. There is also an overriding need to relate what is learned to wider social experience, to recognise the contexts into which that experience can feed, to go beyond the impasse of well-intentioned liberal education approaches which may produce only 'opiniated lethargy'. If this need is not realised, we are in danger of developing 'a generation of worldy-wise cynics who teach others only so that others may be in the know' (Ferguson 1977: 60).

when children engage in real production for real audiences, whether this is writing, performance or media production, then they have an opportunity to learn about their own power as communicators.

(Bazalgette 1991)

How can we find ways of encouraging students to work in this way? First of all, we need to recognise that a great deal of work submitted by students for assessment is missing the important dimension of personal experience and significance.

Far too often, course work folders from a given centre have all been drearily similar. It has been quite clear that a great deal of teacher input has gone into these and very little original creative work by the pupils. It is quite clear that the teacher's input is in every paragraph, and there is almost no personal response . . . there is no attempt to relate to personal experience. There is no subject in the syllabus that is more appropriate to relating to personal experience. We are to some extent teaching a common experience. They *all* have experience of advertising. They *all* have experience of television. And when we see piece of work after piece of work which does not relate to their own experience then we must be suspicious of the way that work was obtained.

(Tony Bisson)

How can we stimulate individual responses in students and avoid such uniformity? It cannot be done simply by inventing new forms of assessment. What students produce for assessment depends on how they work and what they learn during the course. It depends on their taking an active part and being more responsible for their own learning. Apart from potential gains in social and communication skills, group work can involve handling recorded material, making editorial decisions, constructing a perspective and making a product for an audience. It has both a practical and critical dimension.

Practical simulations involving news reporting can usefully lead into a more systematic examination of news values (see Chapter 3 and Grahame 1990: 102–4 for a discussion of simulation as a teaching method). This kind of learning by doing is both more immediate and more demanding than traditional approaches. It also helps students become more aware of what they are learning and enables them to transfer their understanding to other media products and processes. The assignments they produce for course work will then reflect this process.

> We cannot assume that this sort of learning happens by osmosis; we need to actively construct the conditions and practices which will make it explicit for students.
>
> (Grahame 1990: 122)

But practical work need not necessarily depend on using lots of equipment. It can be based on the simplest of technologies like pens and paper, or more complex but accessible ones like audio-tape and word-processors.

> All we really needed was the tape recorder. It was quite an eye-opener for the students just to realise initially that there were different things on the different channels. Then we got into, 'what's the tone?' and 'what type of person is presenting this news?', and I think it made them realise how much the news is constructed rather than being there . . . I set them a task to actually produce their own little news bulletin, choosing the channel and getting the right sort of language (which I felt was valid from a GCSE point of view anyway, because they were thinking about style and audience) and they produced some really interesting news bulletins that showed they'd understood the concept behind the exercise . . . they enjoyed it and had the chance to actually do their own little recording at the end. But even if they hadn't had the chance to record it, I think they got a lot out of actually producing the bulletin because they did it as a team, negotiating 'what is important?' and 'what order shall we have it in?'
>
> (Sue Thale)

At their most successful, such exercises combine both practical and conceptual work, both production and analysis.

> The theoretical skills should reveal an exploration of ideas which should come into the practical work and the practical work should give insights

> which enable the theoretical work to require greater depth and a
> breadth of examples.
>
> (Tony Bisson)

This means a change in the role of teachers. It means learning how to
organise group work effectively and being able to stand back from such
work. It means more one-to-one tutorial work, helping students more with
devising appropriate assignments to take on, with setting goals for themselves, monitoring their work and helping them develop evaluation skills to
apply to their own work. It also means taking more risks than traditional
methods have required. Such work places teachers in a position where they
often do not know the answers and where they are prepared to allow
students to make mistakes.

> Modern teaching techniques, whatever the subject, entail risks for
> the teacher. It's much safer to stand up at the front with the syllabus
> on your table and to go through it chronologically as it were – step by
> step – guaranteeing that the students will give back to you what you've
> given to them. The best ones will give it back to you coherently and
> the worst ones will give it back to you incoherently but everybody will
> have a measure of success. I think something that we have to get over
> very quickly, is that they are going to be allowed to make mistakes.
> There's a tendency with the increasing levels of coursework to assume
> that every time the student puts pen to paper, he or she is being
> tested. They've got to be allowed to do rotten written work and learn
> from it.
>
> (Alec Laurie)

ASSESSMENT PROBLEMS

When the nature of classroom work changes, the traditional essay will
inevitably lose some of its dominance as a form of assessment and a whole
range of new forms will be necessary. But before we can consider the
process of assessment, we need to be clear about what should students be
learning when they study the media.

> Media Studies needs to be a discipline which concentrates on a belief by
> teachers that the cognitive, the intellectual skills of students ... can
> grow, can be used and aren't preset ... that students already have
> experience and will continue to have experience with or without the
> subject.
>
> (Bob Ferguson)

Figure 1.2   Posy Simmonds cartoon

© Posy Simmonds 1986

SOME FORMS OF ASSESSMENT FOR GCSE MEDIA STUDIES

Collages   Promotion packs/Leaflets/Posters
Interviews   Logos
Surveys   Audio montages
Story-boards   Pop-ups
Comic strips   Flow-charts
Forms/Questionnaires

> **Interviews** can be presented as audiotape and give young people an
> opportunity to go to talk to a whole range of other people, including one
> of the most valuable resources, their own grand-parents, who have a
> knowledge of the history of the media which is unrivalled ... We can
> look at *surveys*, which can range in sophistication from just discovering
> what the first year pupils in the school watch most popularly to quite
> sophisticated ideas of notions of pleasure.
>   **Story-boards**, of course, everybody's familiar with ... but allied to the
> story-board and often much more congenial to young people is the
> comic-strip. Taking a comic-strip interpretation of a news event or a
> documentary subject can be quite sophisticated.
>
> (Tony Bisson)

But how can practical assignments be assessed? What kind of criteria are
appropriate for comparing such a wide range of different forms? How can
we make sense of a situation where a student presents, say, a collage of
visual images or a beautifully designed T-shirt?

> Criteria need to be agreed, not just because the teacher has to fill in a
> form to say whether someone has succeeded, but so there is an
> agreement in terms of both the students and the Media Studies teacher
> ... appraising whether they have done what they tried to do.
>
> (Bob Ferguson)

Unless such criteria are built into the work, it is extremely difficult to
assess.

> Some of the early work we had would be, for instance, the very obvious
> 'Images of Woman'. And children had cut out every picture they could
> find of women and stuck them more or less at random on a sheet. It's
> impossible to assess. What are we to make of this kind of work?
>
> (Tony Bisson)

The BFI statement on secondary media work (Bowker 1991) has a helpful
chapter which suggests five main principles for assessment. The Southern
Examining Group has developed a simple framework based on four
criteria: *finish*, *content*, *appropriateness* and *evaluation*.

We evaluate on four criteria. We look at *finish* – the degree of finish, that is. We look at the *content* of the practical work. We look at the *appropriateness*, and we expect the pupil throughout the process of creating a piece of practical work to be engaged in an *evaluation*. This isn't something which should be tagged on at the end when it's all over, it is something that we should be constantly doing and it's very, very important. It does affect the grades.

(Tony Bisson)

But we need more than agreement on clear assessment criteria. It is also necessary for the assignments to make it possible to apply the criteria. That means that the work needs to offer its own indications of what it is setting out to do in the first place.

We're now getting a more sophisticated approach where students will consider aspects of woman, for instance. They'll consider Woman as Sex-object, if you like, Woman as Housewife, Woman as (Paid) Worker. They'll collect images of these and begin to see where these images are to be found. They'll begin to notice differences. They'll notice too that it's quite difficult in some places to get images of Woman as Worker, and so that prompts questions. The teacher's job is to stimulate answers to those questions and very often, in order to clarify the extent to which the pupil has understood, some written component is necessary. But what we've done is free them from the deadening obligation to produce the 500-word essay. Most of it is there, and if you say to the pupil 'Just make clear what you've learned from this, length doesn't matter' the pupil will write, and often write freely and freshly and an understanding grows.

(Tony Bisson)

THE VALUE OF EVALUATION

I think the best piece of work I had last year was actually for 5- to 7-year-olds. It was a piece of work on the dangers of talking to strangers. It took a risk because it was done as a comic and a funny comic, and I was very much afraid that that would have the opposite effect – that it would encourage children to see talking to strangers as something adventurous. But these pupils tested it on local primary schools, they saw that there were dangers in that approach and they explained how they would have revised it with the hindsight of the testing experience. And consequently their evaluation considerably upgraded what was in any case a very commendable piece of material.

(Tony Bisson)

Figure 1.3   Poster from 'Don't Talk to Strangers' project
Source: Alderman Quilley School, Eastleigh

Media Education and Information Technology

Media Education is located by the Cox Report within 'the exploration of contemporary culture' (9.4). It is not surprising then, to find that it also appears in the same context as Information Technology (section 9). Media Education does indeed offer useful approaches to the study of new (as well as old) technologies. This conjunction is therefore promising, as long as we do not mistakenly think of Information Technology as confined to the use of computers. We need to focus on a whole range of technologies which are used to collect, organise, process and circulate information.

Media Education across the curriculum

These possibilities are recognised and pushed even further by the recommendations for National Curriculum Technology (DES 1990a). A similar kind of design and evaluation process is involved for individual and group work and there is the same demand for a degree of self-consciousness about the production process. Useful as this may be, it is not the same as Media Studies. The technology approach certainly includes both process and product, but there is no intended transfer of learning to the mass media. Nor does study of the mass media inform the processes of designing, planning, making and evaluating which form the majority of the Attainment Targets for NC Technology (except, perhaps, at Level 10 of the IT Attainment Target). But there is much overlap here, and strong encouragement to organise the curriculum in a way which enables students to cross subject boundaries and develop their understanding in complementary ways.

> To me, it makes no sense to propose 'the media' as a separate bit of the curriculum ... 'The media' are not a separate part of our experience ... They are inextricably bound up with the whole complex web of ways in which we share understandings about the world, a web which includes gestures, jokes and hairstyles as well as news bulletins, opera and architecture; books as well as television.
>
> (Bazalgette 1991)

Many schools have developed whole school policies for Media Education. North Westminster School in London, for example, emphasises three particular strands:

- Study of the media – their products, the processes and institutions which shape them, and their social and cultural effects.
- Practical work and the production of media.
- Use of the media as educational resources, both in the classroom and for wider communication purposes.

This policy aims to combine practical and theoretical work. Students learn how meaning is made in the media by carrying out small-scale work themselves and relating this to more theoretical work on the mass media (Grahame 1985). Designing a whole school policy is one thing, implementing it another, as a recent study of work at the school has shown (Robson *et al.* 1990: 190). Nevertheless, such developments are encouraging. In the Humanities, for example, such concepts as *representation* are central. Representation is not just a matter of technical coding, it is a process which has deep cultural and historical significance. Understanding the role of representation means realising how it determines the very basis of school curricula and how subjects within those curricula are actually constituted and constructed. Guidance and resources in this area are now becoming more accessible (see, for example, my own work on popular television science (Hart 1987, 1988b, c, d).

> The discourses that are available in Media Studies are extremely interesting because they're about modes of representation. They're about historical representation. They're about what goes on in the real world and what goes on on the television screen. Those discourses are important because they engage with science by asking how science is represented. They engage with history by asking how history is represented. History itself is a representation. Now we've got all those issues to play with and they become extremely interesting [and] exciting. I think you can find ways, however, of not getting carried too high up into the clouds and actually teaching this in such a way that it is manageable in lessons.

(Bob Ferguson)

Media Education offers a more catholic and pragmatic perspective than Media Studies, but the two approaches have many educational aims in common and can be mutually sustaining. Media Education focuses on the central issues of how ideas and knowledge are defined, selected, ordered, presented and evaluated. These are vital areas for every teacher and for every educational process. We shall look in greater depth at opportunities for Media Education across the curriculum and means of grasping them in the final chapter. We now need to look at the main study areas and key concepts of Media Studies in more depth and in terms of what can be done in classrooms.

> You're probably not contemplating Media Studies unless you're prepared to be a fairly exciting teacher, unless you're looking for new fields, unless you're stimulated by the challenge. But even a young and imaginative teacher can easily be frightened by the sheer vastness of this subject. It is a whole way of seeing. It is a way of seeing which even the most analytical of us have in many ways taken for granted and haven't

realised exactly what we're letting ourselves in for. I think you could easily, having tasted it, become frightened by it. In a way, you have to tame it and at the same time you have to ride it and let it take you into directions you hadn't expected.

(Tony Bisson)

Chapter 2

Media audiences

We all belong to many different audiences and we may feel that we know what we like. The best starting-point for understanding audiences is our own experience and that of our students. But getting beyond this may be difficult. How can we study audiences without relying at one extreme on personal anecdotes or, at the other, on masses of indigestible figures?

In this chapter, we shall be examining what we already know about audiences. We shall look at the experiences of students and add to them ideas and findings from audience research. The main focus will be on broadcasting and the press.

We shall be exploring the following basic questions:

● What is an audience?
● What pleasures do the media offer?
● How are media audiences composed?
● How are media audiences addressed?
● How is audience research carried out?
● How do audiences respond to media texts?
● What are the implications of understanding audiences?

WHAT IS AN AUDIENCE?

'Audience' is an inadequate word. Its etymology refers only to the process of *hearing*. Like 'viewer' it focuses exclusively on a single perceptual channel. In the case of a medium like television, this can be misleading because more than one sense is used. But words like 'watching' and 'viewing' also present other problems because they make assumptions about *how* the process occurs. They imply a form of passivity. We have no words to describe the *activity* of attending to television. By contrast, 'reading' suggests a process of *doing* rather than just *receiving*.

Models of audiences

This is not just a question of vocabulary. The words we use come from a history of prejudices about the media which bear little relation to the way we actually experience them. Dominant models of communication as a simple linear process for the transmission of messages have caused researchers to focus on quantitative approaches to audiences. The emphasis has been on what the media *do to* people, rather than on what people *do with* the media. These assumptions are found in current concerns about effects, especially in relation to children and television (DES 1983: 1, 4–5).

The way we think about audiences depends on how we rate what they are doing: audiences *en masse* are often seen as docile or potentially threatening, but solitary readers of poetry are rarely expected to suffer from sudden outbursts of hysteria or violence. There is also a confusion here between imaginative and physiological activity. The fact that television is routinely watched sitting in an armchair or lying on the floor does not mean that it is a passive activity. After all, reading may also take place in all sorts of supine positions.

> There were always people who said 'we don't want the hypodermic syringe view of audiences' – that is that the material from the television set goes directly into their veins and they immediately absorb it and then reproduce it at some later stage – the terrible fear that television could be a propaganda weapon because it might do this. Rather than sitting back in a chair receiving regular doses of television from producers and from actors and from scriptwriters, here were people actively working away, improvising around it, using the television as an occasion for conversation. People even left it on when they went out because they felt that, well it was nice, the house was in some sort of way vaguely populated by all these figures on television, so it wasn't so lonely when there was no one in it.
>
> (Laurie Taylor)

Family viewing

We asked some secondary school students to track their family's viewing over a period of a whole day. They were surprised to find how little actually took place.

> I'm 14 nearly 15, my sister's 20, my brother don't live at home any more so my mum don't need to run around after us . . . so my mum's got more time to watch telly, read and things like that . . . If I ask my dad something, he just takes it all as a joke and starts laughing about it and I get really frustrated with him and I end up getting really mad and just walking off. The same with my sister – she asked some of the questions

for me. When she's at work, she doesn't watch telly or anything, but when she comes home she watches telly and I always thought she watched a lot of telly and that, but she don't. She goes out most of the time, and I always thought she stayed in.

(Amanda Clark)

What was the purpose of this exercise? What did the students learn about their parents' media habits that they did not already know?

It was a good experience for them to actually go home and talk to mum and dad rather than to go home, say 'hello' and sit down have their tea and go out. So that was good for them, and to actually think about their parents as consumers of the media which they don't probably think of. I mean what are their parents' taste in music? What do they like watching ... ? How much do they actually as a family sit down and watch television together or watch a video together or listen to a piece of music together? and that in fact isn't very often. I found that most kids find that through a normal week their contact with their parents as an audience to some part of the media is almost non-existent.

(Mark Prowse)

It may be that family viewing is a thing of the past. The same pattern of separate viewing has been reported in a great deal of recent research into audiences (Morley 1986). Yet the model of the nuclear family sitting around the television set has persisted. The receiver of television programmes is still constructed by most television programmes as a family unit.

On television so often [in] programmes like *Ask the Family*, the family consists of Mum and Dad and a couple of school children. I mean only 5 per cent of the families in this country look anything like that, but nevertheless ... all the people in the household ... would sit down and sit and roar with laughter. Once television becomes fragmented and becomes like all these specialist magazines we lose that.

(Laurie Taylor)

The appeal to the nuclear family is most obvious on public holidays, which are conceived by broadcasters as national family occasions. Viewers are seen as members of a family unit, and ultimately as members of a specific nation with its own social and cultural practices. Because of its intimate manner, television appears to address viewers as individuals. But it actually uses this appeal to mask the generality of its assumptions.

Television has only recently begun to cater for families with more than one television and, perhaps, a video, who may seek different forms of pleasure. Yet newspapers, magazines and radio constantly allow for such differentiation. It may be that television audiences will become more selective and more like readers of newspapers and magazines, choosing from a varied menu of items on offer. There are some signs of this already.

Mixed viewing

Audiences may prefer particular kinds of material across a range of media but they also select a range of different kinds of material within the same medium. This mixed economy of consumption is most marked in television.

> During the course of an evening's viewing we will watch a news programme, we will watch a soap opera, an adventure series, a documentary, for example. And we are used to this kind of mix of programming.
>
> (Steven Barnett)

Television viewing crosses many supposed boundaries between different kinds of programme. Viewers use programmes of different kinds according to particular social contexts and their own needs at a given moment. Some viewers claim that they watch a particular television channel most of the time, but in reality this is extremely rare.

> Most people watch across all four channels. It just simply isn't true that there are predominantly 'BBC2 people' or 'Channel 4 people'. We met people who said 'Oh I'm basically a BBC2 person'. We said 'Why?' and they said 'Well, we just simply watch *Newsnight*'. We said 'Can you tell us what was on *Newsnight* last night?' No, they couldn't. So we said 'Did you happen to see so-and-so?' and they said 'Well I did happen to see that, actually.' We said 'So you were watching ITV?' They said 'Yes'. So really people still go on thinking they really are essentially 'BBC2 people' or possibly 'Channel 4 people', but they're not. They switch around, and the presence of the 'zap-button' has ensured that fidelity to one channel has gone long ago.
>
> (Laurie Taylor)

> It is generally assumed that some programmes, for instance *The Business Programme*, might attract a more up-market audience. Again the research tends to show that while there is a slight skew towards a more up-market audience it is not particularly noticed . . . What certain programmes do is attract audiences which might be deemed inappropriate for that sort of programme. Channel 4 is quite a good example. It will have programmes aimed for example at black people or trade unionists which are watched by a whole cross section of the population.
>
> (Steven Barnett)

Figure 2.1 Television viewing,[1] by social grade[2] and sex

Average weekly hours viewed per person

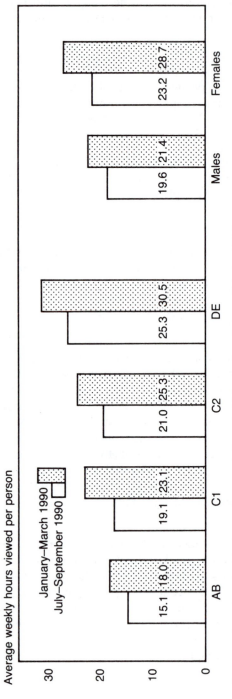

January–March 1990

July–September 1990

AB	15.1 / 18.0				
C1	19.1 / 23.1				
C2	21.0 / 25.3				
DE	25.3 / 30.5				
Males	19.6 / 21.4				
Females	23.2 / 28.7				

Source: Broadcasting Audience Research Board, BBC, Audits of Great Britain, 1990

Notes: [1] Persons aged 4 or over

[2] IPA definition of social grade (see p. 49)

Table 2.1 Soap opera audience profiles, 1988

(per cent of audience in each group)

	East-Enders (week-days)	East-Enders (omni-bus)	Coronation Street	Emmerdale Farm	Brook-side (week-days)	Brook-side (omni-bus)	Neigh-bours (lunch-time)	Neigh-bours (after-noon)	'Average Soap' profile	UK population 4+
Age										
4–15	16	17	11	10	16	18	8	32	16	17
16–24	14	17	10	8	19	18	12	15	13	15
25–34	18	16	14	12	19	18	17	14	15	14
35–44	15	13	12	10	14	12	14	13	13	14
45–54	12	13	13	12	10	12	12	10	12	12
55–64	11	10	14	16	11	11	11	7	12	12
65+	14	14	26	32	11	11	26	9	19	16
Sex										
Male	40	39	40	41	36	41	30	40	39	49
Female	60	61	60	59	64	59	70	60	61	51
Social grade										
AB	12	8	10	9	12	11	11	14	11	17
C1	22	20	19	18	18	18	21	22	20	20
C2	32	33	29	27	34	30	29	33	31	28
DE	34	39	42	46	36	41	39	31	38	35
Average audience										
(millions)	13.4	6.5	16.2	11.2	4.0	2.4	6.6	10.8	8.9	

Source: BBC 1989: 30

A great deal of television viewing may be inadvertent and we should therefore expect many programmes to be watched by 'accidental' viewers. Television viewing *always* involves mixed audiences.

> The high rating soap operas or quiz shows or even news programmes ... tend to be watched by a complete cross-section without any skew towards a particular age or sex or class. And that even goes for programmes like *Top of the Pops*. You get quite a high proportion of the audience ... over 55 simply because they represent a high proportion of the population, and therefore you would expect it.
>
> (Steven Barnett)

Patterns of television viewing do not depend exclusively on the content or quality of the programme. There are many independent and unpredictable variables as well as the more predictable social and cultural ones.

Figure 2.2   Amount of viewing (per head per week), 1985–8, with viewing trend and viewing minus seasonal variation

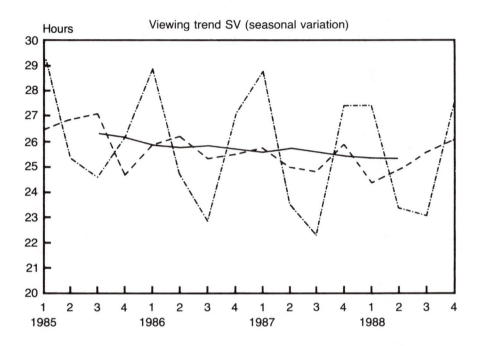

Source: BBC 1989: 42

Different kinds of audiences

Audiences come in different sizes and in different contexts, in large numbers at a live event like a play or a football match or alone at home listening to music. In each case, their roles differ according to medium and context. Variations occur in the way a particular medium addresses its audiences, the way audiences react to the medium, and the way audience members interact with each other. There are clearly big differences between live and recorded events, since live audiences can affect performances in real time. Actors in the theatre or musicians at concerts can modify their performance according to audience reactions. But this is impossible in film, radio or television, since there can be no direct response from audiences to recorded material.

Different media address different audiences and they do so in different ways. But in reality these audiences are not strictly separable. They overlap because people belong to many different audiences simultaneously. They use a variety of media in ways which often interconnect.

You can't take television entirely by itself. You need to read tabloid newspapers in order to understand the way that television is treated, because, for example in a soap opera, this audience sitting watching a soap opera know a great deal about the people who are playing the parts in the soap opera.

(Laurie Taylor)

There are also clear variations in the way audiences relate to different media.

When people listen to the radio it tends to be very much of a background activity – people doing all sorts of things at the same time. They may be doing the housework, they may be driving a car, they may be doing homework, writing letters or whatever. In terms of television, because it involves actively sitting and watching, it is assumed that the process involved is more active. In fact, there is quite a lot of evidence from research undertaken by the IBA to show that when people are allegedly watching television ... they are doing a great many other activities which bear no relation to watching television.

(Steven Barnett)

Radio

Modern radio has the great advantage of portability. This means that listeners can do something else at the same time as they are listening. Many listeners use radio as a secondary medium whilst doing something else like driving a car, jogging, cooking, or reading a newspaper. People usually listen to the radio on their own, often forming a close relationship with particular programmes. Radio is so well integrated into people's lives that it can seem like a friend and companion.

I used to carry my radio with me from room to room, up and down the stairs. So I've got one up now and two down and if I'm doing something in the kitchen and I go upstairs, I immediately put the one upstairs on as well.

(Julie, quoted in Taylor and Mullan 1986: 201)

It was great – it was the best friend I ever had.

(Barnett 1989: 3)

Listening is often thought of as a secondary activity when it is accompanied by some other activity and as a primary activity when it involves sustained concentration. But this basic distinction disguises more subtle variations in attention.

Primary attention:
   (i) Listening and taking notes.
   (ii) Concentrated listening without other distractions.

> *Secondary attention:*
>
> (iii) Listening whilst doing something else such as ironing or driving.
> (iv) Uncommitted listening where the radio provides background noise.

A great deal of radio programming is actually designed to accommodate secondary listening, with material being split up into short segments (more than 80 per cent of BBC Radio output now consists of music and news). But there is evidence to suggest that listeners are still attentive. One market researcher devised the so-called 'Ironing Board Test'. This asked people to test a new spray starch on a pile of un-ironed washing for 15 minutes. While they set about their task a radio was left playing, featuring music, two commercial breaks and a short story. The ironers were unaware that the true nature of the research was to test their recall of the information featured on the radio. The results showed that people remembered much of the information they were offered, despite the fact that listening to the radio was a secondary activity. That research was done to convince potential advertisers of the value of radio as an advertising medium, but it is revealing about the power of radio images, especially when considered alongside other research showing the value people place on radio listening to help them through the day.

> You feel at one with the radio.
> It's life, it's typical. Whereas there's quite a bit of falsity about the television, you feel the radio is genuine.

(Barnett 1989: 3)

AUDIENCE PLEASURES

We can see a great diversity of interaction with the media during the course of a whole day. But some groups, particularly young people, use only a limited range of media. The DES survey of 1983 claimed that school-children spent a large amount of time watching popular television. And a more recent survey of Scottish schools showed that children between the ages of 12 and 15 spent nearly a fifth of their time on television, video, film or music. Put another way, over 75 per cent of their leisure time was taken up by these media (AMES 1986: 16).

Youth audiences

The 16–24 age-group watch only about two-thirds as much television as average viewers. Even though they are likely to be available at the same times as other viewers, they often prefer to do other things than watch television in their leisure time, especially listening to music (BBC 1989: 26).

Table 2.2 Time spent outside school on different media
(N.B. Times given in hours e.g. 1.30 means 1h. 30 min.)

	TV	Video	Cinema	Radio	Record	Newspapers	Magazines	Books
S1 Boys	2.52	0.48	0.09	0.12	0.27	0.11	0.15	0.25
S2 Boys	3.04	0.56	0.17	0.14	0.30	0.10	0.08	0.13
S3 Boys	2.41	0.48	0.15	0.20	1.00	0.15	0.14	0.18
Boys' mean	2.52	0.51	0.14	0.15	0.39	0.12	0.12	0.19
S1 Girls	2.19	0.30	0.06	0.18	0.39	0.09	0.15	0.33
S2 Girls	2.44	0.40	0.08	0.33	1.00	0.10	0.16	0.44
S3 Girls	2.22	0.28	0.11	0.31	0.54	0.09	0.14	0.25
Girls' mean	2.28	0.33	0.08	0.27	0.51	0.09	0.15	0.34

Summary table of time spent per day on media
(Figures in brackets are percentages of total day)

	Audio-visual	Audio	Reading	Total
S1 Boys	3.49 (15.9%)	0.39 (2.7%)	0.51 (3.5%)	5.19 (22.1%)
S2 Boys	4.17 (17.8)	0.44 (3.1)	0.31 (2.2)	5.32 (23.1)
S3 Boys	3.44 (15.6)	0.80 (5.6)	0.47 (3.3)	5.51 (24.4)
Boys' mean	3.57 (16.5)	0.54 (3.8)	0.43 (3.0)	5.34 (23.2)
S1 Girls	2.55 (12.1)	0.57 (4.0)	0.57 (4.0)	4.49 (20.1)
S2 Girls	3.32 (14.7)	1.33 (6.5)	1.10 (4.9)	6.15 (26.0)
S3 Girls	3.01 (12.6)	1.25 (5.9)	0.48 (3.3)	5.14 (21.8)
Girls' mean	3.09 (13.1)	1.18 (5.4)	0.58 (4.0)	5.26 (22.6)

Audio-visual = TV, Video, Cinema
Audio = Radio, Records
Reading = Newspapers, Magazines, Books

Source: AMES 1986: 16

Table 2.3 Other media activities besides watching television, age-groups 16–19 and 20–24, Summer weekdays, 6.00–11.00 p.m., 1988

p.m.	Listening to radio			Watching video			Listening to records/ cassettes		
	16–19	20–24	UK pop.	16–19	20–24	UK pop.	16–19	20–24	UK pop.
	%	%	%	%	%	%	%	%	%
6.00	8	6	7	1	7	1	4	4	1
6.30	9	7	6	1	1	1	4	8	2
7.00	10	10	7	1	2	1	13	7	3
7.30	9	8	5	2	4	2	13	7	3
8.00	11	6	6	2	7	3	13	3	3
8.30	8	4	5	7	6	3	11	1	3
9.00	6	4	4	6	6	3	13	5	3
9.30	10	5	5	7	8	4	11	5	2
10.00	11	5	5	5	7	3	9	4	2
10.30	11	4	5	5	7	3	8	6	2
11.00	11	2	5	5	8	3	6	5	2

Source: BBC 1989: 21

We studied the media habits of some fourth-year students in a Hampshire comprehensive school. They kept a log of a day's media contact and we used this as a starting-point for talking to each of them in more depth by means of interviews. Young people may seem very predictable in their media habits. And in some ways they are.

> Nearly everything I do, except for going to school, is either watching telly or has got music in it ... I listen to the radio in the morning and then I go to school. And then at lunchtime I watch half of *Neighbours* and then when I get home from school I put the telly on and just sit there and do my homework – not really watching it – and then watch *Home and Away* and *Neighbours* and then get ready to go out, listening to *Power FM* and then when I'm at the Youth Centre there's usually [video]tapes on there.

(Amanda Clark)

> When I get in, usually at about quarter past three, I watch telly and that until about 6 o'clock ... If I go out, say, to the Youth Centre, I'll be in about half-ten and I watch telly until about half-eleven, twelve and then I just go to bed.

(Neil Ticehurst)

We shall be examining in Chapters 4 and 5 how readers often react quite individually to different texts. We shall also be looking at how we can make use of the diversity of their responses in teaching about the media in the classroom. But we can note here that some underlying patterns begin to emerge when we look more closely. The verbal accounts the students gave during interview suggest a range of different motives and pleasures in different contexts. Here is an extract from our interview with Stephen Alexander:

When we was on holiday last week I watched telly non-stop all day. I enjoyed some of the morning programmes, 'cause they were in Los Angeles on *This Morning* on ITV, they were there in that and I watched that all week. I enjoyed watching that.

What was it about it that you liked?

They just showed different things. They showed fashion that's in Los Angeles at the moment, things that people do on the beach. They went to Disneyland and all different things like that.

Does it make you want to go to those places?

Yes, I want to go to Los Angeles. I want to go to the beach, 'cause everybody's different there and they're all doing different things ...

Do you have a favourite 'soap'?

It used to be *Neighbours* but I'd say *Home and Away*, 'cause they're always in the sun and it looks – it's more interesting than being stuck indoors . . . all the time.

And you said you watch EastEnders *as well?*

Yeah.

Why do you like Home and Away *perhaps more than* EastEnders?

Home and Away is a bit more livelier. *Neighbours* – not much happens. *Neighbours* is always indoors and so you don't get to see the sun. And in *EastEnders* not much good happens – they're always – somebody's getting run over by a lorry or somebody's got competition on the market. The only good things is when somebody gets married, or an anniversary, and that's it.

The key words which recur so frequently in Stephen's account are 'sun' and 'different'. They connect with an interest in clothes and beaches and contrast with 'indoors'. Ordinary experience is depressing and relieved only by an anniversary or a wedding. The gloomy confines of mundane experience are set against a world of sunshine and smiles. He is searching for something which will overcome boredom and the 'grotty mood' which teenagers dread. *Home and Away* and Disneyland may banish the shades of *Neighbours* and *EastEnders*.

These fears and desires also connect with Stephen's more general comments about what television means to him and why he chooses particular programmes. Although there are some obvious ironies in the fact that he sits indoors to contemplate his outdoor paradise, to call such desires 'escapist' begs too many questions. We may risk underestimating how repetitive and restrictive teenage experience can actually be. Television can simply trigger a change of mood for viewers. We should also recognise the possibility of connections with deeper levels of experience here. It may be an exaggeration to suggest that this conflict dramatises basic conflicts between light and life on the one hand and darkness and death on the other. Yet there are clearly hints of a deeper level of engagement.

If a programme you like is on it makes you feel happier. If it is a boring programme, if you've been in a grotty mood all day and a boring programme's on, you just get even worse.

(Stephen Alexander)

Uses and gratifications theory

Uses and gratifications theory offers a way of making a more general sense of accounts like Stephen's. It sees audiences as active participants in a transaction with the media. Audiences seek to satisfy particular needs through the media, just as we seek to satisfy our human needs for information or companionship through face-to-face communication. The media may, for example, provide a substitute for real-life companionship through pseudo-interactions with glamorous and powerful 'personalities'. Or they may offer a simple form of organised communal experience.

> We talked to people who ... liked that programme – mainly working class women who were over 55 years old – and they said they liked it because (these were often people who lived alone) it was full of people being enthusiastic and people being cheerful and everybody seemed to be having a good time. Yes, they knew that these people simulated these emotions and perhaps in the studio people got it going, but they didn't mind that, and no, they didn't think it was about greed at all. They weren't interested in consumerism or anything, they just enjoyed everybody having a good time.
>
> (Viewers' comments on *The Price is Right* quoted by Laurie Taylor)

McQuail (1987: 73) has devised a simple typology to explain audience motivation. His framework is based on the general headings: *Information, Personal identity, Integration and social interaction, Entertainment.* These categories also roughly correspond with recognisable characteristics of media texts. But there is a circularity about the uses and gratifications approach, since particular audience uses of media are the only evidence that the wants and needs which the media are supposed to satisfy actually exist in the first place. Assuming that common audience needs are *given* does not help to locate their origins. Nor does it tell us anything about the structure of social relations which the uses and gratifications derive from. Are they generated outside the media system or by the texts themselves? Would such needs exist in the form they do without the media? Does toy advertising, for example, meet children's needs or generate them?

What is more, the approach does not provide an adequate account of the complexities of media texts, or of individual responses to them. It does offer some prospect of differentiating audiences according to the kinds of satisfactions which they seek from the media and the kind of material they prefer. But the audience is still seen as a mass entity or as a marketing construction.

Emphasising audiences' motives has certainly been helpful in leading research away from an obsession with the media as manipulative agents. Yet it has also opened the door to the sweeping and sometimes cynical claim that it is merely a market commodity to be purchased by consumers.

It is sometimes argued that the media are the way they are simply because audiences want them that way. This begs the question of what audiences would want if the media were different. It also confuses an apparent choice between a limited range of products with real choice about the style and content of the media.

HOW ARE AUDIENCES COMPOSED?

> [The audience] is a collectivity which is formed either in response to media . . . or out of independently existing social forces . . . Often, it is inextricably both at the same time.
>
> (McQuail 1987: 215)

Audiences can be seen, on the one hand, as produced by media institutions and texts. On the other hand, they may be specific groups who are defined by particular social and economic relationships. They may also be defined, for some purposes, by their attitudes.

Such groupings are themselves the product of social variables like class, race, gender, age and locality. They determine the particular under-standings which audiences bring to texts. So audiences have a dual function. In a general sense, texts make audiences but in a more precise sense, audiences make texts.

It would be impossible for communication to take place at all if it were not possible to predict who media audiences are, what kind of expectations they may have and in what circumstances they are responding. We have concentrated so far on some of the differences between audiences, on the variations in response between individual members and on some of the unpredictable features of communication through the media. Let us look now at aspects of audiences which can be predicted with confidence by producers and publishers. Because people's habits on a typical day and their basic patterns of work and leisure are well established, the scheduling of radio and television programmes has to work within these limits.

> Every single bit of radio listening is done in the same way across the country whether you're listening to Radio 1 or Radio 2 or commercial radio or BBC local radio. Most people listen to radio in the morning . . . I know how many people we get to each day and I know how many people we get to each week. I also know something about the kind of people we get to. Judging by the mail that I get . . . and the kind of calls we get here, we have an articulate and pretty well informed, if not formally highly educated audience, and we are different from other local stations in that.
>
> (Mike Hapgood)

There are common listening patterns across all services. Audiences peak in the mornings and then reduce throughout the day. Stations featuring

Figure 2.3 Hourly viewing and listening by radio and television audiences[1] throughout the day, 1989[2]

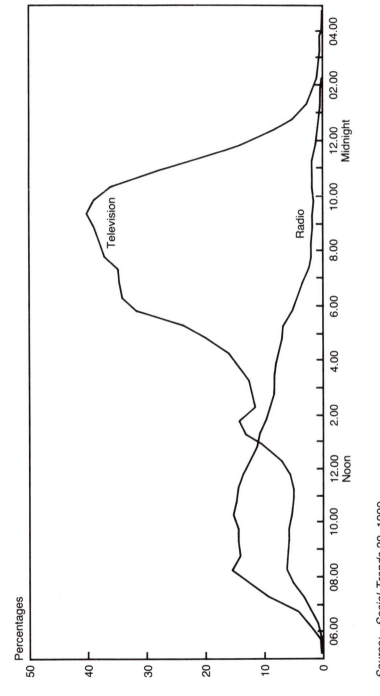

Source: *Social Trends* 20, 1990
Notes: 1 Persons aged 4 and over
2 Average audience, Quarter 2, 1989

popular music in their output have the biggest audiences and the style of music determines age-group of audience. Nearly three-quarters of the population consistently listen to some form of radio each week, for an average of about three hours each.

But audience research also involves complications and uncertainties. The concern of media producers with audiences as quantities has caused some delusions. Knowing the size of an audience is not the same as knowing its composition. A crude estimate of the number of viewers watching any particular episode of, say, a television serial disguises the fact that the actual composition of the audience may change from episode to episode. Similarly, if a programme changed its time of transmission, it would not attract the same audience.

> Although audiences might fluctuate between 16 and 19 million for something like *EastEnders*, it's not the same people watching every week. Only 50 per cent of the audience for one episode will be watching next week's episode. There's a very high turn over ... audiences are unpredictable and watch a specific programme for any number of reasons – many of which have nothing to do with making an active choice about that programme.

(Steven Barnett)

But broadcasters are still able to produce programmes with particular groups in mind and to schedule them so that they are transmitted at a time when the appropriate viewers are available. This is possible because they

Table 2.4 Total amount of viewing by age, sex and social grade, 1987–8

		1987 (hrs:mins)	1988 (hrs:mins)	% Change (+/−)
UK population (4+)		25:25	25:21	0
Age:	4–7	17:17	17:20	0
	8–11	20:15	18:12	−10
	12–15	20:10	20:08	0
	All children	19:20	18:44	−4
	16–24	15:34	17:06	+10
	25–34	24:32	24:07	−2
	35–44	22:52	21:56	−4
	45–54	26:23	26:44	+1
	55–64	33:00	33:07	0
	65+	37:41	37:25	−1
Sex:	Male	23:12	22:56	−1
	Female	27:19	27:28	+1
Social Grade	AB	18:31	17:42	−4
	C1	23:17	22:46	−2
	C2	24:40	25:25	+3
	DE	31:47	31:44	0

Source: BBC 1989: 9

Table 2.5 Average amount of listening, by age, sex and social grade, 1988

(Hrs:mins per head of population aged 4+ per week)

		R1	R2	R3	R4	BBC LR	Nat. Regs	All BBC	ILR	Other non-BBC	All radio 88	(87)
Age	4–15	1:00	0:04	0:00	0:02	0:05	0:01	1:14	0:56	0:02	2:13	(2:06)
	16–24	6:51	0:13	0:02	0:10	0:17	0:02	7:37	3:49	0:16	11:43	(11:26)
	25–34	5:27	0:33	0:05	0:48	0:30	0:04	7:29	3:57	0:10	11:37	(11:09)
	35–44	2:51	1:31	0:11	1:30	0:57	0:09	7:14	3:25	0:07	10:46	(10:20)
	45–54	1:17	3:00	0:14	1:21	1:21	0:13	7:31	2:36	0:05	10:13	(10:03)
	55–64	0:30	3:56	0:20	1:37	1:51	0:22	8:41	1:53	0:02	10:38	(10:23)
	65+	0:49	3:03	0:18	1:50	1:41	0:24	7:32	1:14	0:02	8:49	(8:44)
	All adults	2:50	2:01	0:12	1:14	1:06	0:12	7:39	2:48	0:07	10:35	(10:29)
Sex	Male	2:54	1:42	0:13	0:53	0:52	0:11	6:48	2:41	0:07	9:37	(9:13)
	Female	2:12	1:42	0:07	1:10	1:59	0:11	6:24	2:18	0:05	8:48	(8:32)
Social grade	AB	1:40	1:46	0:32	2:51	0:34	0:12	7:41	1:48	0:04	9:34	(8:59)
	C1	2:33	1:55	0:14	1:24	0:51	0:11	7:11	2:28	0:05	9:45	(9:18)
	C2	3:25	1:37	0:04	0:31	0:59	0:09	6:47	2:51	0:06	9:44	(9:18)
	DE	2:04	1:36	0:04	0:32	1:05	0:12	5:36	2:27	0:08	8:11	(8:08)
	All aged 4+	2:32	1:42	0:10	1:02	0:56	0:11	6:35	2:29	0:06	9:11	(8:51)

Source: BBC 1989: 16

spend a great deal of time and money in finding out about audiences. (We shall be looking at how they and other media institutions do so in the section below on Audience Research, p. 52.) Such research is capable of identifying sub-groups within audiences and relating variables like age, gender and social class to media habits.

Because audiences can be classified in this way, broadcasters can to some extent tailor their programmes for different groups. This can be seen in a very simple way by looking at how television schedules particular slots for children's programmes. Although there is a range of programmes on offer, as there is for adults, programme forms echo adults': children are offered drama, news, quizzes and game-shows. But the emphasis for children is on differentiation according to age-groups rather than on programme kinds. For the most part, they are separated from adult viewing. The Family Viewing Policy reinforces this by prescribing that material not suitable for younger children is transmitted after the 9 o'clock 'watershed'. Hence, much of the moral panic over television content is directly related to the fact that children do in fact watch adult programmes when they are not supposed to, either before or after the 'watershed'.

Figure 2.4   Dimensions of scheduling

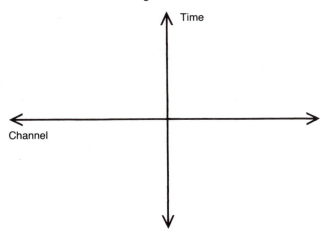

Scheduling has a vertical dimension in time and a horizontal one across channels. Viewers' choices are made in both dimensions. Broadcasters have developed methods of 'hooking' audiences such as 'hammocking' (supporting a programme between two stronger ones) and 'stripping' (showing segments of a mini-series at different times). Viewers equipped with video-recorders and remote controls have responded with 'zapping', 'grazing' and 'multi-channel viewing'. Both seem to be agreed that recurrent serialisation is an effective scheduling method.

It is not surprising that the largest group of viewers for tea-time soaps like *Neighbours* and *Home and Away* is 15 or under. About one-third of the total afternoon audience is between 4 and 15 years old and this group is twice as likely to watch *Neighbours* in the afternoon as any other soap at any other time (with the exception of *Home and Away*).

Like broadcasting, the newspaper and magazine industries have established mechanisms for finding out about their customers. It is easier for them to get clear profiles of their readers, since they often have specialised readerships.

The typical reader is young – 49 per cent of them under the age of 34. They are in the upper part of the community in terms of the jobs that they do and so on. This is measured by the wretched letters A, B, C1 and ... our figure's about 80 per cent, *The Times*' is a little bit more, *The Guardian*, and *Telegraph* a little bit less.

(Andreas Whittam Smith)

Table 2.6 Socio-economic grades in the UK

A	Higher managerial, administrative or professional
B	Intermediate managerial, administrative or professional
C1	Supervisory or clerical, and junior managerial, administrative or professional
C2	Skilled manual worker
D	Semi and unskilled manual workers
E	State pensioners or widows (no other earner in household), casual or lower grade workers, and unemployed

Newspaper and magazine readerships are much more differentiated and specialised than television audiences, but there are trends within television (especially with new satellite and cable services) towards a similar kind of programme targeting. Radio audiences are already more specialised and segmented since, unlike traditional television, different channels attract different listeners.

The audience for Independent Local Radio will tend to be slightly younger, perhaps slightly more down-market. For BBC Local Radio it will be older and slightly more up-market and I think that's almost a sort of caricature that programmers will carry around with them in their head.

(Steven Barnett)

Figure 2.5 Social grade of national daily readers, 1989

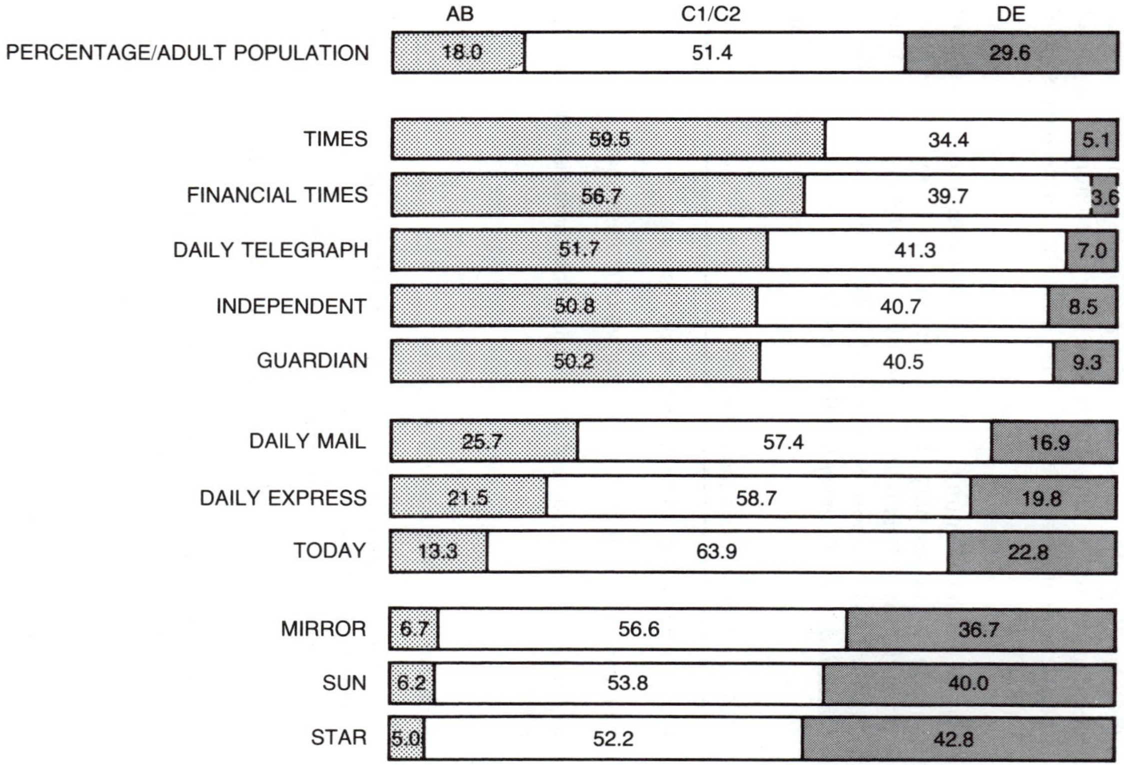

	AB	C1/C2	DE
PERCENTAGE/ADULT POPULATION	18.0	51.4	29.6
TIMES	59.5	34.4	5.1
FINANCIAL TIMES	56.7	39.7	3.6
DAILY TELEGRAPH	51.7	41.3	7.0
INDEPENDENT	50.8	40.7	8.5
GUARDIAN	50.2	40.5	9.3
DAILY MAIL	25.7	57.4	16.9
DAILY EXPRESS	21.5	58.7	19.8
TODAY	13.3	63.9	22.8
MIRROR	6.7	56.6	36.7
SUN	6.2	53.8	40.0
STAR	5.0	52.2	42.8

Source: NRS: Jan.–Dec. 1989

HOW ARE AUDIENCES ADDRESSED?

|| Television doesn't make programmes – it makes viewers.

(Jean-Luc Godard)

The way audiences are addressed is a product of producers' notions of who they are and how they are likely to respond. Audience identity is 'written into' texts in various ways though, for example, tone, pace and vocabulary. Advertising agencies and production companies rely on various shorthand ways of describing the qualities of actors' voices, sometimes even colour-coding them as 'deep brown', 'rich golden' or 'silvery' (see Chapter 5).

Television and radio texts make a special effort to appeal to particular audience dispositions. Audiences are invoked through specific sounds, rhythms and colourings. Children's toys, for example, are advertised on television in ways which are gender-specific. Boys' toys are surrounded by noise and activity, while girls' are quieter, more placid and rely on gentler presentation through fades and dissolves rather than abrupt cuts (Durkin 1985: 29).

How does a local radio station create an identity which its audience can recognise? It depends on the particular mix of programme material they produce, the kind of voices they use and the style and tone they employ.

|| We know that people like a chatty direct style of broadcasting. Every station looks to have a star. If you could go on a listener trip or you talk to a group of people who want to know about the station, the first questions you are always asked are about the stars. We're a 70 per cent speech to 30 per cent music station, so it's a broad policy first of all that says we are the station that will discuss and talk. You will hear a lot of speech on this station. Our music is carefully selected from a range of music. I suppose the easiest way to describe it is 'easy listening'. That helps build identity. To that we add 'jingles' which we hope reinforce both the musical sound and the authority of the BBC.

(Mike Hapgood)

Radio Solent's news 'jingle', like that of many other radio stations, plays a large part in establishing a clear identity for its listeners.

(Dramatic opening music, with percussion)
Strong male voice over: FROM AROUND THE WORLD – ACROSS THE SOUTH – RADIO SOLENT NEWS – FROM THE BBC!
(Dramatic closing music)

|| It's a cracking jingle. What does it tell us . . .? It's obviously a very 'newsy' jingle. It's pregnant with drama. It also says 'BBC' in a highly macho way. The young man who says it is pitching a hard sell there. 'The BBC' gives it authority. We say 'this is all the news you need – from around the world, the BBC's resources draw in all the news. It

spreads it across the South ... Everything you want is delivered to you in our news with the right kind of drama added.'

(Mike Hapgood)

HOW IS AUDIENCE RESEARCH CARRIED OUT?

You take a sample of the population. You install a meter to the television set, and that meter will monitor every single channel. Every time you switch from one channel to another it will record it. Every time the television goes off it will record it – so that's easily done.

(Steven Barnett)

The television industry has its own mechanisms for researching its audiences. The Broadcasters' Audience Research Board (BARB) was set up in 1981 to integrate the separate ratings research carried out by the BBC and the new ITC through the Joint Industry Committee for Television Audience Research (JICTAR). It subcontracts the task of audience measurement to AGB Research Ltd who survey a representative panel of 3,000 computer-linked homes. BARB releases monthly bulletins on gross viewing figures (expressed in thousands) and share of available audience. It also calculates an overall Television Rating (TVR). The panel survey provides a detailed breakdown of viewing by social class, age and gender. Much of this information is fairly easily available to the public.

ASPECTS OF AUDIENCE MEASUREMENT

Average audience: Number of people who watched/listened to a programme averaged over its transmission time.
Programme reach: Number of people who watched/listened to any part of a programme.
Core audience: Number of people who watched/listened to the whole of a programme.
Average daily/weekly reach: Number of people who watched/listened to a radio or television station in a particular day or week.
Audience share: Average amount of watching/listening for a particular service expressed as a percentage of all watching/listening.

The survey can also produce information on regional and scheduling variations which is invaluable to programme planners. Analysis of audience composition by social class shows some significant variations. For example, TVS's regional audience is very similar to that of the ITV Network as a whole at peak-time (7 p.m.) viewing. But the audience normally boasts a greater proportion of ABC1 viewers than the Network and this advantage increases at 'minority' times like Sunday at 10 p.m. This is just the sort of data which can persuade advertisers to select off-peak

Figure 2.6   ITV Network v. TVS regional profiles, 1985–6

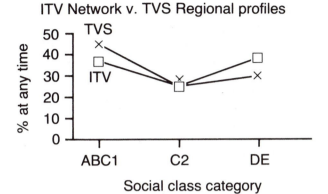

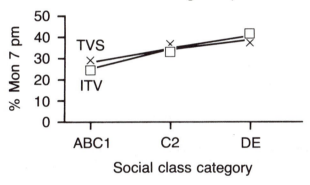

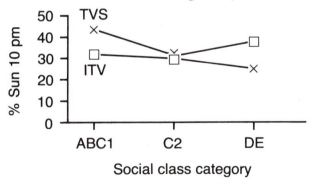

Source: Hart 1988b: 115

spots in which appeals can be made to the better-off viewer (Hart 1988b: 101–16).

Qualitative information about responses and attitudes is also available from the BARB Reaction Service, based on a regular questionnaire to the same panel. This work is subcontracted to the BBC's Broadcast Research Department, although the new ITC also contributes expertise and financial support. Its findings are confidential to the industry. This is partly because collecting and interpreting audience responses is a difficult and expensive process (the BARB Reaction Service costs over £2m a year). Its findings need interpreting with care and so far broadcasters have resisted the pressures of advertising agencies to release them. But broadcasters do take notice of reactions to programmes, so audiences have an effect on programme planning and scheduling.

> BARB is an extremely secret organisation, but commercial television and the BBC have both got the same vested interest, they both want to have very large figures for their shows.

(Laurie Taylor)

The main measures which result from all this activity work in slightly different ways. The Reaction Service produces an Appreciation Index (AI) which gives a sense of audience satisfaction for a programme, measured on a six-point scale, and ultimately is expressed as a percentage. Very few of any channel's Top Ten rated programmes also achieve Top Ten AIs. High AIs tend to be achieved by comedy shows, royalty and animal programmes, while the continuous serials achieve the high numerical scores.

Table 2.7 Appreciation Indices by demographic groups

	Overall AI	Male	Female	Age 12–34	Age 35–54	Age 55+	Social Grade ABC1	C2	DE
Coronation Street	76	71	78	74	74	77	73	75	77
EastEnders	71	67	74	71	70	73	68	71	74
Emmerdale Farm	76	75	78	73	76	79	74	75	78
Brookside	76	73	79	78	72	76	76	75	78
Neighbours	78	74	80	80	75	77	76	79	79

Source: BBC 1989: 34

A programme has clearly succeeded if it registers high viewing figures and high AIs. If the figures are high but the AI low, a regular but indifferent audience is implied. The reverse is often achieved by quality minority programming (often on Sundays). If both measures are low, then something has gone wrong. An AI percentage below 25 is discounted, under 50 is suspect and over 80 is outstanding.

> What's interesting about those audience appreciation figures is that you find the audience appreciation figure out of 100 for Wogan was 64,

> whereas for a serious documentary programme it comes out at about 83.
> Now more people are watching Wogan but it's as though they don't
> think very much of it. Films get very, very high appreciation ratings,
> higher than most programmes on television. All of which confirms the
> idea that lots and lots of people are staring at it but they don't think
> much of it while it is going on.
>
> (Laurie Taylor)

The Appreciation Index has a number of limitations. Firstly, it is a rather
insensitive measure of audience reactions, since it is very hard for a
programme to produce a low figure. Panel members are not expected to
report on programmes they do not enjoy. As a result, 80 per cent of
programmes score AIs over 70 and 60 per cent between 70 and 80.
Secondly, coverage is poor: reactions are registered on only just over a
third of current programmes broadcast. Thirdly, although distinctions are
made between sixteen main and thirteen sub-genres, the same questions
are asked for all programmes, so few programmes can be meaningfully
compared with each other. Finally, and perhaps most important, AIs do
not reveal anything about reasons for choosing certain programmes or
degree of involvement in them. In order to explore these areas, we have to
go to the specialised industry and academic research on responses which is
discussed in the next section of this chapter.

> It's difficult to get a low AI for the simple reason that if you really hate a
> programme you tend to switch it off or to switch over and therefore
> anything below say 60 out of 100 is considered pretty poor . . . Anything
> over 80 is considered to be a very high score. And it's interesting that –
> especially on Channel 4 – those programmes with specific minority
> appeal have often scored very highly because they are being watched by
> a very select group of people.
>
> (Steven Barnett)

Audience preferences

Both the BBC and the ITC (and, more recently, even some of the ITV
companies themselves) have their own Research Departments which carry
out specially commissioned work, often by means of interviews and
discussion groups. Special projects like these can reveal a great deal about
viewer preferences. Audience research can tell producers of texts a great
deal about dominant attitudes towards certain kinds of material which can
help determine the kind of things they offer.

For example, even the crudest public image of particular television
channels can work in favour or against particular programmes being watched
in the first place. This can be illustrated by looking at audience attitudes to
documentary, educational and general science programmes on television.

Figure 2.7 Perceived best channels for science, documentary and educational programmes, 1986

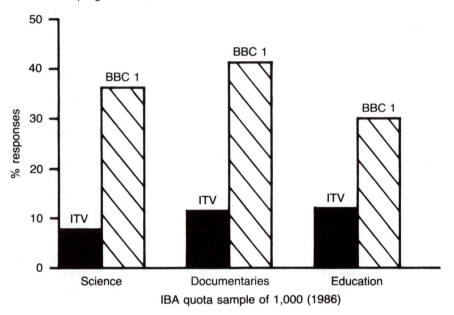

Source: IBA 1986

Belief in BBC2's effectiveness for these kinds of programme is about the same as BBC1's, so there is clearly a very strong predisposition against ITV in this area. Other forms of predisposition are noticeable. Although 60 per cent of adult viewers appear to be interested in science and technology, male or older viewers, those with more formal education and ABC1 social class viewers are disproportionately represented in this group. Watching *Horizon* is not confined to a specific social group, but it is watched more selectively (on the basis of interest in particular editions) than *Tomorrow's World*. It offers different kinds of pleasure and satisfaction, challenge rather than reassurance. Yet nearly everyone (98 per cent) who claims to watch *Horizon* also watches *Tomorrow's World* (Hart 1988b: 139–42).

Much the same sort of qualitative and quantitative research is carried out by the BBC and the Radio Authority for their radio output, through the Joint Industry Committee for Radio Audience Research (JICRARS). The BBC uses its own Daily Survey, based on interviewing at home, JICRARS on diary keeping. There is some debate within the industry about the accuracy of these methods.

With radio listening, of course, it's much more difficult. You can't possibly attach meters. What you have to do is one of two methods. You either have have to ask people, take them through the previous day's listening (what's called a daily recall method) and tick off those programmes that they've watched the day before. Or you give people a

Table 2.8 Circulation of national newspapers, 1988–9

Title	Controlled by	Average circulation 10/88–3/89	+/− On circulation 87–88
Dailies			
Populars			
Daily Express	United Newspapers	1,607,678	− 82,860
Daily Mail	Associated Newspapers Group	1,748,792	− 51,747
Daily Mirror	Mirror Group Newspapers (1986)	3,167,322	+ 79,810
Daily Star	United Newspapers	932,774	−108,874
The Sun	News International	4,214,458	+116,224
Today	News International	565,745	+215,488
(Morning Star)	(Morning Star Co-operative Society)	(29,000)	(1986 figures)
	Total	**12,236,769**	**+178,041**
Qualities			
Financial Times	Pearson	281,249	−17,151
The Daily Telegraph	The Daily Telegraph	1,125,758	−28,260
The Guardian	The Guardian & Manchester News	439,818	−34,199
The Independent	Newspaper Publishing	400,056	+23,306
The Times	News International	442,109	−7,442
	Total	**2,688,990**	**−63,726**
Sundays			
Populars			
News of the World	News International	5,348,576	+196,782
Sunday Express	United Newspapers	2,000,745	−193,001
Sunday Mirror	Mirror Group Newspapers (1986)	2,982,769	+185,490
Sunday Sport	Apollo Ltd	569,119	+569,119
The Mail on Sunday	Associated Newspapers Group	1,959,056	+46,297
The People	Mirror Group Newspapers (1986)	2,707,120	−59,006
	Total	**18,274,505**	**+686,675**
Qualities			
The Sunday Telegraph	The Daily Telegraph	671,386	−59,288
Observer	Lonrho International	712,853	−51,194
The Sunday Times	News International	1,322,536	+15,695
	Total	**2,706,775**	**−94,787**

Source: Hard News 1989
Notes: Circulation figures are those based on the Audit Bureau of Circulation (ABC), a committee of publishers, advertisers and advertising agencies. The actual readership of a national newspaper is estimated to be roughly three times the circulation figure.

‖ diary on a weekly basis and you say, at the end of the day, please just
‖ simply tick the programmes you've listened to.

(Steven Barnett)

The press also has sophisticated research mechanisms. The Audit Bureau
of Circulation (ABC) is an independent body which releases quantitative
data every month on *sales* of newspapers and magazines. These figures are
often supplemented by (unaudited) figures produced by the journals
themselves.

The Joint Industry Committee for National Readership Surveys
(JICNARS) carries out more detailed research on *readership* through its
subcontractor Research Services Ltd. The National Readership Survey
works like the BARB process with a representative sample of 26,000
readers of newspapers and magazines. It gives a very detailed breakdown
by social class, age, gender, and education. Information on how readers
actually manage the business of reading their papers is less easy to come
by. Their practices have not been investigated in anything like the detail
that has occurred with radio and television. Recent data from America
shows that less than two thirds of readers claim to read the whole of any
paper. But 60–70 per cent are known to 'open to the page': this practice
increases with the educational level of readers but decreases with the
physical size and circulation of papers (Bogart 1989: 158–64).

Targeting

The annual Target Group Index, produced by the British Market Research
Bureau, is the largest British product and media survey. It samples 24,000
people to produce such information as numbers of car-drivers or heavy
wine-drinkers, and even brand preferences. Product data is also correlated
with patterns of media use so as to provide information about target
audiences for advertisers. It also produces 'life-style' profiles by asking
respondents to express their level of agreement with nearly 200 statements.
Various schemes have been devised by analysts to categorise these profiles.

Young and Rubicam's 'Cross Cultural Consumer Classification':

Resigned Poor
Struggling Poor
Mainstreamers
Succeeders
Reformers
Aspirers

Specialist magazines rely on similar market data to maintain their
competitiveness. But children's comics are much more 'hit-and-miss'.
Children have little appeal to advertisers, since they are not directly

responsible for consumer decisions, so very little research has ever been done on the comics market.

Table 2.9 Net sales of D.C. Thomson publications for six-monthly periods, January 1988–June 1989

Publication	Jan./June 1989	July/Dec. 1988	Jan./June 1988
*Courier	121,554	121,809	124,551
*Ev Telegraph	45,890	46,211	47,226
Dundee Extra	74,970	74,007	73,683
*Sunday Post	1,306,827	1,356,424	1,392,544
*Weekly News	583,354	641,164	670,502
P Journal	18,258	19,591	21,033
Sporting Post	19,604	20,068	20,676
Secrets	28,000	30,089	34,337
*My Weekly	505,970	516,109	538,561
*Jackie	161,804	182,496	192,976
*Blue Jeans	83,890	71,287	84,895
Teenage Two	245,694	253,783	277,871
Victor	35,855	42,260	47,339
Bunty	53,475	62,342	66,164
Judy	26,841	31,032	35,186
Mandy	31,560	37,947	42,563
Hi	85,468	93,763	**151,059
Girls' papers	197,344	225,084	294,972
Junior papers	233,199	300,104	383,590
Dandy/Beano	445,993	469,857	449,160
*People's Friend	537,556	540,392	566,658
*Scots Magazine	84,591	80,251	80,910
*Annabel	115,757	120,529	123,330

Source: ABC, August 1989
Notes: * ABC ** 16 issues

D.C. Thomson produce some 15 titles for young people ... How are they sold? They are sold through something like 50,000 newsagents up and down the country, each one selling perhaps 10 copies at most. How can they find out what works? In the end they are dependent on 'how many have we sold? Is it making a profit?' Now currently the break-even point for comics is around the 100,000 mark. If it falls below that a title is likely to die. But you can see the kind of pressure they're under. They have got to keep all those newsagents happy, and through them 5 to 10 kids from each. They have got to keep the system producing, and that's hard. And when they launch a new one, they have to think 'do we have any new ideas about what the kids are looking for at the moment?' And the truth is they don't really; they guess, and then wait to see if it sells.

(Martin Barker)

HOW DO AUDIENCES RESPOND?

Audiences, texts and meanings

Audiences work upon texts in complex and different ways, just as much as texts work upon audiences.

(Masterman 1985: 227)

Audiences are crucial to the kinds of representations which media texts generate. Texts need audiences in order to realise their potential for meaning. So a text does not have a single meaning but rather a range of possibilities which are defined by both the text and by its audiences. The meaning is not in the text but in the *reading*. It is only through the interaction of audiences with texts that any meaning is produced at all. Personal experiences and individual identities are diverse and texts therefore have potential for multiple meanings. What audiences bring to texts affects the meanings they take away.

Figure 2.8   Interaction between producers, texts and audiences

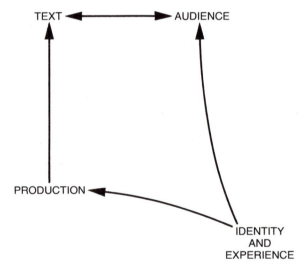

Audiences come to texts not only with existing knowledge and values, but also with experience of familiar forms. As a result, some kinds of text are alien to them. For example, young children are apparently intolerant of adult television news bulletins. They tend instantly to reject the authoritative adult tones of newsreaders. This may be because the content of news is very remote from them. It may also be related to the way in which news is structured.

This situation can be avoided, as programmes like *Newsround* show, by using more child-friendly presentation techniques. Not only are items selected because of their particular relevance for child audiences, but the sequencing of items and the explanation which surrounds them are also specially adapted for them.

Traditional news presentation methods are also a problem for many adult members of audiences. Despite recent innovations in the way news is presented many television news items are difficult for viewers to grasp. Compared with the continuous serial, news fails abysmally. Its 'inverted pyramid' structure (which derives from newspaper journalism) ensures that crucial information is given away early in 'headline' form at the beginning and then repeated for good measure at the end. The most important items are scheduled first so that the bulletin as a whole gets less and less interesting the longer it goes on. At the same time, the overall flow of news bulletins is often erratic. Deciding where to place items is problematic, since it can lead to viewers being confused by invalid groupings or the need constantly to re-focus. It is difficult for viewers to participate in a developing narrative (Gunter 1987: 311–13; Lewis 1986: 205–34; Hart 1988b: 144–5).

Differential readings

A framework for understanding the interaction between audiences and texts has been developed by Hall (1981: 67). He suggests that all 'readings' of texts can be defined within the three broad categories of dominance, negotiation and opposition. Audiences will produce a dominant or *'preferred'* reading of a text if they understand it largely as transmitted. If they read it in a different way by exploiting contradictions within it and subverting its overt meanings, they are producing an *'oppositional'* reading. If, on the other hand, producers and readers do not share the same codes and conventions so that the overt meanings are not easily accessible, then misreading or *'aberrant decoding'* occurs. In practice, most readings are *'negotiated'* between the dominant one and what readers themselves bring to texts.

Understanding responses

Interaction between audiences and texts is not straightforward. It is an unpredictable and sometimes surprising process. Hall's categories are only a logical framework. They do not equate in a simple way with the different socio-economic positions of audiences. There is no necessary correlation between demographic or sociological factors and different responses. But some researchers have tried to refine this approach by exploring the 'fit' between the structural positions of television viewers and their actual responses. They have shown how audiences' responses need to be understood in relation to the subcultural groupings which define them. The way they approach programmes has an important bearing on the meanings which the programmes can achieve.

After viewing recordings of two current affairs series on BBC1, groups with different backgrounds, ages, occupations and political allegiances were interviewed. Five groups of late adolescent students in Further Education, most of whom were female and black, were apparently so alienated from the programmes that there was a huge gap between their culture and what was represented. This resulted in their hardly making any sense at all of the items within the programmes. Analysis of the interviews showed that responses to the programmes covered a very wide range of differences which were not directly related to social class variables but to gender and ethnic differences (Morley 1980). Similar difficulties were experienced by viewers in studies carried out by Buckingham (1987c). In an earlier study, he found that some viewers of the programme 'The Whites of their Eyes' in Thames's *Viewpoint 2* series had difficulty in distinguishing the voice-over commentary from individual views expressed in the programme, and that their failure to understand its basic mechanics meant that they failed to grasp many of the points it was trying to make. As always, the prejudices and opinions which viewers brought to the programme were powerful constraints on the sense they made of it (Buckingham 1983).

Nevertheless, most 'readings' are the preferred or dominant ones for any given text. A recent study of BARB data showed that this was true for TVS's networked popular science series. But only looking in more detail at individual responses throws light on how programmes are actually understood by viewers. Not all readings are equally valid. Some are the result of mistakes, errors and confusions and are better thought of as *mis*readings. Some fourth-year students who watched one programme in the series confused genetic cloning with cleaning and thought that Baltic amber was related to traffic-lights. Similar misunderstandings occurred amongst adults in family viewing contexts, many of whom were unable to keep pace with the programme or make connections between its many different elements. But even these misreadings can offer some insights into the way in which the understanding of a programme comes from an interaction between viewers and text (Hart 1988b: 148–52).

Michael Svennevig's research on *Horizon* for the BBC's Broadcasting Research Department showed very similar problems of keeping pace with rapid shifts of topic and location. Many details of the narrative were lost and the structure was often found to be too complex. Clearly, no viewer can be expected to grasp all of a programme's details, but it seems that some viewers have more problems than producers generally acknowledge. Occasionally, we can see how misunderstandings may begin to form themselves into oppositional readings. It is as if the gaps in the programme are filled with viewers' own material. Sometimes, this material may seem somewhat bizarre, or at least very distant from the focus of the text. Yet viewers' responses can be understood once we begin to look at them in more depth. We begin to realise that programmes are actually assimilated into pre-existent frameworks. These frameworks provide a mechanism for evaluating new information and ideas. Such new data may be completely rejected, absorbed relatively unchanged, or adapted. The material may be so significant that it causes a restructuring of the frameworks themselves and a genuine shift in perception (Svennevig 1984).

Whatever the individual views of audiences, small group discussion of their readings makes it clear that they bring their own views and their own agenda with them. It is these, rather than a blank page, which texts actually address.

IMPLICATIONS

> I think you need to have reliable objective accounts of the way in which people are using television because to start off with many of the other accounts that you've got at the moment aren't particularly reliable. I mean if you go to producers and people who make television they'll paint you a wonderful story of the programmes they're making. If you go to the huge quantitative accounts, all the numbers and the statistics, then these will look absolutely wonderful, But if you go to people and ask them how they're using television, then you find out a completely different picture.
>
> (Laurie Taylor)

Changing media audiences

The Peacock Committee concluded that broadcasting should 'move towards a sophisticated market system based on consumer sovereignty' but with special provision for public service programmes. The 1990 Broadcasting Act has accepted most of its free-market elements but with less specific protection for public service broadcasting (see Chapter 6 for a discussion of its implications). The possible abolition of the licence fee and the introduction of subscription for BBC programmes in the 1990s is a drastic prospect. On top of this, the newly created Broadcasting Standards Council and the prospect of a Fifth Channel have all conspired to concentrate the minds of anyone in broadcasting who might still feel complacent.

Radio audiences are bound to change as a result of more commercial stations and adjustments to BBC provision. Since the end of simultaneous transmission on MW and FM in August 1990, researchers at the BBC have been busy monitoring how audiences have reacted to the changes and to the new-style programmes from Radio 5 on the old Radio 2 non-FM frequencies.

The threat of competition from the new cable and satellite technologies poses further problems for the stability of television broadcasting. New means of distribution and types of programming may prove attractive to financiers and advertisers, but not necessarily with the result of increasing the volume of advertising. The new media may take a share of a limited supply of advertising revenue, especially if they can offer more precisely defined audiences than traditional broadcasting.

Yet there is little evidence as yet of radical changes in the ecology of broadcasting. Cable and satellite take-up has been very slow and traditional broadcasting institutions have proved extremely resilient.

> The real question is, will it take off? Is this actually going to change people's viewing behaviour? The general feeling is that it's not going to be the kind of revolution in television watching that some people have predicted. Most people will spend most of their time, even after twenty or thirty years, watching the core terrestrial channels which give you a mix of programming. But at the margins a peripheral amount of time will be spent watching the individual streamed channels.
>
> (Steven Barnett)

Research methods

> What they have done is they've sat a camera on top of a television watching the audience watching television and people have been making tea, doing the ironing, having conversations, reading the newspaper, all sorts of things – anything but watching the programme that's on.
>
> (Steven Barnett)

Experiments carried out by the IBA and shown on *Open the Box* or the BFI's *One Day in the Life of Television* project (Day-Lewis 1989) produced a great deal of interesting data. But although much of it was intimate, little was sophisticated enough to be worth analysis. If we want to glimpse what goes on inside people's heads, we need to look at more in-depth academic and industrial research, like that carried out by the Broadcasting Research Unit for *The Listener Speaks* (1989) on radio, or for *Keeping Faith* (1988) on Channel 4, or by Taylor and Mullan for *Uninvited Guests* (1986). This kind of work is rare because it is difficult and therefore very expensive. But some aspects of it can be adapted for the classroom.

> We talked to managers of BBC stations, we talked to managing directors of independent radio stations. That was followed by a series of discussion groups where we recruited groups of radio listeners of different ages, different sexes, different social backgrounds throughout the country. We did about forty in all. And finally a full-scale survey which covered a cross-section of the population – a thousand people –

which asked a whole series of questions in a 45-minute interview about their listening behaviour, what they thought about radio, and what they wanted from the future.

(Steven Barnett)

We could hardly really go wandering around bars all over Central London with a tape recorder just taking out a microphone as soon as we heard somebody starting to talk about *Dynasty* or *Dallas* ... So we invited people to join these discussion groups who were fans of particular forms of television. So we had a group of people who were very interested in soap operas ... and then we sat them down and we got them going with questions which we thought would stimulate them. Not 'Do you like it?' Or 'Don't you like it?', But 'Which of the characters in this soap opera would you like to kill off?' Or things, for example, like 'Can you see any resemblance between your family and any of the families in this particular soap opera?' 'Which characters on television are most like themselves in real life?' – to get it going. And then these people would talk away for 2 hours. We'd listen while they talked. We'd tape record the whole thing, then we'd transcribe it afterwards.

(Laurie Taylor)

Different kinds of audience research tell us different things. For finding out about audience pleasures, researchers like Barnett, Buckingham, Morley, Ryder and Taylor prefer qualitative methods. Quantitative and demographic research is very limited if you are really interested in what people are thinking and feeling.

The problem with quantitative research is that you are always going to be confined by the question that you ask, and in the space of a simple 10- or 12-word question your respondent may want to say all sorts of things to qualify their answer but isn't allowed to. You're forced into one of three or four options. During the course of a discussion group you can extemporise much more, you can qualify your statements, you can say 'When I said "yes" to that question what I meant was under these circumstances.' It adds a depth and a quality to what are very bald statements of fact which you certainly can't get through quantitative work.

(Steven Barnett)

On the other hand, to those who take a gloomy view of the future of the media in Britain, examining the minutiae of audience pleasures may seem like rearranging the deck-chairs on the *Titanic*. Clearly, qualitative research has a future in spite of its costs, because it is capable of great sensitivity. Many of its techniques have been developed from market research and it is now as attractive to new media operators like British

Satellite Broadcasting as it has been in the past to advertising and public relations agencies.

Before it merged with Rupert Murdoch's Sky Television, BSB set up two of its own panel of 350 households to research viewer satisfaction and receptivity to pay-television. It has also run a pilot study using a diary system to provide just the kind of detail on viewers' choice, involvement and quality assessment which is lacking in the BARB Reaction Service. In a highly competitive media environment, it is likely that such refined enquiries will increase. It is also possible that they will be seen not just as a form of monitoring, but as a necessary means of assessing markets before large investments are made. This trend inevitably raises the question of whether television could end up like it is in the USA, where research is carried out on programmes which haven't yet been made.

> Every single soap opera, every single adventure series is piloted, is shown to discussion groups, is tested on random cross-sections of the population and constant changes are made in order to make it more appealing to the general audience. That's a road which we're gradually moving down. I think we all have to hope that we don't go too far down it because in the end it emasculates any kind of creativity. Had all programmes been research-led you wouldn't have got a programme like *Monty Python's Flying Circus* because it broke the boundaries, it stretched people's imagination and credibility. It ventured into new ground and broadcasters have to be allowed to do that.
>
> (Steven Barnett)

So far in Britain this kind of market research has had little impact on programme making. But such work can be of great value to programme planners and policy makers. It can tell us what kind of media people like. It has recently confirmed strong support for Channel 4 and public service broadcasting.

Classroom strategies

> The adolescent stage is one of the prime targets for a lot of the media. It is such a part of their lives, such a part of growing up that their conversations are influenced by it. When they come to school they talk about what they've seen, what they've watched, what they're reading and I think they suddenly realise that it is affecting them and therefore it is something that they must be aware of and must be able to comment on. I think we ought to go further than just giving a glib opinion about aspects of the media like 'That was good', 'That was bad'.
>
> (Mark Prowse)

Whatever changes happen in the media, understanding how audiences are monitored and how they sometimes behave in surprising ways is very important. This chapter has suggested that we can learn a great deal about audiences from both formal research and from students. The all-important link between abstract audiences and real people can be made in the classroom by getting students to track their own media usage and their families'. Whatever limitations we might be working under in the classroom, such activity is bound at least to raise some basic questions about methods of enquiry.

Studying audiences in the classroom should go beyond thinking about audiences as victims or dupes and should insist on the vitality of audiences as part of the very media institutions under examination. We should take note of the balanced and persuasive views about the effects of media on audiences and particularly on young people which we have encountered in the research examined here. (We shall return to this topic in Chapters 4 and 5.)

> We don't need to be so worried about our children gawping at the television as we might think if we know that far from gawping they're often playing around and not paying much attention to it and are perfectly capable of discriminating between programmes. We don't need to worry too much about people not reading books or not being stimulated in traditional ways because they are watching television, when evidence comes up from the people themselves that they go out and buy books as a result of seeing television and in fact most of their conversations are often prompted by television itself. So in these ways this slightly finer mesh which tells you about how audiences respond does something to sweep away the stereotypes and the myths which abound on both right and left about what television does – the myth that it has no effect whatsoever and the myth that it has an enormous effect. The truth is far more complicated ... and it's a sort of truth which needs to be taken into account by governments and others as they plan the television of the future.
>
> (Laurie Taylor)

We must acknowledge the evident pleasures which the media offer their audiences, as well as being aware of the dangers. That means having a lively interest in understanding how audiences work as part of media institutions.

> I think we've got to try and help them to develop a sense of inquiry into what they're watching, what they're reading, what they're listening to. What is it that they get pleasure out of watching? Why do they prefer one programme rather than another?
>
> (Mark Prowse)

This process must begin with experiencing the pleasures of the media and extending them across a wide range of texts. Understanding the media should ultimately develop both the understanding of pleasure and the pleasure of understanding.

TEACHING IDEA 1: MEDIA TRACKING

Aim

To find out what media people use in the course of a single day. (The questions below are based on research carried out amongst secondary school students for this book.)

Time

At least two double lessons. Between the two lessons, students need time to collect and examine their data. It could also be treated as a longer project, especially if parents or friends are involved.

Materials

Some means of recording information given by respondents (perhaps including tape recorders); *Radio/TV Times* or other programme listings to prompt respondents.

Method

• Explain to students purpose of exercise. You will be looking at the data together after collection. It would also be useful to discuss what they expect they will find out so that they can compare their predictions with what they actually establish.
• Devise a standard schedule of questions as a basis for individual interviews. For example:
  1 Which is your favourite medium? (*see prompt question below*)
  2 What do you particularly like about it?
  3 Which others do you like?
  4 What do you particularly like about them?
  5 Follow-up questions . . .
  6 What did you learn about the media from your survey of your own media habits?

Prompt question:
If you had to do without all of these *except one* for a whole year, which one would you choose to keep?

Personal stereo	Video recorder	Television
Radio	Cinema	Records
Comics	Newspapers	Magazines
Theatre		

- Students should carry out interviews in pairs, having rehearsed their approach and with clear allocation of recording and interviewing roles.
- Share and discuss findings. Do any common patterns emerge? Are there any unusual variations? What problems were there in collecting data? How could enquiry methods be improved for this exercise?

Further work

Students might track their parents' or friends' daily media use at home. Compare with such detailed surveys as *Daily Life in the 1980s* (BBC Broadcasting Research Department 1984), Sean Day-Lewis's *One Day in the Life of Television* (1989) and other audience research referred to in Chapter 2 of this book. Consider the uses to which such data are put.

Try out different methods of observing viewers watching television. Methods might include live observation, video recording (as in the experiments referred to in Chapter 2 of this book) and audio recording with a microphone fed into a long-play videotape. The following issues will need to be considered:

- Differences between reported viewing and actual viewing.
- Differences between different observational methods.
- Differences between different levels of viewing attention.
- Problems of coding viewing behaviour (e.g. leaving room, doing something else at the same time, talking about programme content or other interactions unrelated to the programmes).

TEACHING IDEA 2: PREDICTING AND REFLECTING

Aim

To explore differences between different readings of the same newspaper article. Students should realise the differences between their first and later readings and between their own readings and those of other students.

Materials

Enough photocopies of a recent newspaper article which includes a headline, photograph and caption (more than one article if you wish).

Time

One double lesson.

Method

- Show students the photograph on its own. Ask them to identify its contents and predict what the story is likely to be about. Repeat the process with the caption and then the headline added. Finally, add the first paragraph of the report and ask once more for predictions about the rest of the story. At each stage, students should write down their predictions individually.
- Compare predictions made by students and relate them to elements in the text. You might draw attention to any dominant or surprising patterns of prediction which emerge (relate these to the Hall scheme referred to on pp. 81–3 of this book).
- Ask students to read the whole article, jotting down quick reactions and comments as they do so.
- Students should use their jottings to make more careful notes under the following headings: 'WHAT I WAS EXPECTED TO KNOW/THINK/FEEL before reading it' and 'WHAT I NOW KNOW/THINK/FEEL having read it.'
- Share and discuss findings. How do final readings compare with initial ones? What does this say about meaning-making? What common patterns emerge? Are there any unusual variations? What does this exercise tell us about the interactions which go on between readers and texts?

Further work

Experiment with changes of structure, vocabulary or presentation in texts to see what changes these produce in the responses of readers.

TEACHING IDEA 3: RADIO LISTENING

Aim

To find out more about what people listen to on the radio, why they like certain programmes and the circumstances in which they listen.

Time

Several double lessons. This work should only be attempted after the class has been familiarised with national and local radio listening patterns and the methods by which quantitative information is collected.

Materials

Radio schedules from local and national radio stations. (See *Radio/TV Times* and local newspapers.) Flip charts, poster equipment, OHP, graph paper, etc.

Method

- Students should decide what information they want to find out about radio listening habits and who they want to find out about.
- Brainstorm as many methods as possible which could be used for collecting information on listening habits and preferences. Discuss with the class the value and problems of different approaches.
- Questions should include listener reactions (how much people enjoy particular programmes or programme segments) and mode of listening (what are audiences doing when they listen to the radio?). Students should also try to find out if people stay with one service or switch stations as TV audiences do. If not, what stops them? Are there any differences here between listening in the car and listening at home?
- Students should then prepare a comparative chart which shows what each radio service is broadcasting throughout the day. This is for ease of reference and memory-jogging when it comes to reporting the findings. (BBC Audience Research might be persuaded to give you a blank copy of one of their forms.)
- The results of the survey should be presented in the most appropriate manner using graphs, charts and pieces of writing. Some interviewing teams might like to present their findings to the rest of the class using OHP equipment and flip charts.

Further work

Students might like to assemble a small group of listeners to discuss one specific programme or feature in detail (e.g. *Our Tune*, Radio 1, Simon Bates programme), along the lines suggested by Laurie Taylor (p. 65 above).

TEACHING IDEA 4: READING NEWSPAPERS

Aim

To find out how people read newspapers and what features about them they enjoy most.

Time

Several double lessons. This work should only be attempted after students have been familiarised with the methods of audience measurement in the newspaper industry and the kinds of information it offers.

Materials

A range of popular and broadsheet newspapers. Graph paper, poster making materials, markers, flip charts, OHP.

Method

- In order to prepare a survey the class and teacher should discuss together how to split the newspapers into easily identifiable sections so that respondents' practices can easily be codified (e.g. sport, news, features, show business, the arts, reviews, etc.).
- Brainstom as many methods as possible which could be used for collecting information on reading practices. Discuss with the class the value and problems of different approaches.
- When the class has agreed an overall strategy, students should split into interviewing teams to work out what kind of information they wish to find out and from whom. Methods might be designed to find out the most popular elements of a newspaper or a series of papers or which sections are read first. Equally, students may want to find out in what circumstances a paper is read (e.g. at breakfast, during a tea break, on the way to work, etc.) and for what period of time. It would also be interesting to find out how many people share the reading of one particular newspaper (the difference between sales/circulation and readership).
- Results of the survey should be written up using graphs, charts, pieces of writing (and OHPs if some of the teams want to present their findings to the rest of the class).
- Discussion should follow on the role of newspapers in an age where electronic information always has the news first.

Further work

There is little work on newspaper reading practices in Britain, but Bogart's *Press and Public* (1989) provides some fascinating insights into how newspapers are read in America. The book suggests all sorts of questions which could be explored with students.

Chapter 3

The formation of facts

We are surrounded by facts. As social beings, we seek them, exchange
them, check them and act upon them. We are all reporters and we handle
large amounts of data in a systematic way. Yet we also rely on second-hand
messages about the world beyond our social experience. These messages
do not come to us innocently. The facts they report are not merely random
fragments which we capture and store. They come to us in patterns which
are largely defined and packaged for us by the mass media.

In this chapter, we show how facts are filtered through the media, across
a range of forms from chat-shows to news, on television and in the press.
We look at where information comes from, how it gets circulated and at
the role of professional public relations agencies. We examine such
concepts as newsworthiness and impartiality and we explore some of the
main constraints on the 'formation of facts' like ownership, the lobby
system and journalistic practices. Finally, we ask what sort of future there
will be for reporting if the trend for personalising issues continues.

We focus on these essential questions:

- How do the processes of selection and editing affect the way 'facts' are
  reported by the media?
- What is the role of public relations agencies?
- How does broadcasting represent the world?
- How does the press represent the world?
- How is news managed by politicians?
- What determines newsworthiness?
- How do the media deal with 'soft' news and personal issues?

REPRODUCING REALITY

The National Curriculum for English places great stress on the need for
students to distinguish between facts and opinions. This concern seems to
derive from a model of media texts as inherently deceptive and manipulative (see Chapter 4 for discussion of this issue in relation to fiction). It

appears particularly in the Statements of Attainment for Attainment Target 1 (Speaking and Listening) and 2 (Reading).

ATTAINMENT TARGET 2 [READING], LEVELS 5–10

Pupils should be able to . . .

(5c) show in discussion that they can recognise whether subject-matter in non-literary and media texts is presented as fact or opinion . . .

(6c) show in discussion and in writing that they can recognise whether subject-matter in non-literary and media texts is presented as fact or opinion, identifying some of the ways in which the distinction can be made . . .

(7c) show in discussion that they can recognise features of presentation which are used to inform, to regulate, to reassure or to persuade, in non-literary and media texts . . .

(8c) show in discussion and in writing an ability to form a considered opinion about features of presentation which are used to inform, reassure or persuade in non-literary and media texts . . .

(9c) show in discussion and in writing an ability to recognise techniques and conventions of presentation in non-literary and media texts, and judge the effectiveness of their use . . .

(10c) show in discussion and in writing an ability to evaluate techniques and conventions of presentation in non-literary and media texts, and judge the effectiveness of their use . . .

(10d) select, retrieve, evaluate and combine information independently and with discrimination, from a comprehensive range of reference materials, making effective and sustained use of the information.

(DES 1990b: 3–11)

Fact and fiction

According to this simple view, facts are things which have happened and fiction is something which has been made (up). Facts are 'out there' waiting to be reported and reflected on. But this distinction is hard to sustain if we start asking some basic questions:

● when does an event become a fact?
● can facts exist in isolation?
● do facts make sense without any context?
● which facts have been selected?
● which facts have been ignored?

All media texts depend in some way on predetermined scripts, whether they are formalised on the page or only floating in producers' heads. But the dependence of different media forms on scripts varies. In fact, we can think of the apparent opposites of fact and fiction as existing on a continuum which embraces *all* media forms. At one extreme is news, at the other, drama. Most documentaries are pre-scripted to the extent that they use fictional techniques of presentation to dramatise factual information. Even when this is not so, documentary makers inevitably approach their subjects with their own agendas and structures, even though they might be unaware of them. Advertising is a highly pre-scripted form but because it also claims to be 'reporting' and offering information about products and services, it also has some of the surface features of documentary (see Chapter 5 on advertising).

Figure 3.1   Pre-scripting reality

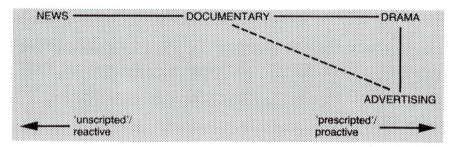

In the arrangement of the image, in the reshooting, in the intervention of the director and the cameraman ... [images] have to speak and to emphasise an aspect of that reality which is claimed to be significant.

(Silverstone 1985: 77)

The media go to great lengths to distinguish factual information from opinion. They also use all sorts of familiar codes to signal when they are dealing with facts. On television, features like Standard English speech, smart clothing and electronic office hardware all assert that we are in the presence of responsible and reliable reporting rather than the realms of fiction or political propaganda.

Selectivity

II There is no fraudulence here. .... It cannot be otherwise.

(Silverstone 1985: 77)

Selectivity and editing are inherent in any act of perception or narration. This can be easily demonstrated by listening to how people describe things or relate events. Their personalities, interests and immediate contexts play a large part in determining what is left out, what is put in and how it is ordered. But when the media report information something else is also happening. There are additional levels of editing which are not directly dependent on the personal views and contexts of reporters. Written journalism often shows traces of the way personality is stamped on stories and newspapers have acknowledged political stances which are usually shared by their readers. Indeed, the politics of newspapers remain a very significant factor in readers' purchasing decisions.

'The Battle of Osgrove'

How can these issues be explored with students? One way is through simulations. Andrew Goodwin's 'Battle of Osgrove' exercise (Goodwin 1988) is a reworking of the 'Battle for Orgreave' during the Coal Dispute in 1984 (Masterman 1984: 99–109). It explores how facts are adapted or discarded to suit the political persuasions of reporters, editors and the papers they work for. The exercise is reproduced as Teaching Idea 1, pp. 110–113 below.

Sarah Hammett used the simulation with a class of second-year sixth-form students on an A-level Communication Studies course at Totton College in Southampton.

Lessons learnt

‖ I think there's no reason why one shouldn't exaggerate in order to make ‖ a point. It's a fundamental technique of teaching.

(Sarah Hammett)

The lesson showed that students were able to use political positions as a filter for the stories they edited. The persuasions of the different papers showed through clearly. The students were also able to point to textual elements in other groups' reports which showed their political positions. They obviously understood what they were supposed to be doing during the simulation, enjoyed doing it and responded well to the pressure of strict deadlines and new information feeds. It was a highly participatory and practical lesson in which the students produced tightly written and carefully thought-out material. Their comments on their own work and that of other groups showed understanding of the editorial processes involved. It was a very useful way of rehearsing, revising and putting into practice concepts with which they were familiar from earlier in their course.

Problems

The lesson raised a number of problems which were apparently encouraged by the simulation. Such simulations are always limited: they tend to oversimplify and exaggerate for the sake of clarity. They can never reproduce the real conditions in which reporting occurs. Students are not professional journalists and can only follow limited stereotyped models of how journalists think and work. There is a danger that this approach to facts can encourage cavalier decisions which are even more irresponsible than the worst excesses of tabloid reporting. There is also a danger that reporting comes to be seen as a conspiracy to deceive.

Subjectivity and objectivity

But there was a more basic problem related to the 'facts versus opinions' distinction. The 'Osgrove' simulation allows students to construct a crude contrast between an objective world of events in which things happen and a subjective world of interpretation through which events are filtered. During the lesson, one of the students contrasted 'what actually happened' with 'the imagination of the reporter'. This dualism is based on a naïve view of the media as distorting agents which introduce bias into reporting. It implies that there is a possibility of unbiased reporting to which the media should aspire. It suggests that in a more honest world political positions could somehow be sidelined so that they do not cause irresponsible reporting. Some students claimed that they were 'trying to make it . . . as unbiased as possible'. They did not recognise that the media are selective in a way which is different from subjectivity. In doing so, they seemed unable to distinguish between fairness, balance, honesty, accuracy, impartiality, objectivity and truth.

A simulation sequence

Figure 3.2   Simulation instruction sheet for the 'Battle of Osgrove'

You are working as a pair/team of sub-editors for a newspaper covering the events at the 'Battle of Osgrove'. This news event concerns the long and bitter national dispute between steel workers and the Government-owned National Steel Board, which began six months ago, when the Government announced the closure of the Osgrove site. Due to what is perceived as 'picket-line violence', in clashes between police and pickets the story has been covered widely throughout the national news media as one that raises new issues of 'law and order'.

This particular story takes place on a day when a mass picket has been organised by the National Union of Steel Workers (NUSW) outside the Osgrove Steel Works, near Birmingham. It concerns an incident which involves the arrest of NUSW leader Albert Jones and his allegations that he was attacked by police.

You will be asked to edit copy submitted by your reporters in the field, from the point of view of your publication. You must also devise a headline for the piece.

Source: Goodwin 1988: 16

The students were given 20 minutes as an absolute deadline for completing their copy. Each group was given the Simulation Instruction Sheet. They were not told to write for a specific audience (as in the original material) but simply for a national daily newspaper. They did not know that they would receive subsequent information, except as indicated in the Instruction Sheet.

Reporter A's 2.35 p.m. report and Reporter B's 3.15 p.m. material were then given to them.

Ten minutes later and with only 10 more minutes of writing time left, Reporter B's 4.30 p.m. and Reporter A's 5.00 p.m. reports were fed in.

Seven minutes later, Reporter A's 6.00 p.m. report was dumped on them and their deadline was extended by another 15 minutes.

Finally, the students were asked to choose a newspaper and rewrite their piece to suit its particular audience.

They read their reports aloud and commented both on each other's writing and on the exercise itself.

Facts and opinions

You may use only the information supplied by your reporters. So you are people working at base, in a newspaper office, and you're getting information sent to you by reporters who are on the scene. And you will know no more about it than you are getting in your bits of paper that I'm going to send round to you. And the idea is that you are constructing a story from the information that you've been given.

(Sarah Hammett)

We're trying to make it generally as unbiased as possible, but it's fairly difficult because we've got two reports so far and they're both very biased in either direction. So we've got to try, without being too vague, to make it appropriate to use as a story. We've got to still keep quite a few of the facts in without getting off the fence.

We're trying to steer away from the graphic details and whittle it down to the facts because some of the language in here is quite violent and we just want to see what actually happened rather than . . . in the imagination of the reporter.

We've been given a trade union paper. So what we've got to do is sort out the information and write it so that it's sympathetic towards the trade unionists rather than the police or anything like that. So instead of saying that some of the papers like the Tory press will be saying that three policeman were seriously injured, we'll be saying that pickets were arrested and some of them were seriously injured. We're leading on the fact that 75 pickets were arrested and 20 were injured, some of them seriously, when a demonstration took place.

(Students at Totton Sixth Form College)

Whatever your audience, they don't want lies. This is a serious story for a serious newspaper presumably. So there's a fine dividing line and it's the one you're finding between selecting the information that seems to you to be most important, and sorting out the information, the fact, the opinion, and what people say and how they contradict one another. And, at the same time, trying to present your audience with the kind of thing that you think they will expect to read, that is a description of the events that have been taking place.

(Sarah Hammett)

Representing reality

Selection and editing occur in every form of reportage. For example, photographs may seem innocent enough but are most suspect precisely at the point where they make their strongest claim to 'capture' or document rather than recreate reality. When words and pictures are combined as *news photos* (often with accompanying captions) there is a powerful conjunction of two systems of selection. The French critic Roland Barthes argued that 'pictures ... are more imperative than writing, they impose meaning at one stroke without analysing or diluting it' (Barthes 1973: 110). But that meaning comes from a series of practical and professional actions at various stages of production. The decisions made (consciously or unconsciously) affect the final outcome at every level of the process.

> **LEVELS OF SELECTION IN NEWS PHOTOGRAPHS**
>
> - *Technical*: constraints are imposed by the technical features of cameras and film (e.g. film speed, light levels, lens range).
> - *Formal*: codes derived from normal ways of seeing enable readers to recognize objects from their everyday world. These codes are basically rules of equivalence which allow us, for example, to represent a three-dimensional image as two-dimensional. They also allow translations of colour, size and contrast.
> - *Composition*: space within photographs is arranged according to artistic/photographic conventions. These determine how foreground and background, centre and margins interact, what different degrees of focus, different camera angles and size of shot mean.

Figure 3.3 What the papers see: the challenge to Mrs Thatcher

How are the meanings of these news photographs determined?
How do the different applications of the codes of selection affect their significance?
Source: The *Guardian*, Nov. 19, 1990

- *Expression*: gestures, expressions and relationships between elements within photographs are interpreted according to variable cultural codes.
- *News value*: people or places within photographs are recognized as *particular* ones already known to readers. A closing down of the range of possible meanings occurs at this level because of the specific identifications made.
- *Frame manipulations*: the processes of cropping, retouching, enlarging all give emphasis to particular readings which have a privileged status because of their news value.
- *Page integration*: codes of sequence and page lay-out place the photograph according to the relative importance assigned to the story it refers to.
- *Anchorage*: captions and headlines are added which finally 'fix' the preferred readings of the photograph.

The first four levels of selection occur in the production of any still photograph. They depend on the competence and skill of the photographer. But at the fifth level, the whole apparatus of news production becomes crucial, for here the routine practices, assumptions and professional judgements of designers and editors come into play.

(Hall 1981: 56–64)

Once we recognise that all media processes are inevitably selective, we can shift our focus towards *how* they select and *with what consequences*. A key concept here is *representation*. It is a difficult concept but it is worth untangling its different senses. Richard Dyer has explained four of the main ones for us:

REPRESENTATION

- A selective *re-presentation* of reality.
  This is obvious in newspapers, where the form is completely different from the events reported, but less so in television serials, which often succeed in creating the illusion of a transparent window on a world which has a similar time-frame and rhythm to our own.
- A typical or *representative* version of reality.
  Media often use stereotypes to typify particular social groups as a form of shorthand. How do the media represent, say, gender or race?
- The process of speaking on behalf of or as *representative* of a particular position.
  Whose views are being put forward in particular messages? Whose voices are being heard?

- The meanings which media messages *represent* for audiences. What do readers bring to messages which affects how they interpret them? What actual sense is made when particular messages are understood?

                                              (Lusted and Drummond 1985: 44)

All media *represent* the world in these ways. In reporting on the world, they make particular, recurrent senses of it.

Opinion formation

Facts are not only the raw material of news reports. They are also central to everyday talk and many forms of public information. Television chat-shows offer a form of 'soft' news which is sometimes thought of in a derogatory way as 'gossip'. They also provide opportunities for publicists and celebrities to promote particular events in an apparently casual and informative way. The provision of information for such outlets has itself become an industry.

> There are in London countless public relations agencies that are forever feeding you with information . . . I have an in-tray that fills up with 40 or 50 or 60 pieces of paper a day telling me that this particular client or that particular client is terribly interesting because . . . and is going to be in the news that week.

                                              (Peter Estall)

Although television producers and editors often emphasise their resistance to publicity bombardment, there is constant pressure to give space and time to personalities and events which are the subject of publicity campaigns. The question then arises of how far such exposure sets the agenda for public discourse.

PUBLIC RELATIONS

> Public relations practice is the deliberate, planned and sustained effort to establish and maintain mutual understanding communications between an organisation and its public.

                                              (Jefkins 1985: 24)

Who uses PR?

Pressure groups, charities, corporations and governments are turning increasingly to public relations firms and advisers for help in presenting information. Almost all human activity is affected by public relations. In 1987/8 about £900 million per annum was spent on public relations in Britain. Government spending through the Central Office of Information accounted for almost £100 million, nearly five times the amount spent five years earlier. With spending on government information campaigns reaching these record levels there is much debate about what constitutes government information as opposed to party propaganda. For instance, critics of the Conservative Government's water privatisation campaign claimed that public money was being misused to promote the water industry, prior to selling it off.

PR consultancies

Many organisations employ their own public relations personnel. But as social and economic issues become more complex, public relations firms have emerged who specialise in areas such as media relations, finance, community relations, marketing, government relations, employee relations and international relations. Also it is now commonplace for advertising agency conglomerates like Saatchi and Saatchi and WPP Group to offer a public relations consultancy along with their advertising services.

Why do people use public relations?

How do companies and organisations create a favourable public image? Using advertising is one way but the most effective image creation happens when the information comes from apparently trustworthy sources such as journalistic features and articles. Consequently, the media receive a plethora of inducements to write or broadcast favourable copy or to get a particular author or personality on to a chat-show. The launch of a new car may well be held abroad with the option of a few days' free holiday for correspondents. Financial and legal journalists could be invited to visit a company's headquarters for a few days in Chicago or Milan, all expenses paid. Nothing is directly demanded for these services but it makes it difficult for journalists to write in a critical manner after receiving generous hospitality.

Advocacy

Those working in public relations see themselves as 'lay advocates'. As specialist communicators, they assess their clients' needs and formulate a public relations strategy with the aim of reinforcing or, in some cases, changing, perceptions about an organisation or group. They are keen to stress that for public relations to be effective, communication has to fulfil certain criteria. Anything else, they say, is propaganda.

PR campaign criteria

- It must have a concern for the truth.
- It must show a concern for the public interest.
- A genuine dialogue must take place.

> You cannot in the long term – by any form of suppression, censorship, emphasis or so-called news management – you cannot in the end distort the picture. The public will find you out.
>
> (Tim Traverse-Healy)

Public scrutiny

PR people present their role as a reasonable and responsible one. It is seen as simply highlighting positive aspects of a particular event or performance and minimising negative aspects. According to this view, public understanding of the truth is safeguarded because they can refer to other sources of information. Having a wide range of other sources of information allows the public to evaluate claims made by professionals. But does the public always have access to these other sources? Are there actually enough easily available alternative sources for the public to be reassured that they are not being deceived? Are the public adequately equipped to make such judgements? Do they sometimes even know when a public relations operation is in progress?

Crisis management

What concerns critics of 'the public will find you out' theory is how long the discovering might take. For many companies, the short term is the most pressing issue. Disasters like the Piper Alpha explosion, the Townsend Thoreson sinking and the Clapham train crash have all caused great public concern. The companies involved naturally tried to limit the damage to their public image. Michael Regester specialises in training companies how to handle the media in the context of such crises (Regester 1987). He emphasises that it is too late to think about public communication after the event. Managements need policies, procedures and training programmes which as far as possible prevent disasters. It is again a matter of performance rather than publicity. But when disasters do happen, it is vital to act fast. The public impression depends on what information is released, how soon and to whom. So a company's crisis management plan becomes a kind of corporate fire drill on what to do in a disaster.

> Our advice to companies that we work with is that they should tell it all, tell it fast and tell it truthfully because the truth will out in the end . . . We're not in the business of papering over the cracks. If we can see very

clearly that the company is vulnerable in some way or another, then our first piece of advice is that you've got to get your house in order.

(Michael Regester)

Two disasters

When the North Sea oil rig Piper Alpha caught fire in 1988 its owners Occidental Oil were so efficient in their crisis management that, in the view of Michael Regester, they came over as an efficient and caring company. He contrasts that with the poor showing by P & O when their ferry, *The Spirit of Free Enterprise*, capsized at Zeebrugge. According to Regester, P & O's crisis management was poor because staff were not briefed on how to cope with the inevitable media attention and top

Figure 3.4 The NASA syndrome

NASA officials, fearful that they could not otherwise obtain congressional funding, mounted an energetic public relations campaign that depicted the shuttle as all things to all people. The agency promised that the shuttle would lift scientific payloads into orbit, provide the Pentagon with access to the 'high ground' of space, and offer an efficient, economical means of launching communications satellites which could turn a profit into a bargain.

Faced with spiralling costs and ever-lengthening delays, NASA cut back its training programme, cannibalized parts from other spacecraft and deferred the spending of half a billion dollars on safety. There was an increasingly wide gap between the facts and the shuttle's glowing image. NASA officials increasingly chose to believe in the image, which, in turn, drifted ever further from reality. The odds of a fatal shuttle crash were variously estimated at one in a hundred to one in a hundred thousand; the *Challenger* mission, the programme's 25th, proved that these odds had been estimated too high.

The justification for NASA's trust in its flawed spacecraft was reduced to the fact that it hadn't blown up yet. As at Chernobyl, the accumulation of an impressive safety record in the past came to be taken as a guarantee that nothing could go wrong in the future.

'The argument that the same risk was flown before without failure is often accepted as an argument for the safety of accepting it again', noted Richard Feynman the Nobel Prize-winning physicist who served on the presidential commission. But, Feynman added, 'when playing Russian roulette, the fact that the first shot got off safely is little comfort for the next'.

It was Feynman who cut through reams of bureaucracy on the O-ring question (which caused the space shuttle failure) by simply immersing a piece of O-ring material in a bucket of iced water during a break in the committee hearings and noting that it grew brittle. The trouble with NASA's belief in its own press clippings, Feynman said, was that nature had not read them. 'Reality must take precedence over public relations', he concluded, 'for nature cannot be fooled'.

Source: Regester 1987: 143–4

management appeared remote and unconcerned. In the short term, Occidental Oil benefited from their efficient public relations, yet at a public enquiry some months later it was revealed that the company had a very poor safety record on the rig. It took longer for the truth to emerge at the North American Space Agency (Figure 3.4).

BROADCASTING

Impartiality

It often takes a disaster to expose the gap between public image and reality. Broadcasting in Britain has regularly played a decisive role in investigating and publicising these differences. Traditionally broadcasting has expressed no editorial opinion but does that mean it is genuinely impartial? ITV is required by the Television Act of 1954 to observe 'due impartiality on . . . matters of political or industrial controversy or relating to current public policy'. The BBC's Charter lays down no such conditions. Instead the BBC adheres to what it calls a kind of unpublished appendix to the Charter and Licence written by the Home Office which requires the BBC to 'refrain from expressing its own opinion on current affairs or on matters of public policy'. BBC policy is also constantly being updated by the News and Current Affairs Index, an internal memorandum which reflects the latest management guidelines on contentious issues.

It seems to me that at a time when the BBC has been pronounced the cornerstone of public service broadcasting, we should regard impartiality as a positive cornerstone of our journalism.   (Redfern 1988: 10)

> **JOURNALISTIC IDEALS**
> - *Balance*: the equal representation of a diverse range of views – sometimes over a series as well as in single programmes.
> - *Fairness*: the proper representation of opinions presented by those most competent to deliver them. IBA/ITC guidelines suggest including a fair representation of the views of those who have chosen not to participate in a programme.
> - *Accuracy*: ensuring that all relevant facts are not suppressed or concealed in any way.

But journalists and programme producers still have to make selective judgements about a range of complex information. Broadcasters argue that it is possible to put aside personal views in order to achieve impartiality in programmes. However, such confident assertions need careful examination.

> The notion of cultural neutrality itself is only workable as an ideal, but in practice it can never be achieved. The very process of cultural selection means that the news is not a mirror image of reality.
>
> (GUMG 1976: 10)

Glasgow University Media Group

In the mid-1970s the Glasgow Media Group carried out a large-scale study of television news. The group suggested that the way television news stories are selected, presented and edited tends to favour those in power. For example, in the reporting of industrial disputes, they claimed that the labour side is looked to for 'events' such as picket lines, demonstrations and mass meetings. On the other hand the management, who often emerge only to make statements, are seen to provide 'facts'. Although, in the pursuit of balance, both sides have been represented the group argued that photogenically the workers often appeared as the source of the discord.

A pro-establishment conspiracy?

Some people saw the Glasgow Media Group's findings as evidence of a conspiracy amongst television journalists to promote pro-establishment views and many broadcasters reacted angrily to having their professional practices called into question.

> As a description of what's on the screen the Glasgow Media Group's work is still the most detailed and thorough work we have ... The problem comes in their explanation of why the things that they've described are like they are ... because they weren't able to do detailed studies of news production they do slip into a kind of quasi-conspiracy explanation. A lot of explanations of news assume that the journalists have some kind of intention to deceive or to present material in a biased way. That isn't the case. What you see on the screen is really the product of a set of routines for getting hold of information and processing it quickly. The problem is the nature of those routines. If you're under a lot of pressure of time, for example, it's a lot easier if you've got a press release that's very nicely prepared that you can just slot in. And that's the primary problem: it's the unequal way in which different news sources present the material and so it's sometimes very difficult for journalists to get a good quote quickly enough from an alternative position. So it's really the way in which the whole system's organised and the pressures of time.
>
> (Graham Murdock)

Despite the controversy surrounding the findings of the Glasgow Media Group it is arguable that their critique caused some broadcasters to review their news production practices.

Consensus

Broadcast journalists work according to a set of professional practices in producing the news. The foremost of these involves consultation with a wide range of 'reliable' sources. But there are always more sources available than are actually used. So they have to be selective and the main criterion for this is newsworthiness. This process of selection controls, amongst other things, which sources are used, how much weight and credibility they are given and how the information is presented. Journalists draw upon a framework of values through which the world is interpreted. But they do not work in isolation. In order to gain attention, stories are presented within the context of the existing values of audiences. So out of the millions of events which happen every day, news items emerge which build on what is already known and which explain the world in a familiar and recognisable way. Where audience knowledge is limited, complex issues are often simplified to provide a ready-made moral framework. Thus, the drug issue is presented as a struggle between the corruptors (pushers) and the corrupted (addicts) with little discussion of society's responsibilities. This process, which journalists see as helping understanding, actually serves to reinforce prevailing beliefs. It creates an implicit consensus which means that the world tends to be depicted as a place where, in the long run, merit is rewarded and villains get their just deserts. This ethical framework:

- reinforces stereotypes.
- provides simple answers to complex problems.
- rarely questions the values of the system.

Working within such a consensus creates a bias of omission because ideas from outside the framework are rarely addressed. And to complicate matters, there are more voices clamouring to be heard.

A new pluralism?

> Post-war British society had accepted a definition of itself as balanced ... Now in the 80s, groups organised around ideas or moral positions compete much more fiercely for full or partial hegemony over civil society than they did in the past.
>
> (Redfern 1988: 54)

New means of distribution (by cable, video and satellite) and new legislation are causing radical changes in the established patterns of broadcasting. But do more broadcast outlets lead to a greater diversity of views being expressed? There is evidence to suggest that the range of opinion available on the airwaves is actually becoming narrower.

When broadcasters do attempt to reflect the complexities of society, authority often tries to restrict them. Programmes which have asked searching questions about the security forces, like Thames TV's *Death on the Rock*, are subjected to official vilification. The BBC was accused of anti-American bias after its reporting of the American bombing of Libya was subjected to intense scrutiny by government ministers. Sinn Fein and other banned organisations were prevented by law from speaking directly on radio and television despite the fact that their statements could be reported in print. At the same time both ITV and the BBC have been weakened by market pressures.

The proliferation of broadcasting outlets means that audiences become fragmented, individual factual programmes command less attention and their budgets are subsequently reduced. Such conditions make broadcasting more susceptible to government influence and ideological control

Figure 3.5 Transcript of illegal broadcast by Radio Arthur during the 1984–6 miners' strike

B: It is not the normal practice of this radio station to read extracts from newspapers, but this particular article has a special significance and highlights the real dangers of privatization, which are to smash trade union power, to make the work force totally subservient, and to close down and asset-strip any section of the industry that does not show enough short-term profits. The article is from the *Times* newspaper . . .

[*Reading of newspaper clip relating to a cabinet sub-committee discussing 'private investment' possibilities for the NCB*]

B: So there you are . . . And that's from the *Times* newspaper. This could well be the economic fate of the Nottingham-shire coal pits – wholesale destruction of the industry. You have been warned! Join the strike now, and help to fight against privatization.

[*More music . . .*]

B: This government is committed to destroying the NUM at any cost and, according to the City of London analyst Phillips Andrew, has spent £15 million a week so far. Truly amazing. Millions of pounds spent on smashing a trade union, while doctors turn away sick people from hospitals and, in some cases, send them home to die in misery for lack of money for the health service. I wouldn't trust these Tories to run a public lavatory.

[*Glory, Glory Hallelujah . . .*]

B: . . We were very pleased to see our brothers from Corton Wood in Nottingham on Thursday August 23. The men from Corton Wood are marching to the TUC Conference in Brighton. We wish them well and Godspeed.

[*Welsh Choir*]

B: . . . To the Nottingham working miners I say this. If you want to save your pits, don't believe the lies that the Coal Board tells you. Don't believe the renegade strike-breakers. Don't be fooled by what you see or hear on the media. Listen to what your union tells you. We care about the mining industry, jobs, the future . . . And now is the time for you to join the strike!

[*Glory, Glory Hallelujah again, building to 'His truth is marching onnnNNN!'*]

Source: Hind and Mosco 1985: 41–3

by individual owners. Broadcasters' traditional aims of achieving balance and impartiality become increasingly difficult. Indeed, there are many people who feel that the new forms of broadcasting should be allowed to present material in as partisan a way as they wish.

THE PRESS

Ownership and control

The ideas expressed in particular newspapers are bound to relate to their basic economic interests. But ownership potentially involves more specific forms of economic control. It allows owners privileged access to public discourse. Such access means opportunities for political or commercial exploitation. It is sometimes argued that this is not a serious problem because readers are aware of such vested interests and therefore do not expect the level of impartiality which they attribute to television and radio. But the ever-increasing costs of starting up a newspaper make it very difficult to enter the market. *The Independent* needed £18 million initial funding and Maxwell's weekly *European* around £25 million. When ownership becomes concentrated into fewer and fewer hands, this can mean less diversity of opinion.

> It's extremely expensive now to start a national paper and although it's possible, as the case of *The Independent* has shown, certain parts of the market like the popular end are extremely difficult to penetrate. You not only need a lot of money to start up a paper, you need a lot of money to keep it in play while you build an audience. What people worry about is the political power. That is because newspapers are private property, and a proprietor has the absolute right to hire and fire whoever they wish working on the newspaper. They obviously have the ability, if they choose to, to use the newspaper as a vehicle for their particular political positions. And since most of these proprietors are both rich and fairly conservative the kind of political positions they adopt are not entirely representative of the full spectrum.
>
> (Graham Murdock)

There are also many other factors which affect the way newspapers report what is happening in the world and the opinions they express (like routine journalistic practices, legal constraints and government restrictions). But it is not easy to unravel how these different factors interact with each other. The relationship between media content and economic interests is complex, dynamic and constantly shifting.

Figure 3.6 Media ownership, 1990

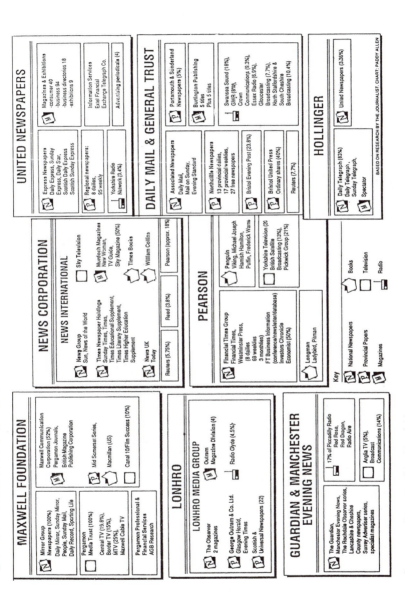

Source: Reprinted in *Hard News*

Concentration and diversification

Two general features are clear:

- Ownership of the British press is concentrated in the hands of a very few proprietors.
- Newspapers are part of larger conglomerates or associations of companies with a wide range of other financial interests.

These features mean that newspapers are subject to the basic need to be profitable in the long term, like any other commercial enterprise. If they do not sell enough copies at the right price, they will not be financially viable. But does this mean that what they print is controlled in the short term by the same profit motives? Does *The Times Educational Supplement* bear the ideological imprint of Rupert Murdoch in the same way as the *Sun*? The fact that it does not is because there are limits to what readers will tolerate.

Market share

What all newspapers have in common is an interest in protecting their position in the market. As well as attempting to maximise sales, they also need stable conditions. Such large sums of money are involved in setting up and running a mass circulation national newspaper that it is very difficult to set up a new paper, especially when established ones use spoiling tactics to protect their own positions. Most new ventures have failed or been taken over. The left of centre *News on Sunday* folded after only a few issues in 1988 and Eddie Shah's SDP-supporting *Today* went right wing when it was re-launched by Rupert Murdoch's News Corporation group.

Commercial interests

Some owners are highly interventionist and may dictate their paper's editorial stance. They may also use them as vehicles to promote or protect their commercial interests. A notable example is the promotion of Sky TV by newspapers in Rupert Murdoch's News Corporation group. At the same time, stories which could damage the other financial interests of a corporation are unlikely to be covered in related papers.

Professional practices

But it is also important to examine how the long-term economic goals of newspapers have to be translated into news stories through the organised process of news production. Journalists learn very quickly by experience to adapt their work to the requirements of their paper. The news values embedded in particular stories are partly a result of routine working practices and expectations.

> When you start as a journalist, obviously what you want to do is to get your stuff onto the front page . . . and you learn by trial and error what stories will get past the editorial threshold and what stories will get a splash . . . But of course the criteria will differ from organisation to organisation: what would be a good story for the *Guardian* or *The Independent* would not be the same in the *Sun* or the *Sunday Sport*.
>
> (Graham Murdock)

Journalists also know that major stories are subjected to rigorous legal examination before they are published. Because legal advisers err on the side of caution, important facts about government departments or individuals may have to be suppressed through fear of prosecution.

Dominant values

But journalists are social beings as well as professionals. They have their own views and values which may be reflected in what they write. They are also tuned in to the dominant values in society which they share with their readers. They recognise a range of cultural and social norms which form a relatively stable consensus. At the level of *writing*, journalists are more concerned with the status of their stories amongst potential readers than with the views of proprietors or long-term corporate demands.

They may exert relative autonomy in their writing but they are working within a system which constrains them. The requirements of those who exercise and delegate power still dominate how they make sense of events and facts through words and pictures. Yet, in spite of all these constraints, some journalists and editors insist that they have a large degree of autonomy. *The Independent* makes such a claim in its title, so it is worth looking briefly at how it operates.

The Independent: how it succeeded

> *The Independent* really reflects the views of me, the Editor, and my colleagues working together as a team trying to decide every day what we think the readers want now. As far as the daily management of the news and the editorial coverage is concerned, the shareholders have never expressed any comments on it, either good or bad. The shareholders are keenly interested to see that their investment pays off and they're much more likely to comment on a lack of financial control, say, than they would be on a particular angle of a news story.
>
> (Andreas Whittam Smith)

By taking advantage of new technology and the demise of restrictive practices in Fleet Street, *The Independent* was able to produce a paper at a fraction of the cost of its nearest rivals. In 1985 *The Daily Telegraph* needed around 4,000 people to produce their paper. *The Independent* carries out a similar process with just over 500, successfully targeting a young up-market audience. Start-up money came from City institutions and pension funds but with a rule that no one shareholder could acquire more than 10 per cent of the share capital.

Table 3.1 The Independent readership profile, 1987–8

	Apr.–Sep. 1988		Apr.–Sep. 1987	
	000s	%	000s	%
Total	1094	100.0	891	100.0
Men	703	64.3	585	66
Women	391	35.7	306	34
AB	531	48.6	494	55.5
C1	337	30.8	236	26.5
C2	150	13.7	95	10.7
DE	76	6.9	66	7.4
15–24	248	22.7	169	19.0
25–34	289	26.4	255	28.0
35–44	236	21.6	205	23.0
45–54	136	12.4	106	11.9
55–64	101	9.2	110	12.3
65+	84	7.7	45	5.1
ABC1 adults	868	79.3	730	81.9
ABC1 20–45	567	51.8	484	54.3

Source: The Independent 1988
Note: The Independent has increased in total readership by 22.8 per cent year-on-year

It is a characteristic of the target audience that they are better educated and more affluent than their parents and that they are sceptical about party politics. *The Independent* recognises this by talking intelligently and objectively about consumer affairs and by maintaining political independence above all else. For these reasons *The Independent* is not party to the parliamentary lobby system, and will accept 'freebies' from no one ... Its stance will always be to query 'The Establishment' and to campaign on issues that arise from its own reporting, analysis and internal debate. By 'The Establishment' is meant the government of the day ... and all other powerful bodies ... The founders of *The Independent* believe ... that good reporting is the foundation upon which *The Independent* will build. Good reporting is accuracy, balance, clarity and style; it is a task that demands a very high level of skill; and it is something that flourishes best in a newspaper that is genuinely independent.

(*The Independent* 1988: 3)

Value-free?

The Independent claims that with no single proprietor, its shareholders are only interested in its financial success and make no comment on its editorial stance. It was one of the first newspapers to refuse 'freebies' and led the way in declining to take part in the lobby system. However, by clever use of the word 'independent' the paper disguised the fact that it was in the process of re-inventing the wheel. It did more or less what rivals such as the *Guardian* were doing but implied that it was somehow more value-free. And despite claims about its own good reporting being a unique feature of *The Independent*, the paper has been caught out in fabricating by-lines for news agency copy from Reuters and passing it off as its own.

If it is impossible for newspapers to be commercially independent of the market in which they operate, can they be politically independent? In this next section, we shall look at how political and corporate sources try to manage information and how the media respond to these attempts.

MANAGING THE NEWS

Choosing the moment

In the late 1950s and early 1960s broadcasters became less deferential towards the establishment and started a trend towards the present-day practice of probing interviews with politicians and leaders of industry. As a result, both government and large corporations have become more skilled in the counter-measures of news management. Such management is particularly noticeable in wartime, when politicians' need to choose the right moment to say something is paramount.

'Yes, Prime Minister'

> We have just learned that the second battalion of the Parachute Regiment has taken Darwin and Goose Green. The Argentine forces suffered casualties, and a number of prisoners have been taken. Initial reports are that British casualties are light and the next of kin are being informed.
>
> (Ian McDonald)

Before any fighting started in the Falklands conflict and with the UK Task Force still on its way to the South Atlantic, the Prime Minister, Mrs Thatcher, was in demand to appear on a wide range of news and current affairs programmes. She chose *The Jimmy Young Show* on Radio 2. Her 20-minute live appearance showed all the signs of being set up at the last minute, in that Young, although well prepared, nervously asked on air how long Mrs Thatcher could spare him. The Prime Minister had the advantage since it was obvious that she could sweep out of the studio at any moment pleading urgent state business. At the same time, by appearing on a light entertainment show she avoided the tougher, more searching approach of a programme like *Panorama*. Young's informal approach made it easier for her to dominate the interview:

Jimmy Young: Prime Minister, can I ask you how long you can spare me, how long you can stay until because . . .

Mrs Thatcher: I've got four and a half more minutes . . .

Jimmy Young: Then we won't have any music 'til after four and a half minutes . . .

Jimmy Young: . . . Now, coming back to the Falklands . . . a Pentagon official said yesterday that you would definitely need air superiority, and in order to gain that superiority you'll probably have to bomb airfields on the Argentine mainland . . .

Mrs Thatcher (interrupting): Jimmy, you are trespassing . . .

Jimmy Young: Would you have to seriously consider that . . . ?

Mrs Thatcher (interrupting): Jimmy – please don't go any further. I never, never say anything about any military options at all. I neither confirm nor deny them. I live every minute of every hour of every day with the feeling that I must do everything to protect the lives of those who are in that Task Force . After all, they're there because . . . we . . . ordered the Task Force to go. They're there to fight for everything we believe in, and their safety – to the greatest extent possible – is my first and primary concern. So I never say anything about any military possibility or comment in any way . . . and, Jimmy, I sometimes wonder if we could ever have won the Battle of Alamein if every blessed shot had been pronounced upon by the commentators . . .

Jimmy Young: Right – can I ask you a non-military question then . . . ?

The interview ended with Jimmy Young playing an Andy Williams record for Mrs Thatcher. The impression she left behind was of a kindly but no-nonsense headmistress, heading off to teach 'the Argies' a thing or two. By referring to the Battle of Alamein, she had been able to appeal to patriotic emotions in her audience and elevate the Falklands conflict to the importance of the Second World War. During such a total war, the government exerted absolute management of all news and information. In a limited engagement like the Falklands, government control was in some ways more difficult to achieve since many news sources were outside British influence. Reports from the battle zone, often delayed by military and government press officers, were upstaged on several occasions by more recent information which British news agencies had obtained from Argentina and Chile. Irrespective of the accuracy of the information from South America, government news management sought to marginalise it as enemy propaganda.

> The Falklands Conflict may well prove the last war in which the armed forces are completely able to control the movements and communications of the journalists covering it.
>
> (Harris 1983: 150)

Mrs Thatcher had insisted that journalists be allowed to accompany the Task Force but it was clear that she expected the media to support Britain (or 'Us'). As a result, the government was quick to condemn organisations which appeared to question British involvement in the war. The BBC was heavily criticised because it insisted on referring to fighting units as 'British forces' whilst its rival ITN and many newspapers called them 'our troops'. By questioning the BBC's patriotism the government put the Corporation at a disadvantage when some of its programmes tried to question government policy over the Falklands.

Changing the rules of engagement

But even when lives are not at risk, peacetime systems of political news management can be equally manipulative. The rules of engagement about getting and keeping control are constantly changing. Broadcasters complain that senior politicians have come to see television and radio appearances as advertising slots. In return for an appearance, politicians demand the last word in a programme or insist that an interview be broadcast in a certain time slot. The public are invariably unaware of this pre-programme bargaining and so are not free to judge the advantages gained by such negotiations. For their part, politicians say that they are often at the mercy of the 'sound bite', when broadcasters ask them to sum up their views on a complicated issue in 30 seconds for the convenience of a news bulletin. Senior Conservative Michael Heseltine has argued that such trends are undermining serious political discussion. He claims he would far rather accept the cut and thrust of a probing, in-depth interview.

The lobby system

This is a means of organising and orchestrating the flow of information from government to the media. It is a twice-daily briefing given to accredited lobby journalists by a press official from the Prime Minister's office. The correspondents are told the 'Downing Street' view of what is going on or they are alerted to political events about to happen. The briefing is 'off the record and unattributable'. It leads journalists to use such phrases as 'sources close to the Prime Minister', or 'senior government sources'. Some newspapers, notably *The Independent*, *Guardian* and *Scotsman*, have withdrawn from these briefings.

We don't belong to the lobby because it has been used, in our view, very reprehensibly to manage the news and to rubbish ministers. It's also had a bad effect on political journalists who at periods (though perhaps not at the moment) have felt that they need do no more than take in what Downing Street tells them is going on and make no further enquiries – they all at least have the same story. Every now and again Downing Street will give a story to our rivals late at night and every now and again we miss something but that is more than made up for by the energetic way in which our correspondents actually locate the news themselves.

(Andreas Whittam Smith)

Some daily newspapers . . . refuse to attend Mr Ingham's briefings. They do their best to find out what Mr Ingham has said then name him as the source. As a result, the press secretary and his staff have not been challenged as forcefully as they should . . . if the lobby was united and all the correspondents were present. This I suspect is leading to more manipulation of the news media. Political journalists on newspapers sympathetic to the government know that when the briefing is over, they can obtain on an individual basis, much of the information they want. Therefore, through selective briefings, the government can secure greater impact.

(Jones 1989)

What happens between politicians and the media often becomes a role model for the media's relationships with other centres of power such as large corporations, trade unions and pressure groups. Most current-affairs journalists and broadcasters see it as their job to represent the public interest by maintaining a scepticism towards these centres of power. And despite the limitations of the consensual framework within which journalists operate, the right to ask questions and get answers is seen as one of the tenets of a free society. But there are other factors at work in determining who asks what of whom and how it gets reported.

NEWSWORTHINESS

Of the millions of events which occur everyday in the world, only a tiny proportion ever become visible as 'potential news stories': and of this proportion only a small fraction are actually produced as the day's news in the news media.

(Hall 1981: 76)

What is it that makes one thing worth reporting and another not?

It has to be an event. It has to be something that has happened, rather than a long process that's been unfolding over time. It has to have happened recently. It almost always involves elite figures . . . News is

not about what ordinary people do, it's about what the powerful do . . .
It has to be an event that has some significance for the country as a
whole . . . and that means that our map of the world which we get
through news is highly partial . . . There are whole areas of the world . . .
which are very sporadically covered in the news. The other criterion
would be human interest: something like a disaster would be automatic-
ally news.

(Graham Murdock)

Gaps in the map

Fleet Street is particularly inadequate when it comes to the reporting of
ethnic stories. The heavy traffic in news items from the provincial to the
national press mysteriously dries up

(Poole 1989: 13)

Criteria of newsworthiness operate together as a framework for what is
reported. As a result, there are information gaps. Some events are under-
reported because they do not fit into the framework. Sometimes the
reasons are related to geography, sometimes to dominant cultural assumptions. Many stories never make the national headlines, while others are
reported because the relevant sources are routinely monitored. This leads
to what are sometimes called 'structured absences'.

There was a fire in which an Asian woman died. A white man was
subsequently charged with an alleged arson attack, and the story was
quite well covered in the local press. And yet it never made it to Fleet
Street. Now, obviously every day of the week there are stories in the
local press that don't make it to Fleet Street. But this was a fire which
was described by the local fire chief as the worst he'd seen in twenty
years in the service. And if you look at the kind of stories that come
through from the regions and the provinces into Fleet Street, very often
stories which are much more trivial but which have clearly come via
local papers are there to see. They reported the murder of a white man
by an Asian shopkeeper who claimed that the man had been stealing
from him . . . I would say that there is an element of racist reporting.

MCLURG'S LAW

One dead Briton says McLurg (who was a legendary news editor) is worth
5 dead Frenchmen, 20 dead Egyptians, 500 dead Indians and a 1000 dead
Chinese.

(Mike Poole)

Determinations

We have seen how political, economic and cultural factors affect the
media's selection of information. We have established that the routine

production requirements of each medium determine the working practices of media professionals. We have also looked at how some of the technical features and conventions of specific media define their typical styles of presentation. All this may suggest a rather monolithic and manipulative system in which there is little freedom either for producers or consumers of information. But such a notion does not correspond at all with our daily experience as readers of the media. If we look from an audience perspective, the media may seem far less powerful and manipulative.

Table 3.2 Summary of main news sources

1 *Sources monitored routinely*
  a Parliament
  b Councils
  c Police (and the army in Northern Ireland)
  d Other emergency services
  e Courts (including inquests and tribunals)
  f Royalty
  g Diary events (e.g. annual events like Ascot or conferences known about in advance)
  h Airports
  i Other news media
2 *Organisations issuing statements and holding press conferences*
  a Government departments
  b Local authority departments
  c Public services (transport authorities, electricity boards, etc.)
  d Companies
  e Trade unions
  f Non-commercial organisations (pressure groups, charities, etc.)
  g Political parties
  h Army, Navy, Air Force
3 *Individuals making statements, seeking publicity, etc.*
  a Prominent people (e.g. Bishops and film stars)
  b Members of the public

Source: Whitaker 1981: 31–2

Audiences

The survival and success of the media depend ultimately on how effectively they can satisfy the right kind of readers to maintain sales and attract advertising revenue. *The Independent* has succeeded because it has found a new readership. It relies on careful market research and communication with its readership to maintain its position. It was a carefully considered decision to include more comprehensive leisure and arts information than could be found in comparable papers. Its Editor, Andreas Whittam Smith, maintains that such material has attracted a young and affluent readership which is attractive to commercial advertisers.

Figure 3.7   Channel 4 News at 7 p.m. daily schedule outline

9.00 am ● The producer of the day arrives in the newsroom. Already, between a third and a half of the programme has been 'blocked off' to make room for expected material. Today, for instance, Trevor McDonald will be sending a report on South Africa. There is also the TUC conference in Blackpool, an event which *Channel Four News* is bound to cover. There are several options for news material. Peter Sissons, the programme presenter, may interview trade union leaders, or reporters may send packaged (edited) material down the line to London.

10.30 am ● Both *Channel Four News* and Channel One (*News at One*, the *5.45 News* and *News at Ten*) hold editorial conferences to decide which 'on-the-day' stories they will cover. *Channel Four News* sends an observer to the Channel One conference to check what the Channel One programmes are doing. *Channel Four News* relies heavily on the *5.45 News* for the 'hard news' for its summary. At the same time, *Channel Four News* will send its own crews on its own on-the-day stories.

2.30 pm ● Editor's conference, attended by the presenters, the home and foreign editors and senior editorial staff. There is a rough running order of items, but the top story is only provisional. Often a story's chances will depend on whether the programme can get an interview. When Dr Allan Boesak was arrested in Cape Town, *Channel Four News* needed to get a reaction from Desmond Tutu. This in turn depended on whether they could get a satellite link. In the event, link and interview went ahead.

4.30 pm ● A running order is circulated. The reporters are returning with their film. Now the process of assembly is underway, as people in charge of captions, slides, graphics, computer graphics, videotape editing and sound dubbing get to work on the 'packages', as the finished news items are called. There are almost 2,000 different sound effects, from oars splashing to cars crashing. The most sought-after effect, curiously, is the sound of silence inside a house.

7.00 pm ● The programme goes on the air. The producer will not have seen how the whole thing looks until this moment. Only the top story is likely to have been rehearsed.

Right up to transmission, *Channel Four News* can deal comprehensively with late-breaking news (this is what really distinguishes it from *Newsnight*). The news of the football disaster at the Heysel Stadium broke five minutes before the producer of the day went down to the control room.

Source: *New Society*, 4 October 1985: i–iv

Figure 3.8 The daily evolution of Channel 4 News

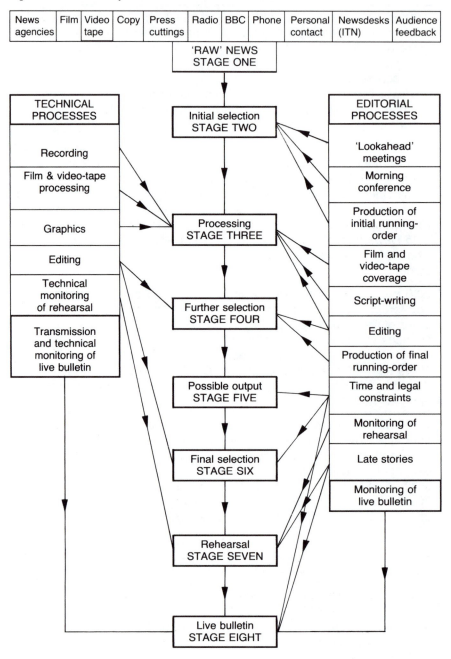

News agencies	Film	Video tape	Copy	Press cuttings	Radio	BBC	Phone	Personal contact	Newsdesks (ITN)	Audience feedback

'RAW' NEWS
STAGE ONE

TECHNICAL
PROCESSES

Recording

Film & video-tape
processing

Graphics

Editing

Technical
monitoring
of rehearsal

Transmission
and technical
monitoring of
live bulletin

Initial selection
STAGE TWO

Processing
STAGE THREE

Further selection
STAGE FOUR

Possible output
STAGE FIVE

Final selection
STAGE SIX

Rehearsal
STAGE SEVEN

Live bulletin
STAGE EIGHT

EDITORIAL
PROCESSES

'Lookahead'
meetings

Morning
conference

Production of
initial running-
order

Film and
video-tape
coverage

Script-writing

Editing

Production of final
running-order

Time and legal
constraints

Monitoring of
rehearsal

Late stories

Monitoring of
live bulletin

Source: Blanchard and Morley 1982

Keeping in touch

Finding out about readers' interests and needs is a vital method of keeping in touch with them and acts as a powerful influence on the paper's form and content.

> You have to start with a very clear view of who your readers are and what are their interests. It's very, very clear in our minds. For me as Editor of *The Independent*, I must constantly remember that very nearly half – 49 per cent is the number at the moment – are 34 years old or younger. That's an extraordinarily young readership and that dominates our thinking about what to publish. The next lesson of course is that there isn't one readership but there are many, and you have to have a sort of feel for these readerships. And we communicate with our readers – or they communicate with us I should say – because they write to us, they telephone us and fairly regularly we try to measure their opinions with market research. You keep your eyes open. You do get a sense. Your antennae are very sensitive to the nuances of news and reaction to news.

(Andreas Whittam Smith)

Table 3.3 National readership profile for the 'Qualities', 1988

	IND 000s	%	TMS 000s	%	GUA 000s	%	DTL 000s	%	FTI 000s	%
Total	1094	–	1117	–	1352	–	2824	–	806	–
Men	703	64.3	649	58.1	832	61.5	1511	53.5	562	69.7
Women	391	35.7	468	41.9	519	38.4	1313	46.5	244	30.3
A	118	10.8	175	15.7	96	7.1	338	12.0	95	11.8
B	413	37.8	497	44.5	524	38.8	1101	39.0	334	41.4
C1	337	30.8	278	24.9	407	30.1	809	28.6	257	31.9
C2	150	13.7	107	9.6	169	12.5	347	12.3	77	9.6
D	45	4.1	36	3.2	91	6.7	127	4.5	44	5.5
E	31	2.8	24	2.1	64	4.7	103	3.6	–	–
15–24	248	22.7	197	17.6	295	21.8	323	11.4	134	16.6
25–34	289	26.4	213	19.1	333	24.6	375	13.3	199	24.7
35–44	236	21.6	211	18.9	279	20.6	491	17.4	162	20.1
45–54	136	12.4	228	20.4	210	15.5	469	16.6	169	21.0
55–64	101	9.2	154	13.8	133	9.8	540	19.1	112	13.9
65+	84	7.7	113	10.1	102	7.5	626	22.2	30	3.7
ABC1	868	79.3	950	85.0	1027	76.0	2248	79.6	685	85.0
ABC1/ 20–45	567	51.8	456	40.8	630	46.6	825	29.2	401	49.8

Source: The Independent Information Pack, 1988

Wallpaper

> And if anyone in the theatre or TV and Radio can claim to have been there, done that, it's my first guest. He was doing chat-shows when God was a boy. He's starred on the West End stage. He's had more successful TV sit-coms than you can shake a Roman Collar at – and there's more! He's about to knock them dead in a little-known soap opera called *Neighbours*.
>
> (Terry Wogan on *Wogan*)

A sense of audience also matters to television producers. Ever since the *Open the Box* series and the IBA's own research with hidden cameras revealed how some viewers behaved in front of the screen, there has been a fear that some peak viewing programmes were not being watched attentively. This is a potential problem even for a chat-show like *Wogan*. So responses from viewers (usually in the form of letters) are noticed and can affect the way the programme operates, as was shown dramatically in 1985 when it changed tack to combat a decline in popularity.

> There's always a great danger that a show that is on three times a week ... will be just on. People will be having their supper, people will be walking round doing whatever in the house. So I hope the show is not like wallpaper ... but judging by the amount of mail we have ... I hope it never will become a flickering colour in the corner.
>
> (Peter Estall)

Gossip rules

Chat-shows are in some ways like news programmes. They use similar selection criteria for the events they cover. Although *Wogan* obviously relies more on personalisation and elite figures, it depends as much as any news bulletin on such criteria as novelty, currency and continuity.

> What we do like to cover are personalities with a great story to tell ... They have to somehow be in the news in that particular week or have a strong current interest ... somebody who has or will be capturing the public imagination in some way ... The information that is coming from them is not information in the same way as the news would give information. It is a gossipy sort of information.
>
> (Peter Estall)

PACKAGING PEOPLE

> The tabloids are full of ... spectres which are haunting this community ... The problem with all of these people is that they're different ... There

are people who are part of us and there are people who are against us
... trying to subvert us.

(Graham Murdock)

We have seen some of the processes which affect the formation of facts.
But how does this give us a better understanding of the media? We can
recognise that selection cannot be avoided and is sometimes highly
desirable. But we need to be able to trace the values and assumptions
which lie behind what is presented to us. We need to be wary, perhaps
sceptical, but not cynical about how 'facts' are formed.

At present our schools largely continue to produce pupils who are likely
to carry with them for the rest of their lives either a quite unwarranted
faith in the integrity of media images and representations, or an equally
dangerous, undifferentiated scepticism which sees the media as sources
of all evil.

(Masterman 1985: 14)

The way the media systematically select their material and present it to us
means that they may present facts too neatly, so that the values and
judgements they contain are not explicit. This tendency to package
information into stories is likely to increase.

News stories are ... little dramatised narratives and they have to have
entertainment value to grab the viewer. So that ups the value of the
entertainment angle on news. What the tabloids do is ... pull out this
consumer personality in the reader and push that ... It's a one-
dimensional appeal.

(Graham Murdock)

Consuming stories

If we see ourselves only as consumers, we are in danger of buying packages
sold without health warnings about the ideas and values they contain.
These values are not always obvious. They are not the result of a
conspiracy to deceive for political or financial reasons. Nor are they simply
the result of information supplied by public relations agencies.

Reporting begins and ends with selection. The trouble with the media is
that the selection is not arbitrary. It follows predictable patterns which are
based on the habits and interests of particular media and their audiences.
Because products have to attract and satisfy audiences, simple story-forms
have evolved as vehicles for information.

Our Tune

Simon Bates's *Our Tune* is a simple example of this kind of development.
Every weekday, for 6 or 7 minutes, Simon Bates extemporises on a
listener's letter. Each week he gets up to 800 of them from people willing to

expose their personal stories anonymously to 10 million listeners. He weaves the fragments of their lives into simple soap operettas. He dramatises a range of problems like alcoholism, bereavement, abandonment, illegitimacy, homosexuality, chronic illness, drug abuse and death. The stories encourage the release of sadness, resentment or joy into a culminating pop song of the listener's own choice.

> Here's a letter from a lady who lives in the South of England by the name of Julie. Now let's talk about Richard who's her fella. Richard – it's kind of hard to know where to start really on this one – Richard she first met in February 1981 and they started going out together and things were good. But there was a background to everything. Richard was very bitter and twisted about his family – not about his father but about his mother. They'd had a fairly happy relationship as children. There'd been Richard, his sister, his mum and his dad. And one day, without any warning at all to the kids – and there had obviously been stresses in the family – one day, Richard's mum got up and announced that she was leaving to go back up North with a fella ...
>
> (Simon Bates on *Our Tune*, 16 August 1988)

Personalising problems

Our Tune packages highly charged personal and social experience into easily consumed stories, a kind of dramatised 'problem-page' which, like classical tragedy, aims to provide emotional therapy. Its basic message is always about facing up to adversity and finding appropriate consolation. The danger is that it can degenerate into a sentimental celebration of stoicism. Unlike traditional 'agony columns', it does not offer practical advice in return. It presents no solutions. It invites identification without distance, emotion without intellect.

The large audiences for this feature suggest that it is serving an important social function. Like soap opera, it offers access to common experience and gives it status at a time when actual communities are being disrupted or disappearing. It has a similar ritual function to a wedding video. It is unique in capturing and commemorating experience in a powerful form. But in some ways it is typical of a widespread development in the media. Such exclusive focus on personal experience across the media as a whole can mean that broader social contexts come to seem irrelevant. Individuals are seen in isolation from each other, disconnected from social, political and economic causes and consequences. The problem is not that such stories are trivial, rather that they are personalised almost to the point of becoming meaningless. The result of allowing facts to be detached from their real contexts is that problems may be presented as insoluble except through consumption.

It is an extension of the 'bias against understanding' in television news which Peter Jay and John Birt complained about in the mid-1970s. They felt that the treatment of issues was shallow and criticised the separation of news from current affairs. Much of this has since been remedied by deeper news coverage (especially by ITN for C4) and the integration of News and Current Affairs departments (as now at the BBC under John Birt). Yet we cannot afford to restrict our attention to isolated improvements in this one area. The problem remains of where most people go for their information. This will be accentuated with the increasing number of competing sources of information in the new media environment and the removal of protection from public service broadcasting.

The problems of how information is processed, packaged and perceived are not confined to news. They are basic to many forms across the mass media and raise serious questions about how well informed audiences can be. Both the quantity of information the media offer and the quality of understanding they promote are at issue. And these issues are central to the kind of democracy we can sustain.

> One of the preconditions of effective citizenship ... is that you have access to all the information and the whole range of arguments that you need in order to make rational political decisions. If you have an information system that is tipped towards entertainment ... and also tipped towards consumerism, that is advertising-supported, then you are distorting the information base of the society ... and you are encouraging people to think of themselves primarily as consumers rather than as citizens.
>
> What consumerism does is to say to people 'If you have a problem, solve it by going and buying something. If you're worrying about the possible threat of nuclear war, go and buy a fall-out shelter for your back garden ... Don't organise, don't discuss, don't lobby your MP ... just go out and buy something and everything will be OK.
>
> So there is ... a fundamental tension in our system between the economics of the consumer system which is encouraging individual solutions to public problems and the notion of a democracy based on collective argument and collective solutions to public problems.
>
> (Graham Murdock)

TEACHING IDEA 1: THE BATTLE OF OSGROVE

This exercise concerns the processes of news selection and asks students to simulate the work of a newspaper sub-editor. Its purpose is not, however, to introduce students to the tasks of sub-editing, but to question understanding of news and news selection. The teacher may need to introduce the exercise with some explanation of how news is gathered and selected, outlining the respective roles of reporters and sub-editors in journalism.

Task A

Students are asked to read the simulation instruction sheet [see below] and the teacher organises the group into pairs or small groups to undertake the task of editing the material. Groups should be assigned to edit the story from a number of different perspectives, such as:

Tory national newspaper
Labour national newspaper
Independent national newspaper
Trade union newspaper
Management newspaper
Police newspaper
 etc.

The teacher should place a time limit and maximum number of words on the story, according to circumstances. Thirty minutes is about the minimum time it will take to do this task; wordage depends very much on how many groups will report back, as you need to allow for everyone to read their finished product to the whole group. The piece could be as short as one or two paragraphs, totalling as little as two hundred words.

Task B

Each group is asked to read out their finished report for class discussion.

Simulation instruction sheet

You are working as a pair/team of sub-editors for a newspaper covering the events at the 'Battle of Osgrove'. This news event concerns the long and bitter national dispute between steel workers and the Government-owned National Steel Board, which began six months ago, when the Government announced the closure of the Osgrove site. Due to what is perceived as 'picket-line violence', in clashes between police and pickets the story has been covered widely throughout the national news media as one that raises issues of 'law and order'.

This particular story takes place on a day when a mass picket has been organised by the National Union of Steel Works (NUSW) outside the Osgrove Steel Works, near Birmingham. It concerns an incident which involves the arrest of NUSW leader Albert Jones and his allegations that he was attacked by police.

You will be asked to edit copy submitted by your reporters in the field, from the point of view of your publication. You must also devise a headline for the piece.

Note: YOU MAY USE *ONLY* THE INFORMATION SUPPLIED BY YOUR REPORTERS.

Reporter A, 2.35 p.m.

THERE WERE VIOLENT CLASHES TODAY AT THE OSGROVE STEEL WORKS, FOLLOWING A MASS PICKET OF SOME 1500 STEEL WORKERS AND OTHER TRADE UNIONISTS OUTSIDE THE PLANT. 60 PICKETS HAVE BEEN ARRESTED, AND 3 POLICEMEN SERIOUSLY INJURED. THE POLICEMEN HAVE BEEN TAKEN TO BIRMINGHAM ROYAL INFIRMARY FOR TREATMENT.

A POLICE SPOKESMAN SAID: 'THREE OF OUR OFFICERS WERE HURT IN THE SAME INCIDENT, WHEN A GROUP OF ABOUT 100 PICKETS ATTACKED OUR LINES OUTSIDE GATE 3 OF THE OSGROVE PLANT. THE ATTACK WAS QUITE UNPROVOKED. I CALL ON EVERYONE TO KEEP THEIR HEADS HERE TODAY, OBEY POLICE INSTRUCTIONS AND PICKET LEGALLY AND PEACEFULLY.'

Reporter B, 3.15 p.m.

OFFICIALS OF THE NATIONAL UNION OF STEELWORKERS (NUSW) THIS AFTER-NOON DENIED REPORTS THAT PICKETS HAD BEEN INVOLVED IN AN ATTACK ON POLICE LINES EARLIER TODAY. NUSW LEADER ALBERT JONES INSISTED THAT THE POLICE SURROUNDED A GROUP OF PICKETS AND CHARGED THEM USING BATONS AND SHIELDS. '20 PICKETS HAD BEEN HURT', HE SAID, 'SOME OF THEM SERIOUSLY'. HE PUT THE NUMBER OF PICKETS ARRESTED AT ABOUT 75, AND ALSO NOTED THAT HIS UNION BELIEVED THERE WERE OVER 4000 POLICE ON DUTY THAT DAY, OUTNUMBERING PICKETS BY A FACTOR OF 4 TO 1. 'THIS IS TYPICAL OF THE KIND OF POLICE STATE THAT HAS BEEN SET UP DURING THIS DISPUTE', HE SAID.

NUSW LEADERS HAVE CALLED FOR CALM AND ASKED FOR WITNESSES TO THE EVENTS TODAY TO COME FORWARD IN SUPPORT OF THE ARRESTED MEN.

Reporter B, 4.30 p.m.

IN AN EXTRAORDINARY INCIDENT AT THIS AFTERNOON'S OSGROVE PICKET NUSW LEADER ALBERT JONES WAS ARRESTED, AND HAS ALLEGED THAT HE

WAS ASSAULTED BY POLICE. JONES WAS WALKING AWAY FROM POLICE LINES AT ABOUT 4PM TODAY WHEN HE CLAIMS HE WAS ATTACKED FROM BEHIND AND HIT BY A POLICE RIOT SHIELD. HE WAS SUBSEQUENTLY ARRESTED AND CHARGED WITH ASSAULT, FOLLOWING AN INCIDENT THAT OCCURRED A FEW MINUTES LATER AT POLICE LINES.

BEFORE HIS ARREST MR JONES SAID: 'I WAS WALKING AWAY FROM THE PICKETING MINDING MY OWN BUSINESS WHEN I WAS HIT BY TWO OF THESE GOONS, TWICE, WITH A RIOT SHIELD. THEY KNOCKED ME DOWN AND I FELL DOWN THAT BANK THERE. I'VE GOT THE BRUISES TO PROVE IT, TOO. THEY ATTACKED ME FROM BEHIND IN A TOTALLY UNWARRANTED AND UNPROVOKED ASSAULT.'

A FEW MINUTES LATER MR JONES CONFRONTED THE CHIEF CONSTABLE FOR THE REGION, MR PHILLIP JACKSON, WHO WAS VISITING HIS OFFICERS ABOUT A HUNDRED YARDS FROM THE SCENE OF THE ALLEGED ATTACK. MR JONES WAS SUBSEQUENTLY ARRESTED FOR A BREACH OF THE PEACE AND RESISTING ARREST. HE WAS HEARD TO SHOUT 'NO WAY! NO WAY!' A NUMBER OF TIMES BEFORE HE WAS ESCORTED TO A POLICE VEHICLE.

Reporter A, 5.00 p.m.

CHIEF CONSTABLE PHILLIP JACKSON HAS DENIED ALLEGATIONS MADE BY NUSW LEADER ALBERT JONES THAT HE WAS ATTACKED THIS AFTERNOON BY POLICE OFFICERS. 'MR JONES SLIPPED DOWN A BANK,' HE SAID. 'I SAW IT MYSELF, AS I DROVE TOWARDS THE PICKET LINE IN MY CAR, ALONG THE ROAD NEARBY. HE SLIPPED AND WAS ROLLING DOWN THE BANK AS I PASSED HIM. HE PROBABLY TRIPPED ON ONE OF THE RAILWAY SLEEPERS AT THE TOP OF THE BANK.'

MR JACKSON CONDEMNED MR JONES' ALLEGATIONS OF POLICE BRUTALITY. 'THIS IS NO WAY FOR A NATIONAL TRADE UNION LEADER TO CONDUCT HIM-SELF,' HE SAID. 'WE NEED MORE RESPONSIBILITY FROM THE UNION LEADERSHIP IN THIS VIOLENT AND UNPLEASANT DISPUTE. NOT THIS KIND OF SENSATIONAL-ISING OF EVENTS.'

MR JACKSON WENT ON TO SAY THAT HE DID NOT IN FACT SEE MR JONES FALL AND COULD NOT SEE THE VERY TOP OF THE BANK FROM HIS VANTAGE POINT IN HIS CAR, BECAUSE THERE WERE BUSHES OBSCURING THE VIEW. 'I SAW HIM FALLING DOWN THE BANK. HE MUST HAVE SLIPPED,' HE SAID.

Reporter A, 6.00 p.m.

THE NUSW THIS EVENING CONDEMNED THE ALLEGED ATTACK ON ALBERT JONES AND HIS ARREST BY THE POLICE. THEY SAID THAT OVER 100 PICKETS HAD BEEN ARRESTED DURING THE DAY'S EVENTS AND STATED THEY HAD EVIDENCE THAT THERE WERE TERRITORIAL ARMY OFFICERS IN UNNUMBERED POLICE UNIFORMS PRESENT AT THE PICKET. THEY ALSO ALLEGE THAT 'AGENTS PROVOCATEURS' WERE PARTLY RESPONSIBLE FOR THE VIOLENT INCIDENT

EARLIER IN THE DAY, WHEN THREE POLICEMAN AND FIVE PICKETS WERE HURT. AN NUSW SPOKESPERSON SAID: 'WE KNOW THAT THE POLICE HAVE ROUTINELY USED SPECIAL BRANCH OFFICERS DRESSED AS PICKETS TO CAUSE TROUBLE ON PICKET LINES AND TO IDENTIFY INDIVIDUALS THEY WISH TO ARREST. TWO SUCH "AGENTS PROVOCATEURS" WERE SEEN AT TODAY'S OSGROVE PICKET.'

A POLICE SPOKESMAN DENIED THE NUSW ALLEGATIONS AND DISPUTED THE UNION'S ACCOUNT OF THE DAY'S EVENTS. 'THERE WERE OVER 3000 PICKETS PRESENT TODAY,' HE SAID, 'AND A SMALLER NUMBER OF POLICE OFFICERS. AS FOR AGENTS PROVOCATEURS – I THINK THEY'VE BEEN READING TOO MANY LE CARRÉ NOVELS, DON'T YOU?'

TEACHING IDEA 2: COAL DISPUTE

Aim

To compare two radio news reports of the same event on different radio stations (Radio 1's *Newsbeat* and Radio 4's *Six O'Clock News*) in terms of language, tone, emphasis and structure.

Time

One double lesson

Materials

Ideally, audio recordings of two reports and accurate transcripts of them, as in the examples below.

Method

- Ask students to specify appropriate criteria for comparison and let them work in small groups on different ones, noting comments on their copies of the transcripts as necessary.
- Ensure that they take note of similar features as well as different ones (e.g. use of named reporter on location and actuality sound).
- Groups report back and discuss their observations.

Further work

What makes this exercise interesting is that these reports are remarkably similar on the surface and do not fulfil common prejudices about differences in style and presentation between the two stations. Try the exercise with other material.

Radio 1: Newsbeat 5.30 p.m. 27 June 1985

1 *Presenter*: Thousands of miners, along with their families and supporters, marched through central London this afternoon in one of the biggest demonstrations seen outside the coalfield since their long strike began. Among the marchers were trade unionists from several industries, notably railway and busdrivers on strike for the day to back the miners. They had already made life difficult for early morning commuters.

2 The marchers climaxed in a mass rally which is still under way. Those who have already spoken include Arthur Scargill, who has praised the young miners and the women who have taken part in the strike campaign. With their support, he said, the miners couldn't lose. On the scene, *Newsbeat's* Mike Gardner.

3 *Gardner*: Police estimates put the number of marchers at around 11,000. Only one nasty incident reported – that came in Lower Thames Street where a derogatory comment about Arthur Scargill on a banner draped from an office window angered a group of about two dozen miners. They broke through a police barrier but three officers prevented them getting into the upper floors of the building. A glass door was broken in the scuffle, though.

4 Here at Jubilee Gardens, they were welcomed by GLC leader Ken Livingstone:

'You have frightened and unsettled this Government more than any other event in the last five years (*applause*) and when ... and therefore there is a duty on the rest of us in the movement to advance every struggle attend to every conflict with this Government, put them into a position where they have to fight on so many fronts that your victory is advanced and the defeat of this Government is advanced. We salute you and welcome you to London, we are proud to have you here.' (*applause*)

5 Earlier, just before the march reached Jubilee Gardens, I spoke with Tony Benn, and asked him what he thought this day of action in the South East had achieved:

'I think probably the most important thing – two most important things that have happened today – are: first of all that the print workers insisted that their statement in support of the miners appear in the national papers and the three newspapers, the *Sun*, the *Daily Mirror* and *The Financial Times* that would not allow the print workers to print their support were not published; and the second thing is that this morning the National Executive Committee of the Labour Party passed a resolution calling for a national campaign with the NUM in support of the miner's case so that today the 27th June carries the progress of the miners' campaign a stage nearer total victory – that's the importance of it.'

Radio 4: News 6 p.m. 27 June 1985

1 *Presenter*: Thousands of miners marched through London this afternoon in support of the pit strike. With them were other trade unionists, their wives and families. The police estimate that 10,000 people were involved. The organisers, the Kent miners, believe the number was nearer 50,000.

2 The occasion was almost entirely peaceful. At a ceremony after a rally on the South Bank of the Thames, wreaths commemorating the deaths of two miners on picket-lines were cast into the river. Joe Paley of our industrial staff followed the march.

3 *Paley*: As the marchers left Tower Hill at the start of their 4-mile walk to the South Bank, they were led by the NUM President, Mr Arthur Scargill, the Vice-president Mr Mick McGahey and two Labour MPs, Mr Tony Benn and Mr Dennis Skinner. It was a peaceful but a lively march (*crowd noises . . . 'Here we go!'*).

4 One incident near Blackfriars Station stopped the march for about ten minutes. An office worker had put an anti-Scargill poster in his window which enraged the marchers (*shouts*). A small group ran over to the building and broke the glass in the locked front door and the marchers wouldn't move until the police had persuaded the office worker to take the poster down.

5 The march then went down Fleet Street and over to the South Bank. At the rally itself, the leader of the Kent pit men Mr Jack Collins, said that the miners would win the strike, and he had this message: 'Oil stocks are getting more expensive, the coppers are getting more expensive and we are more determined. Victory to the miners.'

6 Mr Arthur Scargill praised the young miners and the women for their magnificent support and he said with that kind of determination the miners just couldn't lose:

> 'McGregor and Thatcher and the Government believed they could smash this union and in the process defeat the whole of the British Trade Union movement. Well I've got a word for them, this union are not going to be defeated, we are going to win the fight to keep our pits open, jobs secure (*shouts*) and our industry intact.'

TEACHING IDEA 3: TELEVISION NEWS BULLETINS

Aim

To compare and contrast the different styles and emphases of television news as presented on two or more television channels. By concentrating on the timing and sequencing of news bulletins, this approach encourages thinking about the implicit agendas and hierarchies of news production.

Time

Three double lessons.

Materials

Pre-recorded videotape of at least two news broadcasts from the same day's output on different channels but at similar times, video-recorder and TV set for replay, scissors and paper for constructing sequences.

Method

Preparation

- Record at least two complete news bulletins broadcast during the same part of a single day on two or more television channels.
- Analyse each bulletin in terms of the content and length of each item.
- Transcribe your analysis into a simple diagrammatic form so you can see the bulletins' distribution of content over time easily.
- Write out a slip for each item which briefly indicates its content. Place all the slips for each item within a whole bulletin into an envelope. Do not indicate any time allocations at this stage.

Lesson 1

- Divide class into groups of an appropriate size (up to 5 or 6) for discussion and decision-making.
- Allocate one complete bulletin for analysis to each group by giving them an envelope containing the individual item slips.
- Groups then decide on: (a) the length of each item, and (b) its running order within the bulletin, until they have constructed a complete bulletin of appropriate length which shows timing and running order for all items.

Lesson 2

- Make OHP transparencies of each group's constructions so that whole class can see them.
- Discuss decisions, drawing attention to any selection and significance criteria which may be apparent.
  What basis is there for the sequencing agreed upon?
  What differences and similarities between bulletins are noticeable?
  How can such features be explained?

Lesson 3

- Compare with actual pre-recorded bulletins.
- Discuss how different bulletins relate to different audiences and different channel identities.

Further work

Analyse other presentational features (e.g. title-sequences, music, editing, presenters, use of voice-over, 'accessed voices', use of studio guests, expert commentators, stock film inserts, stills, graphics, animation, tones of voice and editorial angles). Examine how these particular features work to create a recognisable style for each bulletin (see Hartley, J. (1982) *Understanding News* London: Methuen).

TEACHING IDEA 4: A WINDOW ON THE WORLD?

Aim

To explore the role played by the visual track in shaping the meanings of television narrative.

Time

One double lesson.

Materials

Programme script. The extract supplied in script form (Table 3.4) is from a *Panorama* programme of 13 April 1981 which was broadcast in the immediate aftermath of the Brixton riots (10–12 April). It focuses on the 1976 Notting Hill riots as background to the current wave of inner city rioting. The extract consists of old news material re-edited to form a starting-point for studio discussion of the problems of race, violence and public disorder. It was immediately preceded and followed by the presenter.

Method

- Make photocopies of the script supplied (or of your own) covering up the *Camera* and *Vision* columns.
- Explain the context of the extract.
- Explain technical abbreviations where necessary.
- Students work in groups to invent visuals and camera positions.
- Share and discuss different groups' efforts.
- Give out copies of or read through the text of what was transmitted, as supplied on the full transcript.

Further work

What effect do different visual sequences have on the overall narrative? What different expectations or emphases are built into the students' own scripts or the broadcast version?

The exercise would also work well the other way round, i.e. blanking out the SOUND column and asking students to write their own voice-over and sound effects. This would probably be more difficult for less experienced students.

Does it make sense to think of television as simply a visual medium?

Panorama's traditional subtitle 'A Window on the World' is based on a visual metaphor which needs examining carefully. But this exercise should show that the view of the world it provides is also determined by words.

The issues raised here are obviously important for understanding news, current affairs and documentary programmes. It would be valuable to precede or follow this exercise with analysis of pre-recorded extracts from such programmes.

Table 3.4 Extract from *Panorama* programme: *Notting Hill 1981*

Shot	Time	Cam.	Vision	Sound
1.	00.00	Ms, track R. (street-level)	Mixed crowd, (man with wings)	(Music) (and whistling)
2.	00.03	CUs 'inside' view (street-level)	coloured, black and white people moving left to right	The summer of 1976 was hot (Music) In the streets of Notting Hill, the West Indian community staged a massive carnival which, it was hoped, would demonstrate that Britain could relax in real multi-racial harmony.
3.	00.17	WA (street-level) and pan R.	Youths stoning police. Land Rovers moving left to right.	(Heavy crowd noise) Those hopes were quickly crushed.
4.	00.24	2 S (street-level)	Police with batons sorting out crowd forcefully	(Siren noise)
5.	00.28	3 S Fast pan R. and defocus (street-level)	Police and crowd – 1 policeman struggles with 1 black person.	Police trying to arrest handbag-snatchers were set upon by the crowd. (Crowd noise)
6.	00.35	WA (above street-level)	Crowd attacking squad-car. One youth throws pipe (?) through police-car window. Car reverses to escape but is pursued by crowd moving right to left.	(Crash of squad-car window breaking) By the end of the carnival, 546 people had been injured, (325 of them policemen). If it hadn't been known *before*, it was now clear
7.	00.45	MS (street-level)	Overturned car on fire outside basement of house.	that *more* action was needed.

TEACHING IDEA 5: STARTING-POINTS: PR DISASTERS, TV CHAT-SHOWS AND *OUR TUNE*

These ideas might be developed into effective lessons. They are partly based on the idea of applying the conventional criteria for 'hard' news selection to 'softer' more personal areas with the aim of establishing how they work. They draw heavily on the insights offered in Chapter 3 of this book. In each case, suggestions are made which involve active tasks for small groups.

PR disasters

- Invent a suitable disaster and write a press release from an imaginary PR company to the press.
- Devise a sequence of questions to put to a company representative on a radio news programme (perhaps even simulate the interview?).

TV chat-shows

- Write a job advertisement for a television chat-show host. What special qualities and experience are necessary? Peter Estall of *Wogan* listed charisma, friendliness, intelligence, knowledge, memory, writing ability, verbal fluency, confidence, broadcast experience and popularity. What order of priority would you put these qualities in?
- Write a list of selection criteria for choosing guests to appear on a specific show.
- Devise an interview outline for three guests on a specific show:
    Who to select?
    What topics to explore with each guest?
    What order to interview guests in? Why?
    Write a sequence of three questions for each guest on cue-cards for the presenter.
    Write one 'bomb-shell' question for each guest: where and how to slip it in?

Our Tune

- Students listen to broadcast examples of stories on Simon Bates's Radio 1 programme (around 11 a.m.) and discuss how it works.
- Students each write a letter to the Simon Bates programme from the point of view of someone who wants their story featured in the programme and exchange with each other.
- Using the letters as raw material, students turn them into an *Our Tune* narrative in Bates's style (written and/or performed live to other students).

Chapter 4

Some forms of fiction

Chapter 3 was essentially concerned with how 'facts' are presented in the media. It showed that the kind of 'truth' which informative reporting strives to achieve relies on journalistic notions of objectivity. This involves, amongst other things, a respect for the facts. Yet the way facts are presented often owes a great deal to dramatic and fictional structures.

In Chapter 4, we look at how fiction creates a different kind of 'truth'. In its own way, fiction is no less 'true' than factual reporting. Yet the characters, events and language on which fiction relies are all invented. We concentrate on forms of fiction which are familiar to children:

- Media and imagination
- Popular television drama
- Children and media: dangerous liaisons?
- The theatre of the mind
- Magazines and comics
- Literature: reading and responding

MEDIA AND IMAGINATION

When Kenneth Baker was Secretary of State for Education, he wrote a short article (*Sunday Times*, 28 February 1988) which clearly expressed his own views about children, fiction and imagination. He noted with pleasure that Shakespeare is alive and well in theatres, on television, on video and on radio up and down the land. But he argued that none of this could compare with *reading* Shakespeare.

Fortunately, this prejudice has been firmly rejected in the proposals of the Cox Committee on English 5–16 within the National Curriculum (DES 1989). In fact, the proposals go much further than any previous official initiatives in constantly referring to non-literary (or 'media') texts. Media appear in all the Attainment Targets created by Cox and in most of the Programmes of Study for nearly all Levels of Attainment at each Key Stage.

Kenneth Baker's prejudice about non-literary media is worth examining further, since it is one still shared by many others, including some teachers.

> Children watch too much television ... I find this depressing. Literature, the reading of good books, is in many important ways a superior, richer and deeper experience than watching television. A particular feature of the written or spoken word is the unique demand it makes upon the imagination.
>
> (Baker 1988)

> Like travel, television narrows the mind ... The difference between television and literature is fundamental. When we read a book we enter into a secret intimacy with the author, an intimacy ... between strangers. We form our own images in our heads. But when we watch television we all plug ourselves into our sets and collectively receive identical images.
>
> (Holroyd 1982)

The pervasiveness of television in society is now mirrored in schools. Over 98 per cent of primary and 99 per cent of secondary schools have at least one colour television: 78 per cent and 99 per cent have VTRs (BBC 1987). So even though some of the traditional hostility to television amongst teachers may remain, perhaps attitudes are changing (Davies 1989: 119). Whatever an ideal curriculum might prescribe, we have to face the fact that children experience a wide range of media texts, most of which are outside the classroom. This fact needs to be recognised in what and how we teach.

No one would deny the importance of imagination or its potential engagement through literature. But it is a matter of degree, not kind. All media experiences involve children in imaginative work, whether as readers, viewers, listeners, speakers or writers. As the Cox Report reminds us, 'children construct the world through story' (DES 1989: 7.1).

> Once children start to play, fiction is paramount. Play, fantasy, imagination, representation is important to children. It's a way that they use to try and understand the world that they live in.
>
> (Máire Messenger Davies)

POPULAR TELEVISION DRAMA

> Most people spend more time watching various kinds of drama than in preparing and eating food.
>
> (Williams 1974: 59–60)

Continuous serials

Fiction currently constitutes over 35 per cent of peak-time television output. The 'continuous serial' (now most known as 'soap opera',

Table 4.1 National Top Twenty-fives for week ending 15 July 1990

BBC1	million	ITV	million
1 Neighbours (Mon)	16.25	1 Coronation Street (Mon/Wed)	16.87
2 Neighbours (Tues)	14.52	2 Coronation Street (Wed/Sat)	15.34
3 Neighbours (Wed)	14.43	3 Coronation Street (Fri/Sat)	13.98
4 Neighbours (Fri)	14.08	4 Home and Away (Mon)	12.06
5 Neighbours (Thurs)	13.57	5 Home and Away (Tues)	10.98
6 Eastenders (Thurs/Sun)	12.56	6 The Bill (Tues)	10.62
7 Eastenders (Tues/Sun)	12.46	7 Home and Away (Thurs)	10.33
8 Heaven Can Wait	10.99	8 Home and Away (Fri)	10.30
9 Blackadder the Third	10.10	9 Home and Away (Wed)	10.17
10 Desperately Seeking Susan	8.70	10 The Upper Hand	9.42
11 Wogan (Mon)	8.28	11 Emmerdale (Tues)	9.31
12 Six O'Clock News (Mon)	7.65	12 The Bill (Thurs)	8.90
13 News and Weather (Sun)	7.56	13 The Cook Report	8.68
14 Miss Marple: A Pocketful of Rye	7.37	14 Home James	8.47
15 Victoria Wood	7.26	15 News (Sat)	8.17
16 All Creatures Great and Small	7.22	16 Emmerdale (Thurs)	7.99
17 Waiting for God	7.10	17 Island Son	7.95
18 Up to Something	6.93	18 The $64,000 Question	7.88
International Athletics	6.93	19 News at Ten (Mon)	7.87
20 Six O'Clock News (Tues)	6.74	20 Busman's Holiday	7.85
21 Nine O'Clock News (Tues)	6.54	21 Jimmy's	7.22
22 Takeover Bid	6.44	22 News at Ten (Wed)	7.18
23 Six O'Clock News (Wed)	6.25	News at Ten (Fri)	7.18
24 Six O'Clock News (Fri)	6.24	24 News at Ten (Thurs)	7.06
25 Nine O'Clock News (Mon)	6.23	25 LA Law	6.97

BBC2	million	Channel 4	million
1 The Best of Saturday Night Clive	4.12	1 Brookside (Mon/Sat)	5.38
2 Athletics	4.11	2 Brookside (Wed/Sat)	4.35
3 The Travel Show	3.59	3 Brookside (Fri/Sat)	4.15
4 Amongst Barbarians	3.45	4 Cheers	4.09
5 Naked Video	3.20	5 Roseanne	3.93
6 Sunday Grandstand	2.99	6 Countdown (Mon)	2.61
7 Focal Point	2.76	7 The Wonder Years	2.57
8 Gardeners' World	2.55	8 Don't Quote Me	2.51
9 One Man and His Dog	2.49	9 Countdown (Tues)	2.25
10 Rough Guide to the World (Wed/Sun)	2.48	10 Kingdom of the Deep	2.17
11 The Victorian Kitchen	1.94	11 Nuts in May	2.16
Grand Prix Highlights (Sun)	1.94	12 Land of the Giants	2.15
13 We're no Angels	1.92	13 Countdown (Wed)	2.10
14 Underwater	1.88	14 The Waltons	2.06
15 Where on Earth Are We Going?	1.53	15 The Desperate Hours	2.05
16 Cricket Highlights (Sat)	1.51	16 Eat the Peach	2.00
17 Present Imperfect	1.42	17 Countdown (Fri)	1.96
18 The Roux Brothers	1.35	18 Countdown (Thurs)	1.94
19 Under the Sun	1.34	19 Cutting Edge	1.83
20 Horizon	1.30	20 My Two Dads	1.78
Cricket (Mon)	1.30	21 Ramona	1.51
22 On the Line	1.28	Liftin' the Blues	1.51
23 Newsnight (Mon)	1.26	23 David the Gnome	1.43
24 Cricket (Wed)	1.20	Thirtysomething	1.43
Phil Silvers	1.20	25 Check Out (Tues/Sat)	1.40

Source: *Listener*, 2 August 1990

from the early days of American radio) has been one of the great popular successes of television. A total of about 80 million person-hours is spent watching soap opera each week.

Granada's *Coronation Street* has run for over thirty years and has only recently been matched in popularity by BBC's *EastEnders* and the imported *Neighbours*. Such serials are crucial for television companies because they reduce financial risks when compared with single plays or films. They are cheap to produce (because of savings made on recurrent settings and actors) and provide a constant supply of loyal viewers.

What is it that makes soaps so attractive to viewers? Characterisation is limited mostly to 'flat' serial types from three generations, but with more individualised or 'rounded' central characters. The stability of the communities they create, the predictability of plot developments and their recurrent transmission times (with omnibus repeats) are all important aspects of their appeal and help maintain audience loyalty.

Viewing pleasures

Unlike documentaries and detective stories, soaps typically flatter viewers by inviting them to see themselves as 'in the know', with a mastery of specialised social knowledge about characters and events in the serial.

> A significant part of the pleasure of everyday conversation about television derives from the re-living of its narratives, and in particular from the rehearsal of concealed or confidential information which narratives reveal. This re-telling of the 'secrets' which television invites us to share is often referred to, somewhat pejoratively, as 'gossip'. For younger children, this often has a particular fascination, akin to voyeurism. Television may provide them with representations of aspects of adult behaviour which are usually hidden from them, although they may well be aware of their existence. Discussing television may there-fore provide a relatively 'safe' way of acknowledging things which they are normally forbidden to talk about; as well as allowing us to look without being seen, television also allows us to pass comment without fear of reprisals.
>
> (Buckingham 1987b: 163)

One further pleasure offered by soaps has been established only recently through observation of viewers in their own homes and detailed discussions with groups of viewers about television. That is the ease with which television can be used like radio as a secondary medium and allow partial attention to something else (Taylor and Mullan 1986: 154).

Soaps also benefit from their symbiotic relationship with the press. The tabloid newspapers currently employ more than forty journalists as full-time television reporters (Taylor and Mullan 1986: 177). As a result of their attentions, the lives of serial characters are publicised and amplified in the press. And the lives of the actors are implicated in a curious parallel world which is neither quite factual nor entirely fictional.

> They don't only know that this is 'Dirty Den' they also know that it's Leslie Grantham, and they also know that Leslie Grantham has been to prison, so when 'Dirty Den' is in prison, there's a sort of double resonance here. They also know that 'well, that happened to him himself you know'. Now if you don't read the tabloids, if you're sort of upper-middle class and you're sitting there watching it, then you're not really understanding all the little nuances and frissons which are around in soap operas.

(Laurie Taylor)

BASIC CHARACTERISTICS OF SOAPS

Story-lines based on personal and family relationships
Privileged access to intimate secrets of characters
Invitation to moral judgements about behaviour
Multiple story-lines
Speculation about future development encouraged

(Buckingham 1987b: 4)

> If it is a well written episode the writer will try and make the viewer think about the possible ways in which a story-line might or might not go. And if he's structuring it correctly he will time it so that at the end of an episode we don't know whether the story-line is going to go down route A, B or C, and it's left in a sense for that viewer to determine which way he would like it to go.

(Nick Prosser)

Narrative

> Always the same, always changing . . .

(Geraghty 1981: 22)

The appeal of continuous serials is mainly to the known and familiar. But there is much more to them than that. Surprise and suspense are also built into their narratives to raise curiosity and retain interest. Their success depends on a subtle blend of continuity with change.

> You have plural story-lines, tiered one on top of another. Some are short term, some are medium, some long term, some are very light-hearted, some are much heavier. And the good half-hour soap opera is dependent on those actually mixing together well, not to have too many of them, to have the right balance of level between those tiers so that

Figure 4.1   Characters and plot in *Coronation Street*

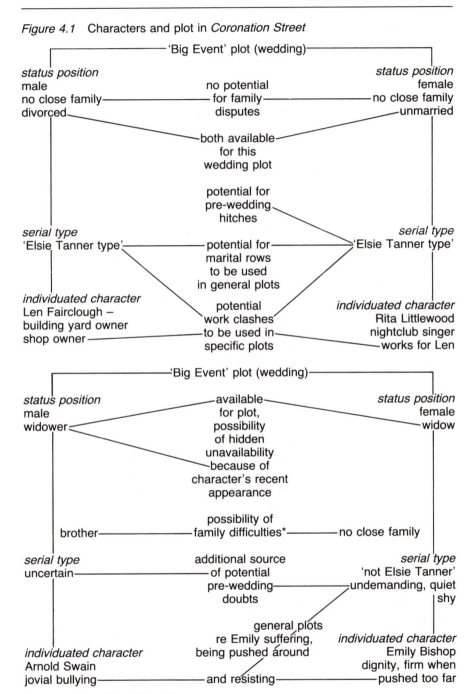

Source: Geraghty 1981: 23
Note: *These diagrams were drawn before the revelation of Arnold's bigamy

> you have a good blend, and ideally that those stories actually link in some way. So you're not just cutting from something in one house to something totally separate in another household.

(Nick Prosser)

The televisual language of British soaps is very much based on naturalist conventions. They rely heavily on the context of the nuclear family in established domestic interiors or communal spaces like shops, pubs and cafes.

> The lighting is usually flat, without harsh shadows; the camerawork is generally static and unobtrusive, with close-ups and tracking shots used only rarely; the editing follows the rules of standard continuity editing.

(Buckingham 1987b: 74)

'EastEnders'

EastEnders was first transmitted at 7 p.m. on 19 February 1985. It initially attracted 13 million viewers and achieved an Audience Reaction rating of 58, climbing to 80 by August (the average AI for British soaps is 70: see Chapter 2). It moved to 7.30 p.m. in September 1985 and was given a 2 p.m. omnibus repeat on Sundays. As a result of thus establishing itself, it reached a viewing peak of 23 million during February and March in 1986 with an AI of 85 (Buckingham 1987b: 21–3).

Text and texture

EastEnders is more complex in its plotting than *Neighbours*. It also has a low frequency of dramatic incidents in comparison with other soaps, but still creates an impression of fast action and excitement. It does so by creating a density of texture in both its content and style. For example, it offers a multiplicity of characters and frequent shifts of location. It often refers backwards, forwards and sideways, not only to restate what viewers already know but make us 'work harder' at reading the text. It has a higher than usual number of major simultaneous story-lines (five or six on average compared with three in *Coronation Street* or *Brookside* and often less in *Neighbours*). The camera work is highly mobile and creates a sense of bustle which is sometimes restless and disturbing (like *Hill Street Blues* or *Making Out*) . This business is also reinforced by the density of atmospheric background sound (again, in stark contrast with the suburban silence of *Neighbours*) (Buckingham 1987b: 54–5).

> Soap operas allow for space for active viewing, so that what viewers are doing in making sense of soap operas is constantly filling in background, recalling what's gone on beforehand, looking forward, making predictions

Table 4.2 Episodic strands in Coronation Street

Episode	1818	1819	1820	1821	1822	1823	1824	1825	1826	1827
Theme										
The Strike	M.T.	M.T.	S.T.	P.	M.T.	M.T.				
Alf/Bet/Renee	S.T.	S.T.	M.T.	S.T.			S.T.	M.T.		
Elsie's return	S.T.	P.				P.	P.	P.		
Fred and Alma			P.	M.T.	P.	P.				
Ena's bed					S.T.	S.T.	M.T.	M.T.		
Emily and Brenda									M.T.	M.T.
Ray vs. Len								P.	S.T.	S.T.

Source: Paterson and Stewart 1981: 83
Notes: M.T. = Main theme
S.T. = Secondary theme as indicated in story outlines
P. = Presence of theme in subsidiary way

as to what's going to be happening in the future, looking across to different story-lines, comparing different characters in similar situations.

(David Buckingham)

Table 4.3 *EastEnders* episode 67 (tx. 8 October 1985): characters and locations

Scene	1	2	3	4	5	6	7	8	9	10	11	12	13	14	15	16	17	18	19
Location	A	B	C	D	B	E	F	DA	F	A	G	H	G	E	G	C	G	A	G
Pauline	x								x								x		x
Arthur	x								x									x	
Michelle	x			x					x				x	x			x		x
Martin	x						x		x									x	
Lou	x							x	x		x					x			x
Nick		x	x			x	x									x			x
Ethel		x		x								x		x		x			x
Dr Legg		x		x															
Debs			x			x	x								x				x
Angie			x								x		x		x	x			x
Wicksy			x		x	x	x				x							x	x
Kathy					x									x		x			x
Saeed						x													
Sue						x		x								x			x
Ali								x								x			x
Ian								x			x					x			x
Lofty		x									x					x	x		x
Kelvin											x					x			
Sharon													x		x	x			x
Den											x		x	x		x			x
Pete														x				x	x
Mary				x													x		x

Source: Buckingham 1987b: 56
Key to locations A = Fowlers' living room; B = Dr Legg's waiting room/surgery; C = Lofty's bedsit; D = outside Debs'/Fowlers' houses; E = Beales' fruit and veg stall; F = cafe; G = Queen Vic; H = laundrette

Like other soaps, *EastEnders* creates a sense of life being lived at normal pace, in parallel with the audience's social experience. Its rhythm and continuity partly depend on a recurrent diurnal structure punctuated by pub opening hours and much meal-taking.

There is a density of naturalistic detail in the background sound and in the design of sets and costumes, and a distinct lack of opulence. Above all, much of the action is resolutely mundane: the characters do their laundry, go shopping, cook and eat meals, go to the lavatory, take their dogs for walks and make endless cups of tea.

(Buckingham 1987b: 74)

Table 4.4 *EastEnders* episode 67 (tx. 8 October 1985): story-lines

Scene	1	2	3	4	5	6	7	8	9	10	11	12	13	14	15	16	17	18	19
Michelle	X				X					X			X	x				X	
Nick/Ethel		X	X			X	x				x	X		X			x		
Wicksy				x		X	x	X		x	X	x		x			x	X	X
Debbie				X				x	X		X					X			
Darts							X					x				x	X		X
Saeed							X												
Angie															X				

Source: Buckingham 1987b: 57
Notes: X = major focus in this scene; x = minor focus

Figure 4.1a   Characters in *Neighbours*

——SOAPWATCH——

Show Houses

Just how neighbourly are the characters in *Neighbours*? BYRON ROGERS tries to put together the pieces of the Ramsay Street jigsaw.

All the homely people, where do they all come from? Ramsay Street regulars (top) and Mrs Mangel's wedding day

PHOTOS: PRESS ASSOCIATION

When my father went to see films, it was to admire chairs. He was a cabinet-maker, and loved scenes in ante-rooms and parlours, the bigger the better: anywhere, in fact, where people waited about and did not get in the way of the furniture. He loved staircases too, and was the last man down our way who could turn a stair. Tarzan he could not abide, or Westerns. And I don't think he would have liked *Neighbours*.

Why wouldn't he have liked it? Well, just ask yourself two questions. Are the dwellings in Ramsay Street bungalows? Those repeated shots of the exteriors make it clear that they are not, yet you never see a staircase in *Neighbours*. You rarely see a bedroom either, and when you do, it is a lonely place where one of the cast goes to mope.

Even more significantly, who lives next door to whom? Ask the BBC's press office, and it is as though you had inquired after a definition of the Holy Ghost. 'Oh, oh . . . gosh . . . Oh God. Well, they do change around a bit.' Even the soap's official fan club, set up earlier this year in Watford, did not know, until they remembered an ancient map that had come out of Australia.

Paul Robinson, motel owner, lives next door to Harold Bishop, cafe proprietor, who lives next door to Jim Robinson, Paul's dad, who lives next door to Des Clarke, a widower. Beyond Des Clarke is a house lived in by Hilary, Jim's cousin, and, beyond that, is the Mangel house. But you try to work that out from your two daily doses.

There is a vagueness surrounding the geography of the close because to establish its topography would require location shots (there is a real Ramsay Street), and everyone knows that *Neighbours*, like the last days of Hitler, takes place indoors. The Red Army forced this on the Führer; with *Neighbours*, it is the accountants of Grundy Television.

Have you noticed, too, how often the curtains are closed? Even in Paul Robinson's office, the blinds are always down. You could be forgiven for assuming that the whole street is deep underground. When its inhabitants do emerge, it is usually under an overcast studio sky. There is the odd expedition, though, to a rather sinister stretch of water they call 'the water hole', beside which they hold picnics or each other's hands, while you wait hopefully for something horrible to emerge from the placid depths.

Apart from that, it is kitchen-diner after kitchen-diner, 'a beige world', as Barbara Cartland would describe it, of varnished pine and bare brown bricks. When the cast of *Neighbours* is not attempting to fix rendezvous for chats with each other ('Can we talk?', 'I'd like to talk', 'This is a good place to talk', 'We'll talk later, I promise'), it has its collective nose deep in the trough ('I'll put the kettle on', 'Some more coffee?', 'I'd better get to the shops or we won't be getting any dessert').

This, of course, means that all the action can take place in the studio sets for the three main houses, among the potted plants, the fitted kitchens, the louvred cupboards, the racked spice-bottles and the rubber gloves.

The rooms in the three main houses are interchangeable, all of them open-plan (so the cameras do not have to be moved), except that the Robinsons appear to have a wall between the kitchen-diner and the lounge (only the Mangels appear to have rooms). But such things are hard to spot, so closely do the cameras focus on the rage, ecstasies and despairs flitting across the characters' faces. In *Neighbours*, they do not like you watching the interiors. Your only real chance comes when one of the babies that appear from time to time decides to do an unscripted runner, and the cameras are obliged to pull back.

The taste is modern-clinical (though the Mangels go in for reproduction furniture), with everything designed to be labour-saving —just as well since nobody ever does any housework, apart from washing-up.

The one touch of eccentricity is Des's Japanese screen, but then you might need reminding that, as a bank manager in Australia, he has Japanese clients (whom he insulted recently). There are none of the little touches you once had in *Coronation Street*, like three plaster ducks that flew through the glorious bad taste of Hilda Ogden's blown-up Pacific sunrise. There is no bad taste in *Neighbours*. What there is is an anonymous, upwardly mobile good taste, as though all the families had materialised in the show houses you get on half-finished housing estates.

Nobody refers to anything. You are not told where any of these objects were bought, the lines of pots, the framed butterfly collections. Nobody dreams of interior decoration. And there is no dust.

At some point in their tangled past, the Robinsons appear to have trekked away from the beige—in their case to anchor in a world of greys and blues, just like the blue ship in the blue harbour on their wall. Again, you have to look quickly, perhaps wait weeks for a glimpse of this or any of the other paintings, none of which you will ever recognise. You might go mad looking at these interiors.

It is all there, perfectly in place, but none of it has anything to do with the people who are supposed to live with it or, in this case, materialise here. Where did they come from? Where, for heaven's sake, did Bronwyn come from, with her further education and her place in close-eyed Henry's bed? Even the fan club could only suggest 'from the country'.

I have been brooding over these sets for a week now, trying to think where I had seen them before, and it has just come to me. Remember the final set in *2001: A Space Odyssey*, when the last astronaut has gone through the Star Gate, crossed the galaxies, and sits in a room which should be familiar but isn't? Everything is in perfect taste but it is no human hand that has assembled it. There are no windows or dust.

That is the world of *Neighbours*. The speeded-up marionettes move through rooms assembled by something which has watched humanity from long-range for its own inscrutable purposes, which may now be watching us, watching its creations. Think about it.

Source: *Listener*, 13 September 1990

Table 4.5a *Neighbours* (tx. 2 May 1988) episode analysis: characters and locations

| Scene | 1 | 2 | 3 | 4 | 5 | 6 | 7 | 8 | 9 | 10 | 11 | 12 | 13 | 14 | 15 | 16 |
Location	O	H	O	H	O	H	D	O	D	H	D	O	D	O	H	D
Kelly	X			X		X		X		X		X				
Mike	X										X			X	X	
Scott	X		X				X		X			X				
Daphne		X		X	X		X	X	X		X				X	X
Helen		X		X	X	X	X		X		X			X	X	
Paul	X		X		X		X		X							
Jim				X	X	X										
Lucy					X	X										
Des																X
Eileen							X		X	X				X		

Key: O = Outside   H = Helen's   D = Daphne's

Table 4.5b Story-lines

	1	2	3	4	5	6	7	8	9	10	11	12	13	14	15	16
Kelly	X	X	x	X	X	X	X		X	X	X		X			
Scott		X							x		X			X	x	
Des									X							
Helen		x														X

Key: X = Major role   x = Minor role

NARRATIVE DEVICES

Cliff-hangers.
False trails ('snares').
Well-kept secrets.
Invited speculation.
Moving across text to link with other story-strands.

(Buckingham 1987b: 62–71)

Representation

ll Soap operas tend to personalise rather than analyse.

(Bob Ferguson)

Whilst some critics argue that soaps only deal with trivia, there can be no doubt that *EastEnders* engages with major social issues. Its very title and location depend implicitly on a concern with class. It constantly dramatises events which arise from the clash between a traditional working-class community and the demands of a more diverse modern society. That society is also a multi-cultural one and so racial issues inevitably arise.

Yet, as with the representation of class, there is a lack of reference to broader structural inequalities. This results in the creation of an apparent oasis of multi-racial harmony. Whilst *Coronation Street* undoubtedly explores different models of femaleness, *EastEnders* is more concerned with examining the traditional masculine roles.

> If it is an issue like race it is very seldom ... tackled on more than a personal level. Now [the] personal level is a very important level, but the issues of racism ... are not issues that are resolvable by what you say to your mate in the pub. They didn't start in the pub and they don't end in the pub.
>
> (Bob Ferguson)

Yet whatever particular concerns are addressed and however fluently they are blended into the daily life of Albert Square, the central questions are about *representation*. How are ambiguities, problems and conflicts actually dealt with in the programme? What overall views of social groups and the role of individuals within them emerge?

> To what extent does *EastEnders* seek to construct an artificially harmonious community, and thereby to efface fundamental differences and inequalities, particularly those based on class and ethnicity?
>
> (Buckingham 1987: 94)

Ideology

> Soap operas have been renowned over the years for occasionally raising certain issues, and when *EastEnders* started, and now with *Brookside* also occasionally, issues like class, unemployment, issues around gender, do come up, and when they do I think they should be welcomed. If you take a broad perspective however, there really has not been in the history of soap operas a great kind of taking on of the social issues of the day.
>
> (Bob Ferguson)

In spite of the popularity of soaps, some critics maintain that their predictability and sentimentality are dangerous. Threats from outside are constantly repelled or neutralised by the internal stability and strengths of the dominant community and its appeal to 'common sense'. If familiar problems are resolved in an unchallenging way, the danger is that the solutions will be ones which maintain the *status quo*. So the characteristic structures of feeling and ideas will be conservative.

But it is not just the way that the characters are presented, the stories structured and the central problems resolved which raises questions about ideology. Equally important is what is *missing* from soaps.

> Young people watching that programme would think black people don't exist in Australia. I wonder though how many of them are learning how

Figure 4.2 'In a lather over soap'

Bob Ferguson, the media studies lecturer who believes that Blue Peter is racist, sexist, royalist, pro-capitalist and removed from the real world, looks at British soap operas.

Now that the BBC has its own 'soap' it is an opportune moment to reconsider British soap opera. This field has been of considerable interest to those involved in media studies and to many media buffs for some time.

I'd like to turn first to one or two comments on the genre which have appeared recently in the British Press. It would seem that apologists for soap are prone to veer towards eccentricity. Peter Buckman in 'The Guardian' November 29, 1984 refers to regular viewers of other than prime-time soap in the language normally reserved for users of heroin; "The addicts need their fix more often and less cut with trendiness than prime-time can give. The prime-time watchers are mere amateurs."

Buckman is fulsome in his praise of the genre, suggesting that it transcends national boundaries, just as myths and morality tales do. He also points out that "the soap fans love tackiness (something the critics can't understand)." But he misses the point that a large number of the critics *are* soap fans. He tells us that the Queen is an avid *Coronation Street* fan, while the Queen Mother prefers *Crossroads*. Just as with heroin, soap opera addiction transcends class barriers as well as national ones.

We do not have very many reliable statistics about exactly who constitutes the vast audiences for soaps in this country. A cynical theory might suggest that it is composed of everybody's friends. What is clear, however, is that soaps are followed with enthusiasm by young and old of both sexes. Julia Smith, the producer of BBC's *EastEnders*, has also suggested that a considerable proportion of the audience is lonely people who live in bedsitters. "If we can give them something to discuss over their shop counters the next morning then it's worthwhile."

It is a moot point whether or not such discussion does take place. What is arguable is that soaps have taken over for many people the function of actual social contact. Perhaps they do not talk about soaps, either over the counter or in the dole queue. What they may do is live privately and vicariously a life which would otherwise not exist for them.

But what about the happy viewers? There must be several million of those who watch *Crossroads*, *Coronation Street* and *EastEnders* who are not experiencing daily pangs of alienation. Why do they watch? Gillian Reynolds of the 'Telegraph' has suggested that it is

In a lather over soap

because they want to know what happens next and to someone else. It will take a lot more research, however, before we can begin to answer these questions.

There are certain presences and absences in soap operas that we can identify and are indeed a matter for some concern. Not that I wish to start a moral panic. Indeed those whose worries might lead along that road should relax. Soap operas neither subvert nor corrupt.

Consider the way class is represented in both *Coronation Street* and the relative newcomer *EastEnders*. How many of the men or women portrayed ever work on the production line or in industry? Do we see them at work or (God forbid) organising?

There has been a lamentable (some would say scandalous) lack of engagement in soaps with the fact that we are now a multi-racial, multi-cultural society.

In relation to representation of gender, it has been pointed out that many of the women in *Coronation Street* have been portrayed as forceful, independent and capable. This is undoubtedly the case and it might have an effect on some of the audience in the long term. It might.

It is certainly the case that *EastEnders* is attempting to raise issues concerning both racism and drugs, but one gets the uneasy feeling that both will be dealt with through the elimination of unpleasant individuals who will thereby be identified as the root cause of the problem.

There are many other absences that cannot be gone into now. Most of them are to do with serious matters, whether social in the wider political sense or concerned with the inter-personal.

A common pull in British soaps is towards nostalgia and those moments in life when a tear wells up. The sense of community they evoke is rooted in a past long gone for the majority. They pull us back to a world that might have existed in order that we may tolerate what exists now. The past goes on for ever. The future goes on till the next episode.

By now the addicts will be setting aside their metaphorical syringes and telling me that soap is just good old fashioned entertainment. I am reminded that I am a killjoy with no sense of humour. As a media studies lecturer I have to remember that there are layers of signification and structures of meaning in soap operas which are worthy of serious study. I need to remember that people want a sense of identity.

But then I need to remind myself, just in case I forget under the weight of argument of righteously indignant addicts, that British soap operas are also first rate ideological binding agents. And, as Lord Reith might have said, "Anything wrong with that?"

I suppose the answer depends upon your line on laxatives.

Source: *Broadcast*, 3 May 1985

> to develop a critique of that and to be aware of how ... lenses are being set up for them as to what the world is about. If all they watch is something like *Neighbours*, then they're getting an incredibly limited view.
>
> (Beverley Naidoo)

The absence of radical conflict and the erasure from the text of disturbing elements which may occur in actual social experience is what gives some soaps like *Neighbours* their particular appeal for children.

> Life isn't always easy and it isn't always reassuring but when you're 8 and 9 the sort of stories that you want are – and that's ... one of the purposes that stories serve in childhood. *Neighbours* obviously works in that way. It's utterly anodyne and reassuring. Nothing goes wrong in *Neighbours* for very long and that's why children like it. Other kinds of soaps like *Brookside* and *EastEnders* I think offer different kinds of gratifications because they are more realistic.
>
> (Máire Messenger Davies)

Yet we cannot be concerned simply with the apparent characteristics of television texts. We need to examine how audiences actually respond to them and make sense of them.

> What is it that one brings to the media which is of such great significance? Of course, one brings one's own daily life and experience, one's own exhaustion, one's need for relaxation and pleasure. One brings all those things. It is also the case that one brings either one's progressiveness or one's reaction to a programme, that the same programme can be read many, many different ways by different people. Instead of suggesting that the programme influences people in that sense what one might say is that the programme may confirm people in their positions. So those racist viewers who see a programme where a black person appears, normal or not, may well be confirmed in their racism.
>
> (Bob Ferguson)

CHILDREN AND MEDIA: DANGEROUS LIAISONS?

> Audiences are not the passive victims of scheduling decisions, and they do discriminate, often in very discerning ways, between different examples of the same genre.
>
> (Buckingham 1987b: 4)

There is no doubt that television is the most popular medium amongst children. There are currently about 9 million 4- to 15-year-olds (about 17 per cent of the population) but at peak viewing times they constitute a third of the total audience. This pattern varies according to the season. In winter, for example, 74 per cent of 4- to 7-year-olds are watching at 4 p.m. on weekdays, while only half that number watch at the same time in summer (BBC Broadcasting Research Department 1984). Children between 4 and 12 watch an average of five programmes each day, and within this age-band the heaviest viewing is by 7- to 9-year-olds in families from social classes D and E. As children get older, they watch less television and, for some reason, develop a preference (most pronounced amongst male viewers) for BBC programmes (Wober 1986).

Children as television audiences

All three of Britain's major soaps are broadcast during family viewing hours before the 9 o'clock 'watershed'. They all (particularly *Neighbours*) have some appeal for children. They all depend on the imaginative involvement of viewers. But soaps are not all the same and their different appeals are reflected in the composition of their audiences. One-third of the *Neighbours* audience, for example, are 15 or under and about half are under 25.

Table 4.6 Neighbours: percentage audience by age, sex and social grade

		13.30–13.50 (Wk 3–4)					17.35–18.00 (Wk 3–4)				
		Mon	*Tue*	*Wed*	*Thu*	*Fri*	*Mon*	*Tue*	*Wed*	*Thu*	*Fri*
AGE	4–7	1	2	2	2	3	10	9	9	10	9
	8–11	1	1	1	1	2	11	12	11	12	13
	12–15	3	2	3	3	3	14	14	12	13	13
All children		5	5	6	6	8	35	35	32	35	35
	16–24	10	9	10	10	10	13	15	14	13	14
	25–34	16	16	16	16	15	13	12	13	13	11
	35–44	15	16	16	15	16	12	12	13	13	12
	45–54	12	14	13	13	13	9	9	9	9	10
	55–64	13	12	13	13	13	8	7	8	7	7
	65+	29	28	26	27	25	10	10	11	10	11
SEX	Males	26	28	27	27	28	39	40	38	40	41
	Females	74	72	73	73	72	61	60	62	60	59
SOCIAL GRADE	AB	13	11	14	13	14	17	18	16	16	17
	C1	19	18	18	16	16	20	21	20	22	22
	C2	26	27	27	25	28	30	30	32	30	29
	DE	42	44	41	45	42	33	31	32	32	32

Source: BARB/AGB (Wk 3–4) 1988

Recent public discussion of children and television in Britain has been dominated by fear of television's potentially harmful effects. The group of teachers who reported to the DES in 1983 were worried that children routinely watched adult programmes containing incidents and values which might be considered harmful to them (see Table 4.7).

Table 4.7 Percentage of total population watching selected television programmes during week beginning 22 March 1982, by age

	Total population	Age 4–7	Age 8–11	Age 12–15	Age 16–24	Age 25–34	Age 35–44	Age 45–54	Age 55–64	Age 65–
Sunday										
Whoops Apocalypse	13	1	6	9	15	20	17	15	11	9
Monday										
Early Evening News (BBC 1)	15	12	13	11	12	12	14	15	17	26
News at 5.45 (ITN)	15	6	9	7	11	11	10	19	25	31
Nationwide	16	14	14	10	12	14	16	17	20	23
Panorama	8	2	3	4	5	7	7	8	12	14
World in Action	14	4	14	9	9	18	16	13	16	17
Police	12	1	2	4	9	19	15	14	18	12
Tuesday										
Early Evening News	13	8	12	10	8	11	13	14	15	24
News at 5.45		7	9	11	12					
Nationwide	11	5	8	8	7	10	10	12	15	19
Emery	18	14	32	19	11	24	19	15	16	15
The Glamour Girls	14	5	7	7	10	12	10	16	22	28
Wednesday										
Early Evening News	13	8	9	9	7	9	11	15	18	25
News at 5.45	17	5	10	12	13	14	10	21	24	30
Nationwide										
Minder	24	3	11	19	22	33	24	28	25	28
Thursday										
Early Evening News	13	9	7	7	7	8	12	15	16	28
News at 5.45	16	5	9	10	12	11	9	19	24	33
Nationwide	11	8	6	8	6	8	10	12	16	18
Tomorrow's World	16	20	25	21	13	19	16	14	14	15
Top of the Pops	25	34	44	33	25	32	28	22	15	11
Kenny Everett TV Show	23	26	36	31	21	31	27	20	12	12
Shelley	20	3	12	12	17	22	18	24	24	30
Friday										
Early Evening News	12	8	9	6	8	8	10	15	16	22
News at 5.45	15	6	11	11	10	9	9	16	23	29
Nationwide	12	8	9	6	8	10	10	13	15	19
Family Fortunes	26	21	25	13	19	23	23	28	34	41
The Gaffer	24	18	31	14	15	24	22	24	25	33
We'll Meet Again	22	7	14	10	14	23	22	26	29	33
McClain's Law	14	3	9	9	9	15	18	17	16	15
Saturday										
Mind Your Language	22	22	20	16	17	21	19	24	27	30
Dallas	23	8	18	16	15	27	21	25	29	35

Source: DES 1983: 5

Note: Figures for *Crossroads* and *Hill Street Blues* are not available as these programmes were not nationally networked at the same time. **Boxed figures** = area of concern noted in the DES 1983 report.

Effects of television on children

Debate has been quickened by hysteria over so-called 'video nasties' which led to the 1984 Video Recordings Act. Similarly, concern about changes in the structure of broadcasting in Britain (especially the role of satellite and cable) has produced the Broadcasting Standards Council. Whilst Kenneth Baker has been concerned with the alleged failure of television to engage the imagination and make demands on children, others have been worried about the dangers of their imaginations being over-involved. This is particularly so with erotic and/or violent material, especially when it is experienced in a normally protected domestic context. The dangers arise, it is argued, because of the special power of visual imagery and the degree of imaginative involvement it produces: children identify with, absorb and imitate the behaviour they see on television. As a result, their own characters and the general social and cultural life of their society are damaged.

> The excessive time spent on watching television creates a situation similar to that of a child living on a diet of one single food such as meat pies or chicken. Whereas meat pies and chicken are good foods when integrated into a complete, nutritious diet, when eaten exclusively they do not provide the variety of nutrients needed for healthy development. Similarly, if children spend most of their leisure time simply watching television, no matter how good the programmes, their growth will be stunted because they are not getting the rich variety of experiences and activities which are necessary for healthy physical, psychological and mental development.
>
> (Horsfield 1986: 53)

The arguments about effects have been running for decades and have never been satisfactorily resolved. Most recently, in the debate over 'video nasties', researchers like Cumberbatch and Barker have shown how careful we need to be in accepting some of the findings of people like Clifford Hill and his colleagues (Barker 1984a, 1984b; Cumberbatch 1984; Barlow and Hill 1985). The so-called Parliamentary Group Video Enquiry suggested that large numbers of very young children were being harmed as a result of watching 'video nasties'. But their methods and data were unreliable. Much of their work was based on problem families listed by the NSPCC. They also relied on self-completed questionnaires which allowed children to claim they had seen non-existent videos. And their use of those titles reported to the Director of Public Prosecutions as a means of categorising 'video nasties' (even though many of these had not been prosecuted, let alone convicted) led them into some bizarre inclusions like *One Flew Over the Cuckoo's Nest.*

> Most people (75 per cent) think that there is more violence on television now than there was about ten years ago. However, most people are

mistaken. Violence and concerns about violence have clearly increased in society in the last decade but this has not been reflected by a proportional increase on television.

(Cumberbatch 1987: 41)

There is a danger of children being exposed to potentially disturbing situations which they are unable to understand and cope with. But there is a greater danger of assuming the existence of effects which are not demonstrable, of ignoring other relevant variables and of making television the scapegoat for all society's ills. We have to ask what consequences we could reasonably expect to occur if television could somehow be magically removed from the calculation.

Television is not all-powerful. It can provide examples of some of life's possibilities for children. It can give them ideas for play and satisfy some of their curiosity for knowledge. But it cannot play for them. Similarly, it can show them how other people, including 'bad' people, behave, but it cannot bring them up to be nice or nasty people. Only families and communities can do that.

(Messenger Davies 1989: 28)

Children's responses

They watch the screen and passively soak in images, words and sounds hour after hour, as if in a dream.

(Winn 1977: 194)

The most recent large-scale research has been carried out by Cullingford. His study was based on the responses of a sample of over 5,000 children from different Western countries and it has received wide exposure in the popular media in Britain. He found that children's television learning styles and strategies showed great subtlety. But at the same time, the differences between their responses were only superficial. Variations in styles of presentation made little difference to these responses. He describes children's characteristic response to television as a 'laconic indifference'. Television promotes, he argues, a form of 'perceptual passivity' amongst viewers. (See Hart 1986a and 1986b for fuller discussion of this study.)

Most of the time children view television with not only an indifference to the meanings or possible meanings being offered, but a palpable resentment that there should be even a hint that they should need to derive significant meanings . . . It is as if their minds were functioning on a different level, below a trapdoor of language, which, when language attempts to describe it, transforms the nature of what is being described.

(Cullingford 1984: 150)

The effects of television lie not so much in the content but in the actual conditions of viewing.

> The acquisition of the habit of subconscious inattentive viewing, half-hearted attention sustained over long periods, an indifference to information and the casualness of boredom are all part of children's response to television. The effect itself lies in the act of watching.
>
> (Cullingford 1984: 176)

There are undoubtedly large variations in individual learning styles and strategies. It is therefore important to relate the study of children's responses to television more closely to relevant general theories of learning. These would then provide a sounder basis for conducting effective research.

> It is not the medium itself which imposes social norms as much as the individuals responding to the medium.
>
> (Cullingford 1984: 179)

According to Cullingford, content and style are only marginally relevant. The medium is the message, not as a result of the total submersion and participation of viewers in the process, but for precisely the opposite reason, that they remain aloof, indifferent and untouched by it. If Cullingford's findings were valid, we would not need to be in any way concerned with the effects or influence of television. But his account of children's responses is as suspect as that of the Parliamentary Group Video Enquiry on 'video nasties'. It lacks any convincing account of how children make sense of television. Cullingford's analysis of children's responses is written as if he had actually had access to what was going on in their minds. In reality, he is merely speculating on the basis of data from postal questionnaires (although he is understandably reluctant to mention this important methodological fact).

Interactive viewing

Thinking of the viewing process as an interactive one requires a shift of focus away from medium and message towards children as viewers. It demands that we see them as active participants in the making of meaning. Meaning becomes the product of an interaction between programmes and viewers rather than a fixed property of the programmes. Traditional effects research focuses on audiences as passive objects. But this approach emphasises the role of audiences as informed subjects who respond actively to what they see.

> Television, like other media, does not necessarily work in directly observable ways to have an influence and it may take time for the constant exposure to creative ideas to have an effect.
>
> (Messenger Davies 1989: 66)

Other researchers have found that children's responses are active, thoughtful and sophisticated (Hart 1986b, 1988; Palmer 1986; Hodge and Tripp 1986).

> They act like it's really happening, they get really into what they're acting ... they don't just stand there and say something ... They act it and they sort of feel it, and so you feel it as well, so you get into the show with them.
>
> (Annette (11) on *Sons and Daughters*, in Palmer 1986: 42–3)

> Television elicits direct responses from children which, on the whole, are favourable and trusting, creative and positive. Children rarely complain or criticise in their spontaneous responses to the medium, and when they are asked for specific contributions, like artwork or competition entries, they give them in impressive numbers and with great imaginative diversity. Although the children who write, or send contributions, in response to programmes are a self-selected sample and thus cannot be assumed to be typical of the whole population, the extent to which their response is positive is impressive – particularly when contrasted with the mainly negative responses of adults (also a self-selected sample). But there are other ways which indicate how children respond to television – ways in which they take programme commercials and their messages and put them to use in other areas of their lives. Television does influence the activities of children – but not always in ways which we would expect or predict.
>
> (Messenger Davies 1989: 164)

Figure 4.3   An interactive model of how meaning is constructed

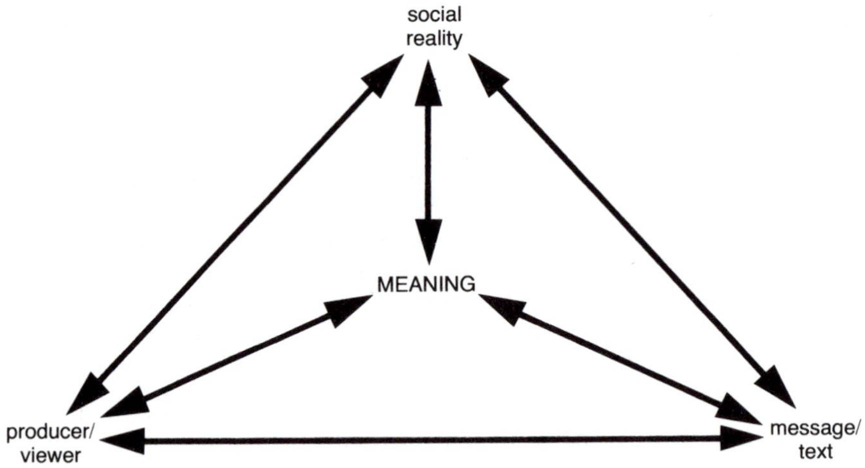

Source: After Fiske 1990: 4

THE THEATRE OF THE MIND

Children should experiment ... with dramatic improvisations of the stories they read and write; they should experience and take part in the performance of poetry; they should listen critically to radio plays.

(DES 1989: 7.8)

To imagine that more than a handful of young people are listening to radio plays is at best wishful thinking and at worst naïve. A common-sense view tells us that young people's use of radio is largely confined to listening to popular music presented by fast-talking DJs. This kind of radio is not generally seen as presenting the range of fictional forms which we have noted in television. And yet a closer look at the schedules for Radio 1 or an average local commercial radio station would reveal the use of a whole range of story forms which appear to have strong audience appeal. Programme trails, advertisements and public information campaigns often use short narrative forms to underscore their messages. And large audiences have been achieved by DJs, able to create a good running story as a back-drop to the records, from Jack Jackson in the 1950s to Steve Wright in the 1990s. Furthermore, the conventions of soap opera are used in one of Radio 1's most popular features, *Our Tune*, where DJ Simon Bates extemporises tales of tragedy and romance woven from letters sent in by listeners. As we showed in Chapter 3, *Our Tune* is a kind of 'mini-soap' characterised by gossipy accessible language, careful scene-setting, detailed narration of dramatic moments, essential bridging passages and simple moralising. Such examples show how popular radio can provide a useful and easily accessible source of fictional forms. Understanding how these forms use the radio conventions of words, music, sounds and silence in order to stimulate the theatre of the mind, could be the starting-point for more complex work on radio.

Radio and imagination

Hardly anyone studies radio in school, not because they they think it's depraved or dangerous, but because they can't imagine what they'd do with it.

(Bazalgette 1991)

The vital ingredient in the success of any radio programme is the imagination of the listener. It is often said that radio has better scenery than television because listeners are required to provide their own pictures. Radio uses a wide range of fictional techniques to help create these pictures, from the reading aloud of literature to the presentation of minimalist modern drama. Unseen characters and situations materialise in the mind of the listener, stimulated by a description of a scene or by hearing it acted out. Scenes can change quickly, allowing a strong narrative drive, as in popular serials like *The Archers*. Exclusivity and intimacy is maintained with the audience since everyone has their own version of what characters such as Phil Archer or Nelson Gabriel look like. Attempts by broadcasters to fill in these details which are normally the preserve of the listeners' imagination are not always popular. When the BBC published a map of the mythical village of Ambridge in the *Radio Times*, many listeners were dismayed to find that it did not accord with their version of the village.

Radio offers the dramatist the opportunity to develop characterisation and use words in a visual and evocative way. *Under Milk Wood* is still one of the most famous examples of this special power of the medium and Dylan Thomas has been described as having 'the ear of the listener, not the eye of the reader'. Radio is also good at presenting reflective plays which reveal the innermost thoughts of characters. The critic Ronald Hayman described radio drama as 'the dramatisation of consciousness' and some modern plays for radio like Harold Pinter's *Victoria Station* have taken full advantage of this strength in order to experiment with narrative. The play concerns a taxi driver who is being told by his control to go to Victoria Station. The normal conventions of radio tell us this as our imagination begins to build a picture of what the character looks like. But the story remains unresolved. We are told someone is asleep on the back seat but little else. In each of the many pauses, our imagination attempts to complete the story, but the play never moves towards a resolution of the narrative and so we find ourselves painting in plot as well as scenery. The conventions of radio have allowed Pinter to present our imagination with an even greater challenge.

Language and conventions

Consider how the imagination works on this short extract from an evening on Radio 3.

Continuity announcer: And that ends our recital recorded here at Broadcasting House by Noemy Birankyer.
(*pause*)
Continuity announcer: On January 26th an exhibition opens at the Hayward Gallery here in London featuring the work of Leonardo Da Vinci. 480 years after his death he remains the supreme example of a man for whom there was no gap between art and science. This evening, Sydney Anglo, formerly Professor in the History of Ideas, University College Swansea, considers what was until recently a neglected aspect of Leonardo's genius.
(*pause. FX Indistinct scratchy recording sounding like Italian (30 seconds)*)

Professor Anglo: That fragment of speech must, I suppose, be the most remarkable in the entire history of recorded sound – Leonardo Da Vinci holding forth into his own Echo Mechanica roughly 480 years ago, and explaining his own philosophy of experimental science. The academic dust stirred up by the recovery of this and other wax cylinders, cut by Leonardo in the early years of the 16th century, has at last started to settle. And while the debate concerning their content, precise dating and identification of the various interviewees must inevitably continue, no one now seriously doubts their authenticity.

That 'talk' went on to provide further recordings of Leonardo interviewing his contemporaries supported by dramatised translations. It had all the hallmarks of a serious documentary programme yet it was the beginning of a play called *The Leonardo Cylinders* (BBC, 12 January 1989) produced for Radio 3 by Piers Plowright. Just as Orson Welles convinced large numbers of listeners to a radio play in 1939 that a Martian invasion was imminent, so this piece of fiction had many listeners fooled. The straight-faced use of documentary codes meant that, initially, some thought they really were listening to genuine recordings of Leonardo, despite being some 300 years ahead of the invention of recorded sound.

Looking at how such a convincing context was created provides a useful insight into the language of radio. A classical music concert has just finished and the continuity announcer is reading the credits in well-modulated Received Pronunciation tones. This is followed by a pause. Even if we have no previous knowledge of Radio 3, we are conscious of listening to a channel which treats information seriously, so we have no reason to doubt the truth of what is being said. In the same authoritative manner, the announcer then introduces the programme about Leonardo, authenticated by reference to a genuine exhibition which is taking place at the Hayward Gallery in London. Another pause adds gravity and provokes anticipation. This is followed by 30 seconds of unintelligible recording. Such a lengthy extract suggests a desire to inspect evidence in a minute way. Professor Anglo's voice has a quiet, academic authority and his references to 'dust settling' and 'debates . . . concerning precise dates' are the stuff of academic discourse. The use of such conventions causes us temporarily to misread the form. We think we are listening to a documentary. But as more information is revealed we start to realise the impossibility of hearing recordings of Leonardo's voice. Our minds switch to reading the material as a drama which requires the willing suspension of disbelief. This playing around with the conventions of drama and documentary has arrested our attention by making us work harder to interpret the opening of the play. The producer has also created an appropriate context for a play which presents information about Leonardo's life by imagining how he would have used a recording machine.

Such a play on Radio 3 is unlikely to be of interest to the majority of young people but its conventions have many features in common with more popular programming. The words carry the primary message but our impressions are shaped by the use of music, accent, pauses and sound effects. Understanding this can provide a way of looking at the way radio news is presented, how stations package their identities and even how DJ patter affects the mood of programmes.

Consider how the DJ uses this short station identity jingle to create an air of intimacy with his listeners:

DJ (over up-beat music): It's exactly six o'clock – good evening.
Sung jingle: This is South Manchester's radio . . .
DJ: It certainly is . . .
Sung jingle: K-F-M

The DJ speaks confidently over the up-beat music with a gritty but friendly Mancunian accent. He knows just when to stop speaking in order to give way to the pre-recorded sung jingle which identifies the station's area of interest, and he also squeezes in the words 'It certainly is . . .' between two lines of music. The whole thing takes 15 seconds and acts as a station identification signal. By his spontaneous intervention the presenter has added his own confident performance to help us make sense of the jingle. Without any further information being spelled out to us we know what sort of music the station is about to play, that the DJ is confident and knowledgeable about his material and that the station cares about its image in the community because it employs local people.

Getting the message across

The extracts from both *The Leonardo Cylinders* and KFM Radio use codes and conventions which invite the audience to interpret the material as authentic. In both cases the mood was helped by the previous reputations of the two broadcast institutions. Audiences expect Radio 3 to offer serious discourse, whilst a local pirate station like KFM would be looked to for cheeky, local chat. In both cases the dialects and delivery of the presenters played a part in helping create impressions of authenticity. But how do other forms on radio represent reality? The popular radio soap opera *The Archers* creates a surface realism by using naturalistic settings. In addition, it often incorporates current rural issues into its story lines to add a sense of realism, just as *EastEnders* often takes up social issues. The producers claim that the information can be socially useful but its main function is to help maintain the illusion that events in the serial are currently happening. But how far is it possible to include social messages in radio drama without alienating the audience? The issue is well demonstrated by *The Merseysiders*, a twice-weekly soap opera on BBC Radio Merseyside. The serial attracted a range of sponsors including adult education agencies, community groups, the Health Education Authority and local crime prevention organisations. The influence of such groups is sometimes easily detectable.

(FX Door closing)
Sarah: Oh hello Celia – come in.
Celia: I though you were out when I saw the window open – I got a bit suspicious.
Sarah: No, its OK, but thanks for keeping your eye out, though.
Celia: Anyway, why aren't you at college – it's your first day back isn't it?
Sarah: I wasn't sure about going back, you know, with all the problems over Christmas. Have you got time for a cuppa?
Celia: Yes love.
Sarah: Well, to be honest Celia, I haven't even started all me work for last term.

They go on to discuss how Sarah can resolve the problem of being late with college work whilst still coping with a family. Then, later in the same scene:

Celia: Ooh ey look – there's that cat again – I wonder who it belongs to?
Sarah: I don't know – I put some food out for it a few times. It's dead friendly – here you are, let it in.
Celia: Ah come on – puss, puss puss.
Sarah: Ah isn't it lovely?
Celia: I think it's a stray. All it needs is a good home.
Sarah: Well why don't you take it in?
Celia: Mm – I suppose I could do. I tell you what – I'll take it round to ours and then I'll feed it and if it keeps coming back then I'll look after it. You wonder why people get pets then not bother looking after them.
Sarah: Yeah.
Celia: Oh listen – have you got any tins of food for the old people?
Sarah: Well I haven't got much but you can have some soup or something.
Celia: Oh anything will do – thanks Sarah – we're going round checking on the pensioners in the area making sure they've got food and that they're keeping as warm as possible.

Later in the same episode the main character, Sarah, is involved in a bitter argument with her husband about whether or not to have an abortion since her pregnancy might interfere with her studies. Such a concentration of social issues from lost cats to abortion is common in *The Merseysiders* and it demonstrates the key difference between this kind of soap and series like *The Archers* or *EastEnders*. In *The Merseysiders* the plot is largely determined by the social and educational concerns of the sponsors. Although it is a form of fiction, it exists mainly to promote socially useful messages. This can have a limiting effect on the material and be unsatisfactory on two counts. Firstly, it could be so dull that it fails as drama and, secondly, if audiences become too conscious of educational messages in the text, then the material risks alienating them as being too preachy. Whilst messages of social relevance are often included in soaps like *The Archers* and *EastEnders*, the primary function of these programmes is to entertain through telling a story. Concern about social issues in such programmes is secondary and largely exists to add authenticity to plots and perhaps allow programme makers to claim social relevance.

Radio comedy

It is unlikely that many young people will have listened regularly to *The Archers*, although it may well provide useful classroom material when studying narrative structure or the use of naturalistic conventions in popular fiction. But an even more accessible source of material is radio comedy. It is probably within the experience of most young people since it is popular on Radio 1, either in episodic form or used as part of the patter of some DJs. In addition, both Radio 2 and Radio 4 include a wide range of comic programmes in their schedules and radio advertising often features short comic vignettes, written and performed by famous comedians. So it is worth spending some time looking how radio comedy works.

From *ITMA* onwards, comedians have recognised radio's potential for surprise, fast-changing scenes and rapidly shifting dimension often ending in nonsense. With no need to make pictures, other than those in the imagination, radio is less tied to the conventions of naturalism. *The Goon Show* and *Round the Horne* were pioneers in placing characters in totally absurd situations, such as crossing the desert in a leather omnibus or having actors play impossible roles like that of a volcano. This is not to say that all radio comedy has been constructed in this mould. Programmes such as *The Clitheroe Kid*, *Meet the Huggetts* and *Life with the Lyons* were the 1950s equivalents of today's television situation comedies. They often achieved audiences as high as 16 million with their theatrical conventions of story-telling. The success of episodic situation comedies was developed by classic programmes like *Hancock's Half Hour*. It made full use of radio's ability to engage the imagination and enabled the writers, Galton and Simpson, to go beyond the straightforward plots and create a character who caricatured the suburban dweller's fight against the encroachment of a hostile world. Hancock's speeches to an imaginary audience of the citizens of East Cheam became slightly surreal dramatic monologues which were never equalled on television. They relied on parody and the listener's own pictures of this preposterous little man. Later in the 1970s, the cult series *The Hitch Hiker's Guide to the Galaxy* again used both the conventions of situation comedy and those of the absurd to create humour. It featured a traditional slowly unfolding plot, interwoven with parodies of life on earth and absurd notions such as asking a computer to work out the meaning of life. The answer it finally gave was 42. *Hitch Hiker* became one of the more successful transitions of radio material to television but it only existed in the first place because of the kind of experimentation made possible by radio. The relative cheapness of the medium means that more risks can be taken with unproven material. And it appears to be more willing to test out contentious material.

The Radio 4 programme *Loose Ends* has provided a forum for new material such as that written by Victor Lewis-Smith. Absurdity, parody, and satire feature in his 6-minute comic presentations. They are delivered at break-neck speed and packed with complex sound effects as he moves in and out of several themes. The pieces acknowledge the greater ability of modern audiences to cope with fast-moving information. In one sequence which satirises the BBC (BBC 1989) the captain and bosun represent BBC censors, looking for jokes in the material but ready to interrupt if anything too shocking happens.

(*FX: Fast spooling tape*)
(*Music: Constantly repeating motif*)
Voice over: The two phrases 'Smug bunch of hypocritical bastards' and 'BBC Management' are very unlikely bedfellows. As are the phrases 'the BBC charter forbids advertising' and 'there now follows on BBC1 a 45-minute programme on the making of the films *Moonwalker*, *A Fish Called Wanda* and *Roger Rabbit*.' You may be right in suspecting that these are nothing more than shameless plugs made and paid for by the companies involved. As for freedom of speech on Radio 4 just try interviewing the IRA or talking about animal cruelty or homosex . . .
(*FX: Fast spooling tape*)
(*Music: SEASCAPE*)
Captain: What the hell is going on bosun?
Bosun: Captain – he's on his soap box doing over the BBC again sir. Visibility down to 5 yards.
Captain: Oh dear – right, start bailing out the old material.
Bosun: Aye Aye sir.
Captain: Now here's a cracker, bosun!
Bosun: Yes sir?
Captain: What do you call a judge with no thumbs?
(*FX: Fast spooling tape*)
(*Music: Constantly repeating motif*)
Voice over: Justice Fingers. As for freedom of speech, Radio 3's audience consists of intellectual grown-ups and consequently is able to say what it likes on the grounds of artistic licence whereas Radio 4's audience is geriatric and needs to be protected from real life. To pursue this analogy, if Radio 3 has an HGV licence then anodyne Radio 4 is licensed

only to drive invalid carriages, motorised tricycles and lawnmowers under 2cc, which is why this is the most dangerous thing you will ever hear on Radio 4.

Despite its sometimes self-congratulatory tone the material attracted a cult following. Audiences who identified with the humour were making a statement about themselves and their political attitudes. Spotting the sophisticated cross-referencing going on in the piece (e.g. the captain and the bosun represent the BBC, and the BBC building in Portland Place is said to resemble a battleship) served to increase audience feelings that they were part of an in-crowd who appreciated the deeper levels of humour. But on a more basic level the comedy is achieved by traditional means. The speed of delivery and constant surprise serve to disorientate the listener and there are elements of stand-up comedy as well as a sprinkling of old jokes.

Discussing comedy in this way has much in common with traditional ways of understanding how texts make meaning. Although satirising the BBC may well appeal to the more adult Radio 4 listener, a large amount of radio comedy appeals directly to young people because, like *Monty Python*, it takes the standard codes of the medium to extremes and breaks them through parody and absurdity. Victor Lewis-Smith's humour appeals because it creates a bizarre, fantastical world full of child-like, zany humour. Lewis-Smith was first heard on Radio 4 but was later given a slot on Radio 1, probably in recognition of this appeal. But such humour, with the ability to turn the world upside down, has long been available to young people through the medium of comics and has represented a source of great pleasure to them.

MAGAZINES AND COMICS

Every single new medium for children that has appeared over the last 150 years has at its first appearance been a topic of a wave of panic. It happened with music hall, it happened with the penny dreadfuls, it happened with film, it happened with television, it happened with comics and it happened with videos. On every single occasion there has been this wall of protectiveness quickly thrown up round the medium to save children from imputedly dangerous impact.

(Martin Barker)

Comics and magazines have come in for almost universal condemnation by those in education. A 1973 survey showed that teachers were ten times more likely to introduce TV and newspapers into the classroom than comics (Murdock and Phelps 1973). In the 1950s horror comics produced a moral panic similar to that caused by the TV and 'video nasties' in the 1980s. Through their use of easily accessible images and restricted codes, comics and magazines stand accused of trivialising both language and human experience and of failing to engage the imagination of children. Yet they continue to be popular. According to one survey, 54 per cent of children under 12 read at least one comic a week (AMES 1986: 6).

Comics and magazines have traditionally fallen into three age ranges:

- Pre-school comics such as *Twinkle* and *Jack and Jill*, usually approved of by parents.
- Juvenile comics such as *The Beano*, *Dandy*, *Whizzer* and *Chips*, only just tolerated by parents and teachers.
- Adolescent comics/magazines displaying a sharp gender divide, featuring sport and war action for males and romance for females. Some of these publications provoke outright hostility from parents and teachers.

The gender divide is seen as a precursor to adult formula-reading so competition for readers is fierce between the two publishing giants D.C. Thomson and the International Publishing Corporation. They dominate this market by virtue of their size, expertise and easy access to national distribution. Despite the large number of titles produced, the formula remains fairly narrow and attempts by smaller independent companies to extend the range have often ended in financial disaster. But more recently, fringe publishers have begun to make an impact in the cult comic market by promoting comic conventions and selling through mail order and specialist comic shops.

Comic appeal

> I am sure that part of the pleasure for children in comics is knowing that they're only just approved of by parents. They're only just accepted by adults. Kids actually know that comics are mildly subversive. They ask difficult questions, they probe and prod and do things that are slightly embarrassing for parents. And part of the pleasure is precisely in that unacceptability.
>
> (Martin Barker)

Comics such as *The Beano* present a totally exclusive world which a child can understand and enjoy without adult help. Characters are often easy stereotypes with names to match (*Dennis the Menace*, *The Bash Street Kids*, *Lord Snooty and his Pals*) and the stories always finish as they began with the initial situation and relationships restored. Along the way, however, all forms of absurdity and anarchy are possible and strips like *Dennis the Menace* and *The Bash Street Kids* are able to turn the world of home and school upside down. Barker maintains that such stories attract children because they impose a child-like logic on the complexities of the adult world. The play and fantasy of the comic strip help them come to terms with the rules of adult power. So even when Dennis the Menace seemingly loses in the power game by invariably getting the slipper from his dad, in another sense he has won because his antics have usually subverted the status quo and brought adults down to a child-like level.

> His Dad thinks he's always bad but Dennis the Menace is just out to have some fun which is normally like children nowadays. The adults think it's all wrong and they forget when they were children.
>
> (Neil Ticehurst)

> Always in these comics the children win as they lose. Just at the moment when they are being hauled back into line they are proving by the fact that they bring adults down to their level that they're actually winning. In other words the adults have their mystique stripped away. No adult appears serious or proper in the *The Beano*.
>
> (Martin Barker)

> Dennis is late into school to find teacher's setting the class the job of writing a poem. And as he walks in the teacher looks up sternly and says 'Dennis'! Whereupon Walter the Softie thinks that he must want the poem written about Dennis and proceeds to write this scurrilous poem attacking Dennis' good name. Dennis can't let this pass and so over the next page and a half he seeks his revenge on Walter by lassooing him and calling himself the 'poet lariat' and quoting a poem about Walter being
>
>   ... the softest of the softy breed,
>   you are a nasty little weed ...
>
> and setting about walloping him really hard. But at the precise moment when he's going to take his revenge, who should appear but Dad with a poem written on the bottom of his slipper. Whereupon, as Walter 'tee-hees' about poetic justice, he lays him over the log and wallops his bottom. Now does Dennis win or does he lose? In this one sense he loses because he gets a good walloping but in another sense, he set out at the beginning to subvert the entire idea of poetry from being a school curricular thing into being something that kids could take over and use for themselves. So what's happened at the end? Dad has had to join in the subversion of poetry by writing absurd lines on the bottom of his slipper. Dennis has won.
>
> (Martin Barker)

Adolescent attractions

Exclusivity and secrecy continue to play a role in the appeal of magazines and comics catering for adolescents. The gender divide means that males are fed action and sport along with magazines catering for exclusive

Figure 4.4   Some rules from 'The Game of Tricks 'n' Jokes'

The A–Z of powers and strategies for children

The aim of the game is to have fun, despite everything. Fun is had in particular by winning or losing with the maximum absurdity. Therefore almost every rule below may be broken, provided only that the effect is ridiculous enough. The winners are those who score the most points in this way. Points are directly cashable as reader-loyalty. Government Health Warning: *You are warned that anyone playing should suffer fantastic injuries. This game is therefore not suitable for those with weak imaginations.*

Rules:

1. All real players are children. All other players are on sufferance and, if possible, to suffer. The only hope for other players who want to avoid pain is to pretend to be a child.

2. Each player must adopt a character which tells him or her how to behave. Preferably choose one whose name warns others what you're likely to be like. Once chosen, you must behave like that – or else.

3. Failure to observe Rule 2 will bring the sky down on your head. Behaving out of character is extremely dangerous, and you had better have an extremely silly reason for doing so. Any attempt by another character to make you act out of character will bring the sky down on *their* heads.

4. Any player who looks or acts the least bit pleasant, or rational, is a cissy, a softy and a teacher's pet, and has only him/herself to blame for what happens.

5. Players play tricks on each other. The first one to play a trick will get his/her comeuppance, unless s/he is clever enough to get away with it. (NB Players who get away with it too often run the risk of appearing too clever. See Rule 10 for what happens then.)

6. You score points by making comeuppances happen appropriately. The more appropriate absurdities you can build into the punishment, the better.

7. No player behaves rationally. Any player caught behaving sensibly will be immediately flogged, beaten up, or otherwise hospitalised. Alternatively Rule 10 may be cited immediately.

8. Everything happens too fast. All true players suffer from hyperactivity and minimal brain dysfunction. Being slow is a symptom of a sickness known as adulthood; any adult players are advised to hide their advancing slowness.

9. Any adult permitted to play should be as horrible as possible, or else should simply pretend to be a child. Adults who play at being children will receive all known punishments, but will also have fun.

10. More points are deducted for being boring than for anything else. Any player caught being boring several times, will cease to be ...

Source: Barker 1989: 89–90

interests like computers or BMX bikes. Females, on the other hand, are provided with magazines like *Jackie*, which feature romantic photo-stories coupled with advice on fashion, make-up and how to get boyfriends. The attraction of such publications is that they allow girls to experience thoughts about love and romance in private, away from the possible embarrassment of having to admit interest in these subjects to parents and teachers. Similarly, young males presented with war action stories are interested in how characters cope with personal difficulties relevant to their own background or personalities. So a kind of contract is formed. The readers bring with them a curiosity about life experiences which the comics acknowledge. They do this by providing stories which talk to young people about the things they want to hear and in ways they can understand. But such accessibility means that stories are generally based on easy stereotypes.

Values

Such stereotyping appears to be the source of most adult concern over comics and magazines (Hemming and Leggett 1984). Girls are encouraged to accept passivity while boys are invited to be active. But we have also established that audiences bring different experiences to reading. This means that texts cannot be judged on their face value. Some young people may be capable of enjoying the secrecy and exclusivity of comics and magazines while still recognising that they deal in stereotype and fantasy. They are more likely to be able to do this if they have started to develop their own critical framework by experiencing a range of reading matter beyond a diet of popular fiction. If we accept these arguments, then any study of comics and magazines will have to recognise the pleasures they bring to young people. If students feel these pleasures are under attack they may react negatively to any attempts at analysis or merely parrot what the teacher tells them.

> Comics have for so long been a respite for kids. They have been one of kids' ways of getting away from teachers, so that I think you have to start by letting the children talk about their pleasure in them. You have to find outlets for them to say for themselves 'I like this', 'I don't like this', 'This would make a good comic', 'That would make a good story', not 'What images can you find in here girls and boys?' That would be the worst possible way to start and unfortunately it has tended very often to be the way in which they have been used in the classroom.
>
> (Martin Barker)

Action – a case history

Barker's study of *Action* (Barker 1989: 17–61), which ceased publication in 1976, is helpful in understanding more about how comics are read. *Action* was part of a new wave of boys' comics. These featured hard-hitting adventure stories along with magazine-like features representing broader interests. *Action* followed the simple stereotyping habits of other titles but it was anti-authoritarian. Its characters were often fighting against the odds. The comic openly acknowledged that they were living in an unfair world. It was also very violent. Almost immediately *Action* attracted heavy criticism from consumer protection groups, MPs, magistrates and the Responsible Society. Its publishers IPC were subjected to hostile coverage from the press and broadcasting. It was described by one critic as an 'invasion of childhood'. After much protest the publishers bowed to pressures to clean it up and eventually withdrew the title altogether after pressure from the distributors W.H. Smith.

But Barker's research shows a variety of adolescent readings of *Action* most of which differed considerably from adult interpretations. Committed readers found the comic 'more grown-up, sarcastic and cynical' or they said 'it made you think, that says it all'. Others felt it 'dealt with the seedier side of things, yet still moral!' and one fan recalled, 'It was just better, a friend.' Clearly these readers were interpreting *Action* differently from the way adults were experiencing the comic. Barker maintains that the case of *Action* shows a disturbing gap between the language of the critics and what is revealed by the comic and its readers. *Action* melodramatised problems with authority thus providing a way for some readers to deal with the concepts of authority and power. Teaching about comics then needs to acknowledge these differences and look further at the expectations they offer their readers.

The furore over *Action* epitomises the problems facing teachers and parents thinking about what kinds of material children should be encouraged to read. There is no doubt that some childish (and adult!) pleasures involve the consumption of formulaic, pulp-written material which is often mindless and sometimes potentially dangerous or disturbing. Such material cannot be ignored and yet the type of hysteria noted earlier, which the so-called 'video nasties' provoked, is neither helpful nor appropriate. Learning how to make mature judgements about a range of fiction is an important part of growing up. Media Education can help, by encouraging students to develop a language through which they can begin to understand their own responses to texts. So first of all we need to acknowledge the validity of young people's individual responses to fiction and to accept that, in the case of comics for example, these will differ from adult interpretations and vary from person to person. By experiencing fiction in this way young people begin to develop their own value systems. So good Media

Education should provide an opportunity for students to talk about their understanding of texts and to recognise the features of different kinds of material from *The Beano* to *The Diary of Anne Frank*. In this way students can develop their own evaluation of texts and a language through which to express it. The wider the range of material to which they are exposed, the greater their understanding is likely to be. Of course at every age there are judgements to be made about the appropriateness of material but these need to be thought out in a context which acknowledges the fact that children's individual tastes and pleasures vary and that their responses will almost always differ from adults'.

We need to accept the validity of the special meanings which young readers create through comics and magazines. Only then can they begin to grow into readers who can make their own judgements about texts. Ultimately, they should be able to speak with confidence about the characteristic forms and pleasures of a whole range of different texts independently and autonomously.

LITERATURE: READING AND RESPONDING

Literary fiction immediately invokes notions of pleasure rather than danger or subversion. Many teachers feel on much safer ground when dealing with literature. Yet it is not meant to be safe. A genuine engagement with the experience of others could never be that.

> When I'm writing I'm thinking of areas in which I can reach into the experience of the children I'm writing for and then using that and then moving beyond that into a whole range of other experiences, adventures . . .

(Beverley Naidoo)

> An active involvement with literature enables pupils to share the experience of others. They will encounter and come to understand a wide range of feelings and relationships by entering vicariously the world of others, and in consequence, they are likely to understand more of themselves.

(DES 1989: 7.3)

The Cox Report is curiously ambivalent about non-literary fiction. It seems to assume (if only by omission) that non-literary texts are dangerous or worthless. There is an isolated reference to radio plays and an appeal to approaches developed by Media Education. Non-literary texts are also included in the reading profile component and the Report embraces Michael Benton's emphasis on a reading and response-based approach to literary texts (DES 1989: 7.8; 7.23; 9.9; 7.22). But then why not consider seriously the television texts which we know most young people enjoy and respond to? Here we want to look at what such an approach to non-literary texts involves and explore how it can be applied equally well to them.

What is reader-response?

> Reader-response is really giving the literature back to the readers . . . trusting the reader . . . starting where the reader is . . . signalling to the young reader that whatever they say in speech and in writing, negative or positive – because negative responses have to be accepted – whatever they say about the story or the poem is valid as a starting-point and is valued by you as a teacher.
>
> (Michael Benton)

Many studies have been carried out on how individual and small groups of children read and respond to writing. Reader-response approaches have provided many insights into reading processes and imaginative responses among children. These approaches have already been adopted in some schools as good classroom practice in the teaching of literature as well as being recognised formally within National Curriculum English (DES 1989: Appendix 6: *Approaches to the Class Novel*).

Reader-response approaches are based on the notion that readers are active meaning makers who use a range of strategies (introspection, retrospection, anticipation) to travel in the 'secondary worlds' of fiction. Every text offers 'gaps' which readers are invited to explore and fill with their own speculations as the text unfolds. Every reader embarks on a journey of discovery which involves such processes as prediction, surprise, shock, accommodation, integration, disappointment and the satisfaction of fulfilled expectations.

Beverley Naidoo's children's book *Journey to Jo'burg* exemplifies the process of interaction between reader and text vividly. Her protagonists, Naledi and Tiro, are faced with a crisis when their baby sister becomes dangerously ill. So they decide to set off in search of their mother.

> through this journey, she had begun to find out so much . . .
>
> (Naidoo 1985: 65–6)

The novel is a classic psycho-physical journey (in some ways like Conrad's *Heart of Darkness*) in which every step taken, every barrier overcome is also a growth in knowledge.

> Naledi and Tiro went to Jo'burg to find their mother. They had no idea what the city was like, there was so much they didn't understand. But in this strange and frightening place they found something else.
>
> (Naidoo 1985: dust-cover)

The documentary basis of the story is emphasised in the Longman edition by a selection of photos, newspaper reports, a map and the dedication to 'two small children who died far away from their mother ... and to Mary, their Mma, who worked in Jo'burg.'

> Before this journey to fetch Mma, she had never imagined that all this land existed. Nor had she any idea of what the city was like. She had never known a person like Grace before, and she had never known her own mother in the way she was beginning to know her now.
>
> (Naidoo 1987: 48)

> the journey becomes a learning process, as the nightmare complexities of apartheid in the wider society are revealed to them.
>
> (Naidoo 1987: 43)

It is impossible to capture readers' immediate responses. But some insight is offered in letters to authors, as in this extract from 11-year-old Asma Rahman's letter to Beverley Naidoo. Although this is a considered and reflective response, it still carries traces of her initial reactions as she struggles to find the words which will express what she wants to say.

> I don't know why some people think books like *Journey to Jo'burg* are wrong to have in schools and colleges or to have films, commercials, TV and radio programmes illustrating things like that. I personally think it is an excellent idea. Why shouldn't young people learn what is really happening on Earth? I mean kids our age only learn about the good things, but we never learn the facts ... I sometimes wonder why the world is like this. I just don't understand how people can be like this, how they can be so cruel. Why do people think they're more superior than others? What can we do to change this? How did it start in the first place? I'm always searching through my brains to find the answers.
>
> (Asma Rahman to Beverley Naidoo, 13 May 1987)

Although Asma went on to suggest a sequel to *Journey to Jo'burg*, she must have been even more disturbed by the grimmer and harsher events of *Chain of Fire* (1989) in which Naledi and Tiro are forcibly relocated, along with the rest of their village, in what the authorities call their 'homeland'.

Several techniques have been developed by researchers to record secondary responses to poems and fiction and some of them are also usable in the classroom. For example, readers can 'map' their own reading routes, tape-record a running commentary on their reactions as they read, write notes around poems or draw diagrams. With novels, it can be done by stopping at pre-determined points to make jottings or record initial reactions to a sequence or make predictions about how the narrative is likely to develop. In addition, it is possible to extend this into group discussion or more extended and reflective personal writing.

Michael Benton's work has helped a great deal in the study of how

Figure 4.5   Elizabeth's initial responses to 'Frogs in the Wood'

At the end - everywhere I've lived I've had my
own private little place where I can be alone -
sometimes inside the house sometimes outside
where I go to think or just to be alone
- after first reading &
last verse

Frogs in the Wood   (13) Shadows but not
   (1) good to be lost?   scary

(2)   How good it would be to be lost again,
no way ── Night falling on the compass and the map
out   Turning to improbable flames,   (3) Sunset reflected
           Bright ashes going out in the ponds.   then dying

           And how good it would be
           To stand bewildered in a strange wood
(4)   Where you are the loudest thing,
excitement Your heart making a deafening noise.

           And how strange when your fear of being lost has subsided
           To stand listening to the frogs holding
(5) Sounds Their arguments in the streams,
& nature   Condemning the barbarous herons.

           And how right it is   (6)
           To shrug off real and invented grief   freedom
           As of no importance
           To this moment of your life,
                (14) physical   (7) finding yourself
           When being lost seems
(9) likes So much more like being found,
being   And you find all that is lost ── (8) problems worries
alone   Is what weighed you down.   lost

           (15) mental   Brian Patten

(10) not silence - friendly noises distant enough
     to remain undisturbing and in the background

(11) happy - surprised - relieved   (12) light - airy

Source: Benton 1988: 43

Figure 4.6   The movement of Elizabeth's responses to 'Frogs in the Wood'

Initial Responses

Elizabeth 'Frogs in the Wood' *Eliz, IRs 1–15*

1   good to be lost
2   no way out?
3   sunset reflected then dying
4   excitement
5   sounds of nature
6   freedom
7   finding yourself
8   problems worries lost
9   likes being alone
10 not silence – friendly noises distant enough to remain undisturbing and in the background
11 happy – surprised – relieved
12 light airy
13 shadows but not scary
14 physical
15 mental

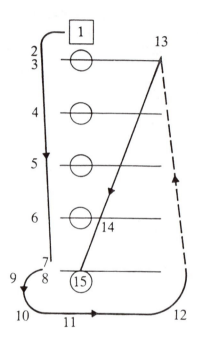

written at the top of the page:

At the end, everywhere I've lived I've had my own private little place where I can be alone. Sometimes inside the house sometimes outside where I go to think or just to be alone. After first reading of the last verse

Source: Benton 1988: 44

Figure 4.7   Reading and responding to poems: a flexible methodology

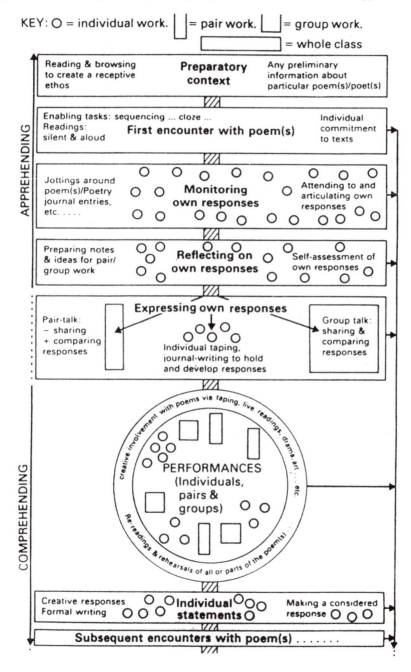

KEY: O = individual work. | | = pair work. |__| = group work.

|___| = whole class

APPREHENDING

Reading & browsing to create a receptive ethos   **Preparatory context**   Any preliminary information about particular poem(s)/poet(s)

Enabling tasks: sequencing ... cloze ... Readings: silent & aloud   **First encounter with poem(s)**   Individual commitment to texts

Jottings around poem(s)/Poetry journal entries, etc. . . . .   **Monitoring own responses**   Attending to and articulating own responses

Preparing notes & ideas for pair/ group work   **Reflecting on own responses**   Self-assessment of own responses

Expressing own responses

Pair-talk: – sharing + comparing responses

Individual taping, journal-writing to hold and develop responses

Group talk: sharing & comparing responses

COMPREHENDING

creative involvement with poems via taping, live readings, drama, art, ... etc.

PERFORMANCES (Individuals, pairs & groups)

Re-readings & rehearsals of all or parts of the poem(s)

Creative responses Formal writing   **Individual statements**   Making a considered response

Subsequent encounters with poem(s) . . . .

Source: Benton 1988: 205

children respond as readers, although he acknowledges how difficult it is to track primary responses.

> Whenever anybody reads a story or a poem or looks at a painting for more than a few seconds and then tries to reflect upon the experience, we all know ... that there are things that simply cannot be caught in language, that language is a very poverty-stricken instrument for capturing those feelings and fleeting impressions that we have.
>
> (Michael Benton)

Responses to other media

There are clearly formal and presentational differences between literature and other media. Some researchers argue that these differences explain how and why attention is given or withheld. Literature and television both rely on signs and codes which are apprehended visually (although television of course has an additional auditory channel). Clusters of words on the page or patterns of dots on the screen are the material forms which generate meaning. But is there an essentially subjective imaging process which occurs in reading which does not occur in viewing? Does it actually matter that some of the signs used by television are already themselves visual? All media allow some degree of freedom to choose what to attend to within the text, so that variations of response will occur. At the same time, it cannot be denied that audiences come to every media text with their personal memories, some of which are activated by viewing, listening or reading, so that meaning is inevitably a matter for negotiation which will differ between individuals.

There is no doubt that television narratives and other forms of popular fiction found in comics and magazines have a powerful formative influence on children's writing. If we want to know more about the sense which they make of soaps, for example, and how they incorporate them into their personal agenda, we can look carefully at the narratives they create for themselves. Increasingly, they show the marks of a genealogy from television soaps. Some teachers will disapprove of writing based on soaps because they find it derivative. But the use of such models does not necessarily mean thoughtless reproduction of formula fiction or enslavement to a fixed set of values. Instead of making automatic assumptions about the inferiority of such forms, we could be helping children to write authentically by recognising and understanding the codes and conventions which they draw upon.

Media Education and fiction

Just as English has much to learn from Media Education, so too reader-response approaches can be effectively used with other media. We looked in Chapter 2 at a number of studies which explored television viewers' responses and understandings in depth. Other recent studies have shown increasing critical powers amongst children who have been taught in a constructive way about media (Davies 1989: 131). The role of Media Education, like that of English, is to help children to enjoy a wide range of media and to be aware of how they work. This process necessarily involves them in becoming more active media readers and audiences. As they become increasingly able to create a critical distance between themselves and the media texts they value, they are moving towards the kind of autonomy which is the main aim of Media Education.

> we should broaden our notions of what constitutes useful and interesting writing, and include within that writing based on popular fiction. Once we start to take [it] seriously, there would be other consequences for our practice. We could encourage children to articulate what they already know about how such fictions work and help to refine that knowledge . . . This might involve using some of the critical strategies commonly associated with Media Studies, asking such questions as: How does this piece come to have meaning? What is its purpose, and how has it been produced? But we would do this for different reasons. Rather than using such questions to focus pupils' attention on how they are being manipulated or worked on by the text . . . the point would be to enable pupils to manipulate the rules of the text's construction for themselves.

(Moss 1989: 117–18)

If one of the purposes of literature is to challenge readers to travel beyond themselves and, perhaps, to be disturbed into 'critical thinking about existing stereotypes and values' (DES 1989: 7.4), there must also be a place for such challenge by non-literary texts.

> Distressing and violent events on television can also help children to come to terms with their own fears and emotions – just as fairy tales and folk tales have always done.

(Messenger Davies 1989: 93)

When Damon Grant of Channel 4's *Brookside* was stabbed to death in the street, many viewers were horrified. Máire Messenger Davies's 8-year-old daughter Elinor was devastated by it and discussed it for weeks. Yet with help from other members of the family, she found her own way of dealing with it. She was aware that it was 'only' a soap opera and she knew of the problems such programmes have of writing out long-standing characters. This understanding clearly balanced and encompassed her grief, and she was able to distance herself from it, as her letter to her mother (in the next room) showed.

Dear mum

I think that Damon dieing in Brookside was awful I was crying because of it the script writers should have thought before they had writen the script I know Damon wanted to get out of Brookside but they dident have to kil him out of it Damon and Debbie could of gone to America to get out of it and stayed there anyway lets change the subgect because I am crying here did you see Bread on sunday I did it was really good it was funny too I watched ever Decreasing Circles you could not of watched it because you were at Dad's coire concert Today I am ill and I am at home I have got a cold and cough I saw Brookside last night and it was sad OoOoopps Iam getting back on that subdject

Yours Sincerly Eli Davies

TEACHING IDEA 1: RESPONDING TO TELEVISION

Aim

To demonstrate some of the active imaginative processes involved in television watching.

Time

One single or double lesson.

Materials

Video-recording of short (less than 5 minutes) television drama.

Method

- Select the video sequence carefully so that it will appeal to the class, but find something which they are unlikely to have seen.
- Show the class a single frame of the narrative by pausing the video at any appropriate point of interest (do not show them any of the sequence before the single frame).
- Ask them to write down in note form (either individually or in small groups) what they see in the frame (individuals, locations, clothing, gestures, expressions, interactions, emotions). Discuss their answers.
- Ask them to note down their guesses as to what kind of drama it is, what is going on in it and who it is about. Discuss their answers.
- Play a section of the extract long enough for the students to grasp what kind of drama it is and stop the tape at a moment of suspense. Discuss how accurate their guesses were.
- Ask the students to write down their predictions for the ending of the episode or drama. Discuss these and explore their reasoning. How is such prediction possible?

Further work

Adapt the 'Reading and responding to poems' diagram (Figure 4.7 p. 161) for use with television drama.

TEACHING IDEA 2: SOAP NETWORKS

Aim

To explore and clarify some of the basic conventions of the soap opera form.

Time

At least one double lesson.

Materials

Video-recording of one complete episode of a familiar soap (preferably recent).

Method

- Ask students to group all characters into (a) family groups; (b) work relations; (c) other relationships.
- Display some of the information on the board or OHP.
- Watch selected episode, asking students to note which networks appear.
- Discuss the importance of different relationships. What sort of community does this serial present?
- Is this serial's use of such networks similar to other soaps? If not, what differences are there?
- Discuss *why* such networks are so important in soaps. Do they create a sense of community and make the serial more convincing or do they just make story-telling easier?

Further work

Each of the following questions could form the basis of a double lesson. They are put in an order here which tries to postpone the question of realism until some consideration has been given to formal and content details.

- How many different segments/plots are present in this episode? How many of them are initiated/continued/concluded in this episode? (See diagrammatic methods shown in Chapter 4 of this book.)
- What period of time is represented in this episode? What sort of time compressions take place?
- What sort of locations are featured in this episode? How important are they to an understanding of the serial as a whole?

- How are women represented in this episode? How do they relate to each other and to men?
- What values and beliefs are embedded in the community the serial presents? What ideas on work and leisure, men and women, age, class and race does it offer?
- How real is the world of this serial in the light of your own daily experience?

TEACHING IDEA 3: RADIO AND THE IMAGINATION

Aim

To explore the narrative conventions of the audio medium and to understand how they stimulate the listener's imagination.

Time

At least three double lessons, although it may take considerably longer, depending on the level of student understanding.

Materials

Radio recordings using short narrative sequences (e.g. advertisements, comic sequences, short section from a radio soap opera) which use a range of audio conventions in telling their stories. This would include accent, tone of voice, incidental music, pauses, sound effects and fade-outs.

One portable cassette player and microphone between two students and cassette tape. (Get the class to bring in their own portable machines from home.)

Method

- If the class is new to such work be careful to choose a relatively short and straightforward piece to begin with. Repeat as often as necessary in order to build class confidence in understanding the codes and conventions. Ask them to bring in recorded examples from their own listening.
- Listen to the recordings of the short narrative sequences and get the class to write down the impressions they form of certain characters or write a short description of the place where the scene is happening.
- Discuss the ways in which their impressions were formed and the devices, other than script, which were used to convey the information.
- Split the class into pairs. Ask each pair to plan on paper a story lasting about 90 seconds which can be presented on audio-tape. No more than ten words of dialogue are allowed and the rest of the story must be constructed from sound effects, pauses and use of natural ambient sound available in school. Get them to write a detailed plan of what they hope to do and why they think it will work.
- After the planning process allow pairs to collect their material. They should assemble it in narrative order using the pause button between sequences. This avoids the need for complex editing.

- When this process is complete, listen to the results either as a whole class or in small groups. Listeners should be asked to describe the pictures that each production has established in their minds.
- Discuss which production methods achieved the most response and understanding from the audience. Compare the methods used with those originally heard at the beginning of the cycle.

TEACHING IDEA 4: UNDERSTANDING COMIC CONVENTIONS

Aim

To develop understanding of some of the codes of comic story-telling.

Time

At least two double lessons.

Materials

A collection of comic strips which feature children getting into trouble with adults, e.g. Dennis the Menace, Bash Street Kids, Minnie the Minx. These should be copied so that each student can look at the same strip.

Method

- Look at the various strips together with the class. Then split into pairs and ask each pair to discuss and write down their answers to the following questions:

  How can you tell what each of the characters is like? (e.g. facial expressions, dress, what other characters say about them, what they do).

  Which are your favourite characters and why? How does the strip convey feelings such as anger, exasperation, guilt, pleasure, pride, snobbishness, innocence, stupidity, toughness?

  How does the strip convey movement (e.g. speed and slowness) and noise?

  How does the strip convey tone of voice?

- Depending on the level of students' experience, it may then be possible to go on to discuss how each plot works – where the story starts, what happens to disrupt the status quo and how are things brought back to normal again? Who wins? Dennis the Menace, for example, or his dad?
- After studying the form of comic strips, the class should then write their own stories for Dennis the Menace or another comic strip. The more adventurous could make up their own characters. The story would need to be capable of being told in about sixteen frames. After getting the plot worked out, students would need to specify the details of each picture. These could be drawn or written.
- Discuss with the class the restraints and opportunities offered by the comic-strip format.

Chapter 5

Promotion and persuasion

This chapter examines the role of promotion and persuasion in media products and on our own perceptions. It concentrates on the advertising and pop music industries. Media Studies teachers have traditionally focused on hidden persuasion as the key to understanding the media, so advertising has been central. It has often been seen as a manipulative process – what Marshall McLuhan called an 'onslaught on the unconscious' which affects our basic ways of seeing.

We all know that both these industries try to sell us things and shape our attitudes. But traditionally we expect clear boundaries between promotional material and editorial content. Yet in the new media environment, promotion and persuasion are achieving a new power. Deregulation has encouraged television and film producers to seek finance through sponsorship, product placement and merchandising deals. Sponsoring television weather forecasts, for example, may seem innocuous enough, but such trends may compromise programme making. In the world of pop music, the fabrication of stories has become so routine that it is sometimes hard to distinguish news reports from promotional material.

But are audiences necessarily the victims of the values which are promoted? This chapter proposes a new and quite different view of how we respond to promotional texts which is based on the fact that readers bring their own meanings to their readings. It is divided into two main sections:

- Advertising and persuasion
- Pop and promotion

> Masters of our own universes, of all we see and hear, circles of which the centres are everywhere and the circumferences are nowhere. At the still point of our own turning worlds. Neither flesh nor fleshless, just music and image, neither from nor towards, just the here and now.
>
> (Woolley 1989: 20)

Figure 5.1a Finished storyboard for Pirelli's P6 'Double Indemnity' commercial. A tale of an adulterous wife, fixed brakes, attempted murder. And a 'torture test' for the product

'DOUBLE INDEMNITY' STORYBOARD

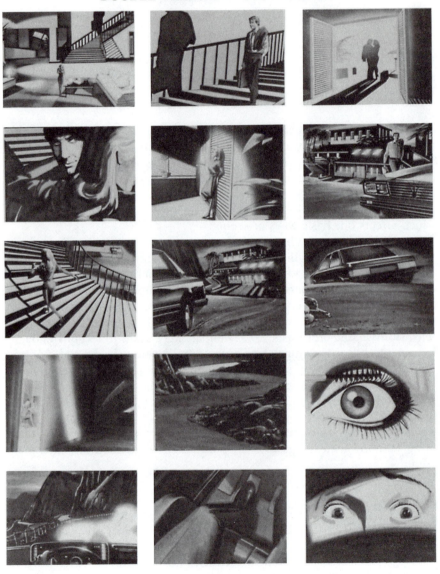

Source: Evans 1988: 52–3

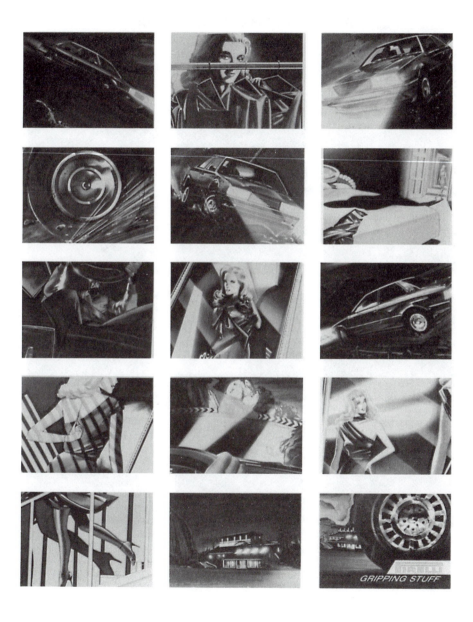

Figure 5.1b   A series of stills from Pirelli's 'Double Indemnity' broadcast
commercial

'DOUBLE INDEMNITY' COMMERCIAL

Source: Evans 1988: ii

ADVERTISING AND PERSUASION

It is important for media teachers to move beyond the traditional position of considering advertising as a separate or discrete sphere, with quite distinct boundaries which mark it off from television programmes or newspaper articles, and to begin to see media content and advertising as inextricably bound together.

(Masterman 1985: 106–7)

Consumers are protected by statutes such as the Sale of Goods Act (1979). They are also protected by the advertising industry's own voluntary self-regulatory body, the Advertising Standards Authority, with its familiar slogan 'Honest, Decent, Legal, Truthful'. The Independent Television Commission is responsible for the control of television and radio advertising. Between them, these bodies ensure that standards of truthfulness are clearly established and monitored.

WHAT IS AN ADVERTISEMENT?

A message specified by its originator, carried by a communications system and intended to influence and/or inform an unknown audience.

(Fletcher 1988)

Whatever its measurable effects, advertising clearly matters to advertisers, since huge sums are spent on advertising budgets and spending has trebled over the last decade. Its primary function is, of course, to sell goods and services. But since advertising uses powerful images to promote its products, it also incidentally promotes *'life-styles'*. Some advertisements, like those for public utilities and environmentally sensitive industries, are solely devoted to promoting public images of themselves (see Chapter 3). These images and life-styles are created mainly by telling stories with an immediate human interest.

Advertising only holds a mirror up to the way society is. It doesn't lead trends . . . it doesn't create needs where they currently don't exist. And I guess if your problem is with society as it is then advertising will always offend.

(Rita Clifton)

Advertising stories are not just series of events in time. They involve structures of cause and effect. This means that they also have values. Advertisements for items like cars or computers speak of status, style and success more than the actual features of the products. The kind of values portrayed and the way they are presented are important factors in creating the ideologies which envelop the products. The famous Pirelli tyre advertisement, for example, invites us into a glamorous but dangerous world of *haute couture*, cosmetics and barely negotiated chicanes.

> The 'content' of a medium is like the juicy piece of meat carried by the
> burglar to distract the watchdog of the mind.
>
> (McLuhan 1973: 26)

Advertisements do not lie. At least, not in an obvious way. But they do
offer a highly selective form of truth-telling. There are clear differences
between the frontal 'hard sell' approach which makes direct claims about
products and urges audiences to behave in specific ways and the more
subtle 'soft sell' which leaves audiences to do more imaginative work
themselves. Stories usually demand this kind of imaginative work from
audiences, so we need to focus our attention on how they work.

> People grossly overestimate the sort of things that advertising can do.
> Consumers aren't stupid and ... people are very literate as far as
> advertising is concerned ... They use advertising very intelligently. In
> many ways they actually participate in the communication process in
> advertising and tell us in research that they enjoy doing so. So clearly it's
> not like an insidious or subliminal persuasion. People are willing
> participants these days in the way advertising works, and again actually
> enjoy part of the process.
>
> (Rita Clifton)

Television advertising

Television programmes are scheduled according to relatively fixed time-
slots, but together they form an almost continuous flow. Programmes are
linked together by continuity, by styles and, on ITV, by advertisements.
The same actors and voices often appear in both the advertisements and
the programmes around them. George Cole appears as Arthur Daley in
both *Minder* and a building society advertisement. Certain kinds of
programme (like *The Clothes Show*) unashamedly feature commercial
products or create an ambience favourable to consumerism. Independent
radio, newspapers and magazines show the same sort of integration of
editorial and advertising material. 'Advertorials', advertisements which
masquerade as news stories and features specifically designed to attract
relevant advertisers, have all become commonplace.

> The walls which have historically divided advertising from programming
> so that advertisements are clearly marked as such, will begin to dissolve
> and possibly to disappear so that you will get a new kind of advertising
> where the advertising pitches are actually integrated into the pro-
> grammes themselves.
>
> (Graham Murdock)

On a more general level, the viability of a proposal for a new television
programme may be measured in terms of the richness of the 'spin-offs' that

can be generated from it. This obviously creates a number of problems because some forms of programming don't really allow themselves to be exploited in this kind of way. So they may not get made in the future. There is also a danger not just that some programmes don't get made but that commercial thinking infiltrates media production in a way which people don't notice. So it becomes more difficult to answer the basic questions, 'Who is communicating with whom and why?' and 'how has the text been produced and transmitted?' (DES 1989).

> What advertisements are – and all forms of promotion – are a particular way of talking about and looking at the world. And the more you have a media system that privileges that perspective the less space you have for alternative ways of looking and talking so that it actually reduces the diversity of voices and perspectives which are in play in the media system. The more the system depends on advertising and is saturated by it in all different kinds of forms, the less space there has to be for other ways of speaking.
>
> (Graham Murdock)

The main characteristics of television advertisements can be summarised fairly simply. They combine factual information about products with fictional characters and settings. They also provide an ambience with which they wish to associate their products. This is achieved by a variety of standard forms of presentation (Williams 1990: 69):

- rapidly dramatised situations which relate products to ordinary situations;
- use of simple entertainment techniques like song/dance routines adapted to products;
- insertion of products into leisure/sport/travel sequences;
- use of television performers (in and out of role) to recommend products.

Television advertisements have much in common with the programmes around them. Yet they also differ in some ways. Their messages are highly compressed because of time-constraints. So much money is spent in their production that they are often more immediately attractive than the programmes themselves. They need to be, because they are bound to be seen many times by the same viewers. Their production values are usually extremely high in order to maximise their shelf-life.

Children often find television advertisements more engaging than the programmes around them. Many adults fear this results in their being manipulated and exploited by manufacturers of children's products. But it is not that simple. Children can certainly identify goods featured in particular adverts and can remember, often with a great sense of enjoyment, jokes, music and story-lines from a wide range of adverts. This is true not only for products which are immediately relevant to them but also for others which they could not possibly wish to purchase. In any case, it is arguable that influencing children is not a very effective way of selling products, since they have limited control over parents or family expenditure. Children are sometimes more interested in the adverts themselves than in the products they feature. This is simply because adverts have very basic messages to offer and they express them in very memorable, often humorous ways. Some of the most popular adverts amongst children (e.g. Anchor butter, British Telecom, Carling Black Label and Mates condoms) are curiously irrelevant to them.

> Humour, an amusing story and clever effects [appeal] to children, with the story being incidental . . . just because [they] like and enjoy adverts, there is no really strong evidence that this attractiveness automatically translates into children wanting or buying things they wouldn't otherwise have wanted.
>
> (Messenger Davies 1989: 187–90)

Imaginary worlds

In many cases, advertisements offer their products as solutions to problems. But they can also create dissatisfaction with the way things are. What if you cannot afford what is on offer and what if it fails to fulfil its promise? By offering products to aspire to in a mythical future, advertising may create discontent with the here and now.

> The period into which we are moving is one . . . in which there is going to be a situation of absolutely finite resources. It is very significant that we are hitting this with things like water, with things like energy, indeed with things like capital at the very moment when we are still celebrating as if we were children . . . happy consumption of pleasant objects that we all enjoy but which are trivial compared with those basic wants.
>
> (Raymond Williams)

Advertisements often promote feelings of dissatisfaction or desire amongst audiences which the products claim to remove. This is most often done by the creation of a mythical ('Martini') world which is offered as a superior form of existence. The purchase of the product becomes the key to entering this mythical world. So advertising has effects beyond stimulating the need to buy.

> Ideally, advertising aims at the goal of programmed harmony among all human impulses and aspirations and endeavours . . . it stretches out towards the ultimate electronic goal of a collective consciousness. When all production and consumption are brought into a pre-established harmony with all desire and all effort, then advertising will have liquidated itself by its own success.
>
> (McLuhan 1973: 242)

Selling life-styles

> We don't just suddenly think up an idea. We go through very strict
> planning disciplines: 'who are you talking to?' 'what are you trying to
> say?' 'how should you say it?' and also critically 'where should you say
> it? ... There are so many products, so many brands competing for
> consumer attention and also competing for a share of the consumer's
> pocket that clearly advertising is necessary from our point of view to
> be able to build differences and to express differences and to sell
> differences ... between different products, that actually in many other
> ways might seem to be rather similar.
>
> (Rita Clifton)

The function of advertising is to deliver audiences to the market. So how
do advertisers decide who to aim at? In a society fragmented into many
different groups, they have had to use detailed market research from
discussion groups and questionnaires. But mass communication also allows
them to build up particular class, age and gender-related constituencies
whose habits can be recognised and thus make the task of promoting
products and services more cost-effective.

Some agencies have come up with what is called 'life-style' advertising.
A good example is the mini-soap approach in the Nescafé Gold Blend
advertisement. The agency who made the advertisement, McCann Erickson,
produced a report on perceptions of women. One of the categories of
women it created was the 'Lively Lady':

> She likes men, she likes going out, she likes having a good car, credit
> cards, having fun. She is comfortable with success. She likes certain
> perfumes. She reads the *Daily Mail*.
>
> (Jo Vale)

The 'Lively Lady' is just one example of how advertisers make sense of
products for consumers. In order to create such life-style images they need
to find out what we as audiences are thinking and feeling. So when market
research uncovers new social trends advertisers are feeding back to us
versions of ourselves.

> Consumers have to want it to happen, and clearly if we've done our
> homework properly, if we've done our research properly and involve
> consumers in that research process, we are going to give them things
> that they want and actually talk to them in the way that they want to be
> talked to.
>
> (Rita Clifton)

In the 1980s, images of thrusting, self-satisified, high-consuming 'yuppies'
were rife in advertising. For the 1990s, agencies suggest that the
dominant images will be more socially and environmentally sensitive.

'Greed', they say, will be superseded by 'Green'. But how can advertising be used for socially desirable ends like promoting green issues? Is there not a danger that concern for the environment is being translated into just another 'life-style' label? Some advertising agencies have predicted a number of new labels for the 1990s which are a strange concoction of 'Greed' and 'Green'. They include people who are 'carers' but not 'sharers' and 'money-grabbing ecologists'.

The Volkswagen Passat advertisement (1989) is a good example of these paradoxical formulations. It reiterates Volkswagen's long-standing claim for the reliability of its cars, but in a novel way. At the centre of its story is a young Shirley Temple look-alike who is rescued by her father from an inner-city nightmare. The urban jungle is polluted by danger, crime, and exhaust fumes. He leads her away to his powerful car where the mother is waiting to whisk her away. It offers a fairy-tale solution of private security against public squalor. A form of escape is being recommended which only some people can afford and which works to the detriment of others. Ironically, the motor car (which is arguably a major factor in urban migration and inner-city decay) is seen as providing a kind of privileged escape. It presents a contradictory and very private kind of ecology.

> On the one hand there is the belief that the new wave young who are about 20 at the moment, who've been brought up to consume goods and see consumption as a form of expression, who are very individualistic and are not concerned about society as a whole, that they are going to set tomorrow's trend and we are continuing into a more selfish society. On the other hand there is the belief that we're about to enter into a form of collectivism which is not an old-fashioned socialist idea but a new idea which has emerged from our growing concern about the environment.

(Jo Vale)

But audiences and consumers do not respond to abstract ideas. They need to relate directly to the images, voices and environments in which they appear in advertisements. So the imaginative contact must be concrete and immediate. Audiences must make literal sense of situations before they can make imaginative sense of them. Only then can they begin to respond to the product's specific appeal. So image, voice and style are crucial. The producers of advertisements are sensitive to the different appeals which their clients need to make and which audiences are likely to respond to.

> I think the voice is very important to the whole commercial . . . voices that the consumer can identify with. The sort of words that are probably most used are 'friendly', 'mumsy', 'hard-edged', 'fruity' . . . probably the most important word that's asked for or used at the moment is 'natural'.

‖ Everybody is looking for very 'natural' [voices]: boy-next-door/man-next-door/housewife-next-door . . .

(Anne Dawson)

Sometimes the images which advertisements present become part of everyday conversation (like Paul Hogan's lager adverts). Not only does this help to disseminate the advertisers' messages still further, but it also shows that audiences see themselves as part of the communication process. When audiences are involved in this way with familiar advertisement stories they are more likely to become sympathetic towards the products. It also means that they may be drawn in to the imaginary world of advertisements and share in their values.

‖ They are selling us ourselves.

(Williamson 1978: 13)

Advertisements actually do *three* things:

• They sell goods, services and corporate images.
• They create brand identity, discrimination and loyalty.
• They create structures of meaning.

The story forms which act as vehicles for the products are likely to rely on enigma and suspense. The product is often revealed as coming to the rescue of a harassed victim of circumstances and its identity concealed until the last possible moment. The satisfaction which these stories offer includes the pleasures of both suspense and reassurance.

Story structures

Advertisements have distinctive styles and surface features. The texture of their stories constantly varies, especially on television when they have a texture which can be very dense. Yet many advertisements are based on very simple story structures and these can be broken down into a few basic elements. Several different schemes have been devised which claim to unlock the secrets of narrative. They do so by finding their underlying structures.

This kind of analysis can be very useful as a way of exploring some basic *principles* of story-telling. It can reveal some of the patterns which commonly underlie advertisements, whatever medium they are presented in. Noticing and defining these patterns can help us to become more aware of how advertisements work. There is no particular virtue in any individual scheme, but there are clear advantages in applying one that fits as many cases as possible without having to distort the text.

This scheme is based on research into how a large number of subjects told spontaneous stories in response to the same stimulus (Labov and

Figure 5.2   Labov and Waletzky's five stages of narrative (modified)

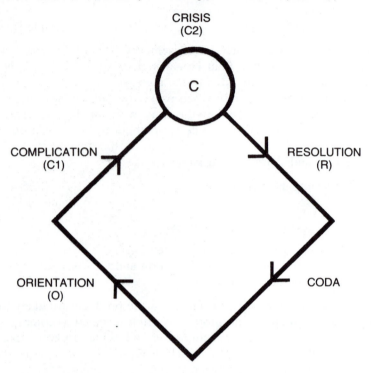

Source: After Ryder 1982: 75

Waletzky 1966). The stories showed recurrent patterns in the way they organised time. Comparing how events were organised in the stories with how they had actually occurred, the researchers were able to build a general theory of narrative. They concluded that such stories consisted of five main elements (not always in this order):

Orientation – scene, time and participants introduced.
Complication – one or more cycles of events unfold.
Crisis – pivotal point in story on which resolution turns.
Resolution – cycle(s) of events confirm/deny previous expectations.
Coda – optional sequence where story-teller 'signs off', sometimes relating story back to present context.

(after Ryder 1982: 74–5)

Dramatic form

We should be wary of applying such schemes to all story forms, however attractive they may seem. Written or spoken stories use a range of verbal techniques and sequencing principles to surprise or reassure their audiences. These techniques can also be seen at work in television, radio and the press. But media stories are different from the kind of stories which much research has focused on. They rarely have *narrators*: they are *dramatic*.

Looking at advertisements in terms of their dramatic story form is helpful because it focuses on how audiences participate in the process of persuasion and how that process actually works. Traditional ways of telling stories depend on a story-teller who frames and mediates between audience and action. But the stories used by television, radio and press advertisements are rarely narrated. They are *enacted*. As in the theatre, the only framing devices are the physical properties of the media themselves. These properties are sufficiently 'transparent' and self-effacing that audiences are able to experience the 'action' directly and immediately. High quality reproduction of images and use of naturalist codes and conventions make the illusion of participation easier and enable more personal involvement.

Home and romance

Newspaper and magazine advertisements have to rely for their story-telling on words and pictures which are fixed in time. But they can still be dramatic. They are still able to provide situations with a past and future as well as a present. They can still use 'characters' who are involved in the action of the story. Some advertisements also use narrators, as in conventional story-telling.

> Characters in ads are always locked into a moment, the narcotic perpetual-present of consumption ... that has nothing to do with the main currents of human behaviour.

(Saynor 1990: 38)

Asking some simple questions is an effective starting point for exploring how advertisements work. With the DishwashElectric advertisement, for example, we could ask:

- What has just happened in the picture?
- What is happening now?
- What will happen next?
- What messages are being exchanged within the picture?
- What messages are offered to readers by the picture as a whole?
- In what sort of publication would you expect to find the picture?

These are necessary as preliminary questions before we can go on to examine more fully how the story is constructed.

Figure 5.3   DishwashElectric advertisement

"I was getting to know the dishes better than my family."

There's nothing I like better than preparing a meal for the family. And there's nothing they like better than eating it.

But when it comes to the washing up... no-one wants to know. So guess who always does it?

I began to feel I knew the people on our willow pattern plates better than my own family.

So it was touch and go: we either stopped eating or we bought a dishwasher. Now we're the proud owners of a dishwasher – and none of us would be without it. "I'll do the washing up" they say as they stack it full of plates and pans and glasses and knives and forks and dishes and casseroles. "You go and sit down."

And that's exactly what I do, leaving them to argue over who presses the button that starts the machine rinsing and washing and finally drying up everything bone-dry and shiny-clean.

The only thing I miss is my willow pattern love story. I hope it still ends happily ever after.

Please send me a copy of your DishwashElectric leaflet.
Post to: Electricity Publications,
PO Box 2, Feltham, Middlesex TW14 0TG.

Name _____

Address _____

Postcode

DISHWASHELECTRIC
THE ELECTRICITY COUNCIL, ENGLAND & WALES
D8/210

Source: The Electricity Council, England and Wales

Figure 5.4 DishwashElectric advertisement showing the Labov-Waletzky stages of narrative

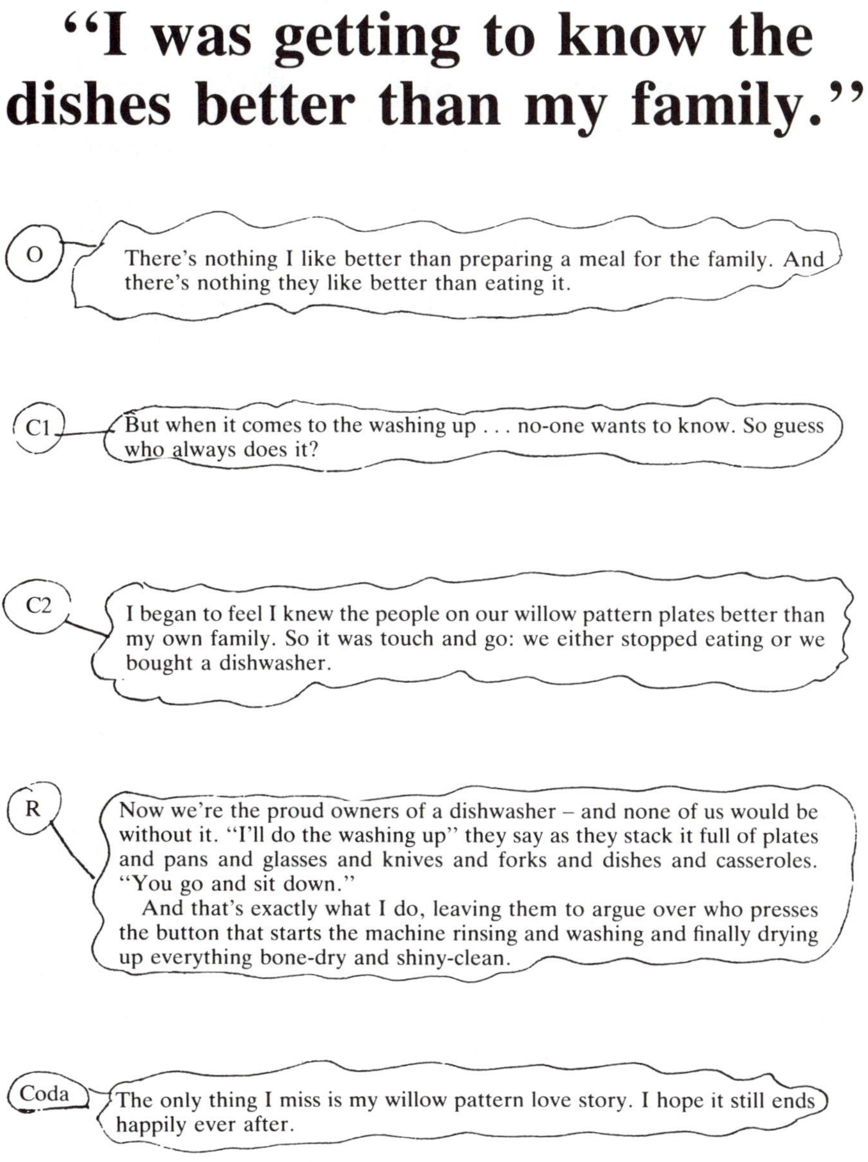

"I was getting to know the dishes better than my family."

O There's nothing I like better than preparing a meal for the family. And there's nothing they like better than eating it.

C1 But when it comes to the washing up . . . no-one wants to know. So guess who always does it?

C2 I began to feel I knew the people on our willow pattern plates better than my own family. So it was touch and go: we either stopped eating or we bought a dishwasher.

R Now we're the proud owners of a dishwasher – and none of us would be without it. "I'll do the washing up" they say as they stack it full of plates and pans and glasses and knives and forks and dishes and casseroles. "You go and sit down."

And that's exactly what I do, leaving them to argue over who presses the button that starts the machine rinsing and washing and finally drying up everything bone-dry and shiny-clean.

Coda The only thing I miss is my willow pattern love story. I hope it still ends happily ever after.

Key: O = Orientation, C1 = Complication, C2 = Crisis, R = Resolution.

This advertisement is unusual in having a narrator. The voice is clearly that of the woman in the picture, the housewife and mother who has a problem with washing dishes and at the same time being with her family (although the voice could theoretically be the man's). This tension between different family responsibilities is captured vividly by the carefully positioned images of the family playing *Monopoly* and the dishwasher. It is also dramatised by the headline quotation from the mother: 'I was getting to know the dishes better than my family.' Both of these elements summarise the essence of the advertisement's message at a glance. When coupled with the information about the product in the bottom-right corner of the page, the suggested solution to the problem is clear.

So why does anybody bother to read the rest of the text? No doubt many readers do not, but those who do are probably attracted by the offer of a story, with its promise of intimate revelations from a particular fictional character. The character also has a strong general appeal through its stereotyped traits. The story is cast in a form of popular romantic fiction most often associated with women's magazines. Much of its language both helps to characterise the speaker and to signal the way the story should be read. This formal function is clear at the very end of the story in 'I hope it still ends happily ever after.' So the product is actually credited with providing not only time for the family but also particular forms of domestic/romantic pleasure for the wife/mother.

Underneath the individual surface features of the text, the way the story is told clearly exemplifies the Labov-Waletzky scheme explained earlier. The pictures, headline and opening paragraph are the *orientation* element. They tell us about the mother's pleasure in preparing food, the family's in eating it and the mother's dilemma with the washing up. The next three sentences ('But . . . So . . . I began') are the *complication* element. They present a series of problems: no one wants to do the washing up, so the mother does it, but this creates a new problem which puts her in danger of separation from her family. The *crisis* states the need for a solution to be found: stop eating or buy a dishwasher. The *resolution* element presents the family as magically transformed by possession of the dishwasher ('Now we're the proud owners of a dishwasher . . .'). The problems listed in the *complication* are now reversed as the rest of the family queue up to stack the dishwasher while the mother relaxes and the machine does the work. The final element is the *coda*. This refers us back to the willow pattern plates in a neat transformation: the fantasy of the happily ever after ending has been realised within the family. It is incorporated in the fantastic powers of the dishwasher.

An office of my own

The Epson PX-8 computer advertisement which appeared in one of the Sunday colour supplements also tries to integrate the product into a simple dramatic framework. It uses a narrator, film and television producer Verity Lambert, in the specific setting of The Meridiana, a fashionable London restaurant. Information about the product and the manufacturer is provided on the 'bottom line', as in the DishwashElectric advertisement, but there is also a slogan 'It's the only way to work' which was used throughout the campaign. It acts both as catch-phrase and as witty summary of the story which surrounds it. The product is also displayed in action on the restaurant table.

As with the DishwashElectric advertisement, there is much more happening than the story-line. The characterisation of Verity Lambert is much fuller than that of the anonymous housewife. She is constructed as somebody special. Her job is seen as distinctive and attractive, with a certain mystique (in contrast with 'the straight business community'). Yet she began her career as a secretary with ABC. She can thus claim to be both unique and typical, so that the life-style she represents ('a bit swankier ... envious glances') can be associated with the product she is advertising. While the waiter's movements in the photograph are deliberately blurred, she sits and confidently addresses the onlooker just as directly as her voice speaks to the reader in the accompanying text.

The story she tells follows exactly the same scheme as the Dishwash Electric advertisement. The *orientation* is provided by the headline, the photograph, the 'by-line' and the first two autobiographical paragraphs in the text. The *complication* comes with the rise to fame via Thames and Euston films, for this brings with it increasing responsibilities and more paperwork. The *crisis* element is signalled by 'Which can lead to problems' in the next paragraph. It is implied that she is not very keen on paperwork. The *resolution* covers a series of successes with the product, in spite of Verity Lambert's computer incompetence and general scepticism. The *coda* signs her off with a similar tongue-in-cheek comment to that in the DishwashElectric advertisement. The fantastic powers of the product have been so 'proven' by her personal testimony that she imagines hordes of business executives competing for table space in fashionable London restaurants.

Both of these advertisements draw on powerful conventional ideas about the role of women in relation to home and work. Both female figures are stereotypes but they offer rather different conceptions of women in relation to technology. It is very productive to ask why the dishwasher is presented by an anonymous housewife while the computer is distinguished by a 'Career Woman' (an early version of the 'Lively Lady'?). Both of them contrast work with leisure and acknowledge the tension between simply enjoying life's pleasures and having to work hard for them. In both cases, the product advertised appears forcefully at the centre of the *crisis* sequence in the advertisement. Both achieve a miraculous resolution of potential conflicts through the powers of modern technology. The structure

Figure 5.5 Epson PX-8 advertisement

Source: Epson Corporation

Figure 5.6   Epson PX-8 advertisement showing the Labov-Waletzky stages of narrative

An office of my own

BY VERITY LAMBERT, FILM AND TELEVISION PRODUCER.

O

Ever since I started as a secretary in ABC Television back in 1961 I've worked in some pretty unconventional offices – but then I am in a business where being unconventional is one of the rules of the game.

It did make me wonder why the Epson corporation chose me to give their new portable computer a whirl though. Despite the claims of computer types that we'll all be hooked up to the things by the end of the decade or risk being social outcasts, I'd always imagined I might just manage to struggle on without one. I'd also imagined computers were most at home in accountant's offices, but Epson seemed to think they could prove me wrong. They might have succeeded.

When I joined Thames Television as Controller of the Drama Department in the mid 'seventies, I'd grown used to the idea that offices were places you got trapped in. Things haven't changed over the years. Thames was very good for me; producing series like 'Rock Follies' and 'Edward and Mrs Simpson' and plays like 'The Naked Civil Servant' was a great experience. Tough but great.

C1

When I became a member of the board at Thames with the help of what I'd learnt in the intervening period at Euston Films developing series like 'Minder' and 'Fox', life did get a bit swankier. I now had an office with a sofa in it. Unfortunately, with the sofa came more paperwork and less time to sit down and do it.

C2

Which can lead to problems. Television and film production requires that you have some sort of affinity for paperwork and, I suppose, a fair amount of ruthless determination to tie up loose ends. Without that you don't stand a chance, which brings me back to the Epson PX-8 computer you see me with in The Meridiana.

R

The Epson was introduced to me as one of the smallest, most powerful, portable computers in the world. "Great," I thought, "they've given the state of the art portable to someone who's mechanically subnormal and a complete computer illiterate". The promise was that with it, I'd be able to work anywhere, anytime, independent of my office. Hmmm. Well, I've only had the computer a couple of weeks but it's fulfilling its promise. I expected to be dredging half submerged mathematical equations out of my schooldays to operate it. No such thing. On the first day I put my diary for the next month into it – turned up at a meeting and caused a bit of a stir, (and surprise, surprise, generated envious glances from some of my colleagues) by calculating the costs to complete one of our current films right there in front of them. The word processing has proved invaluable. Wherever I am, be it a meeting, a train, a cab – or a restaurant – I can get on with things I'd normally have to do in the office. That's in two weeks.

Coda

Against all my prejudices, I've become a fan of a computer. I shudder to think what might happen when the straight business community get hold of Epson PX-8's. There'll be nowhere left to eat in London for a start . . .

Key: O = Orientation, C1 = Complication, C2 = Crisis, R = Resolution of this kind of advertisement is clearly akin to popular fictional forms. The woman in the Dishwash Electric advertisement is clearly a fictional construct. Verity Lambert may be a real person, but neither the words used in the text nor the heroic feats achieved with such startling immediacy on her first day of using it are hers. But the appeal of the stories is so great that we are expected to indulge the fantastic claims made for the products.

An office at home

The television version of the Epson PX-8 advertisement goes even further in presenting attractive life-styles to surround the product. It creates a similar world of elegance and luxury, but it is a speechless world in which communication is by posture, glance and movement. Like the print element in the same campaign, it plays around with conventional conceptions of the role of women in relation to technology. This 60-second advertisement dramatises the situation of a woman who goes out to work while her man works at home. It uses all sorts of visual and musical techniques to tell its story, yet its basic narrative framework is the same as in the two magazine advertisements.

The story is told (in twenty-nine shots) as a series of contrasts between natural and artificial ways of living, between domestic comfort and the harsh world of work. Home is seen as a warm, protective and luxurious refuge, while going to work means entering an alien world which is full of noisy and hostile traffic.

Orientation (00–14 seconds)

The advertisement begins with Vivaldi strings over a complex close-up of the computer (accompanied by sound-effects of its alarm signalling morning) which pans and refocuses on the man's face. He rises, opens the window shutters and flinches at the harsh entry of sunlight. Outside, we see and hear noisy and congested traffic. This is contrasted with an unusual aerial shot of the man leaning across the bed over the woman (she wears a wedding ring) who lies there. His eyes turn away from the erotic potential of this scene to look at the computer screen displaying 'FRIDAY MORNING' and bleeping once more.

Complication (15–28 seconds)

They have to go to work and make their preparations. The Vivaldi music increases in tempo as if in response to the urgency of this call to work. Both partners begin to move around the room as they dress, alternating balletically between foreground and background positions. Their movements are intercut with shots of the portable computer being closed and put into a brief-case, as if ready for work. Various erotic images of her lips and lipstick, legs and stockings culminate (surprisingly) in *her* departure for work. They kiss on the doorstep, leaving him at home drinking coffee and wryly shaking his head as if at her misfortune. The sequence creates a further *complication* by suggesting a *ménage à trois* involving 'his' computer. A subtle equation is made between the charms of the computer and the woman by their positioning and by the identical colouring of her lipstick and some of the computer's keys.

Crisis (29–35 seconds)

A radio voice refers obliquely to traffic on the roads as the man lays out his suit on the bed as if for work. Again he shakes his head (this time at the suit) scratches his chest, puts on a casual shirt and takes the computer out of the brief-case. He has decided to work at home. Just as this sequence is finishing, Ian Holm's voice-over delivers the product information. This links it with the story so far and runs right through the *resolution* and *coda* sequences to the end of the advertisement (line endings indicate shot changes):

Epson, one of the biggest computer companies in the world, have just developed one of the smallest, most powerful computers in the world.
The *Epson PX-8*.
The Epson works anywhere,
which means you can too.
    (FX *Traffic noise*)
The *Epson PX-8*.
It's the only way to work.

Resolution (36–50 seconds)

The Vivaldi music continues at matching tempo right through to the final shot of the *coda* sequence but here continues briskly as a sequence of shots displays the portability and versatility of the product. The man operates the keyboard as he sits on a luxurious sofa or at a desk and even walks around carrying it until he is interrupted by the squeal of tyres and noise of car horns outside.

Coda (51–8 seconds)

The woman reappears from behind the man on the balcony where he stands, computer in hand. She winds her arm around him in a 'come hither' caress which strangely echoes his relationship with the computer. He is surprised but pleased to see her. The final shot (the 'pack shot') displays the computer alone in a different setting with a telephone number for further information superimposed.

The remarkable achievement of this advertisement is that it manages to naturalise a highly artificial product. At its most basic, its appeal is similar to advertisements which eroticise cars for male conquest. Yet it also creates a more subtle identity for the PX-8 amid the opulent pleasures of a luxury flat. It domesticates the computer into an exclusive, self-contained and childless world whose smartness is marked by the elegance of baroque music. In its attempts to create new images of work and leisure, this advertisement finally moves from simple fiction on to the level of mythology.

Home and away

Radio offers stories within advertisements with a similar degree of human interest and comparable basic structures. It can also use dramatic forms, as in the advertisement campaign for Kleenex tissues which incorporates a strong romantic theme to gain our attention. Each advertisement has only 30 seconds to tell a story and sell a product, so it uses the radio convention of sketching in a dramatic framework and relying on the imagination of the audience to fill in the detail. In the example discussed here, voice quality quickly establishes the scene, music common to a whole series of Kleenex radio and television advertisements underscores the mood, words are carefully chosen but kept to a minimum and maximum use is made of pauses to convey meaning:

> **PHONE CALL**
>
> (*Romantic music: Intermezzo from Mascagni's* Cavalleria Rusticana)
> *Him*: (*at the end of a telephone*): Hello it's me . . .
> (*pause*)
> *Her*: It's two o'clock in the morning. What is it in Bonn?
> *Him*: Listen, erm (*pause*) will you marry me? (*pause*) Please?
> (*slight pause*)
> *Her*: Oh, Oh darling of course I will – yes.
> (*music swells*)
> *Him*: You will? Really?
> *Her*: Yes, yes, oh . . . (*begins to sniffle*) Oh . . . hold on I need a **Kleenex tissue.**
> *Him*: Oh that's great, because I didn't go to Bonn – I'm in a phone box round the corner.
> (*as music resolves*)
> *Male voice-over*: **Kleenex Tissues** – softness is our strength.

The framework devised by Labov and Waletzky for analysing stories can also be usefully applied to this sequence. No single account of its structure can be definitive, since it is possible to place the transitions from one phase to another differently. For instance, where does the crisis occur? Should reaching for the tissues be seen as providing help at the moment of crisis or as playing a part in the resolution of the problem? Does the crisis come after the man has asked the woman to marry him or after his plaintive 'Please?'? Whatever conclusions analysis suggests, its main purpose is to increase students' awareness of how the advertisement works as a narrative. At a simpler level, analysing voices in terms of the impressions they make is a simple, practical and effective way of beginning to understand how advertising works for audiences.

The use of romantic music and a voice on the telephone saying merely, 'Hello, it's me . . .' tells us a lot. The caller is obviously known intimately as he does not have to say his name and his husky tone suggests that we are hearing a conversation between lovers who are temporarily parted. The swirling music underlines this romantic theme and the violins hint that we might be about to hear something important. This is followed by a pause which increases audience anticipation about what will happen next. It also represents the slow reaction of someone getting a phone call in the middle of the night. When she says, 'It's two o'clock in the morning. What is it in Bonn?', it confirms and extends our impressions. It is obvious from the text that they must be lovers who are temporarily parted since no one but intimates would call each other so late without recrimination.

Complication (7–11 seconds)

The story develops dramatically as he hesitantly asks her to marry him. Even in a single line, audience anticipation is increased by the use of two pauses. The plaintive 'Please?' at the end of the line makes him sound genuine and asks us to sympathise with him. During the slight pause that follows, the music quietly ends a phrase in anticipation of the answer.

Crisis (12–17 seconds)

A crisis has been created and becomes the fulcrum of the story. Will she accept or reject him? Her breathless answer is accompanied by the strong main theme which is easily recognisable and which tugs at our emotions. His 'niceness' is further reinforced by the fact that he appears genuinely surprised at his good fortune. He is grateful that she has agreed to marry him and it invites us to conclude that she made a wise choice. He does not take her for granted.

Resolution (18–26 seconds)

As she reaffirms that she will marry him she starts to cry but help is at hand in the shape of a Kleenex tissue. The product helps her out in her moment of need. She is helped further by a neat twist in the story. He is not in Bonn but in a phone box round the corner and will no doubt be round to comfort her very soon. As we smile at the deception, we realise that we are already thinking of them as a couple rather than as two individuals at the end of a phone.

Coda (27–30 seconds)

Just as we are left celebrating this newly found union a reassuring voice-over relates the qualities of softness and strength to Kleenex tissues and the music quietly resolves itself.

The romantic story and the mildly humorous twist in the tail make it possible to listen to this advertisement several times without getting bored. At the time of broadcast, listener interest was extended still further by featuring the same two characters in a linked series of advertisements for Kleenex tissues. Using the same simple, compressed structure the other advertisements dramatised events in the lives of the couple after their marriage. (The same music was used in the parallel television advertisement over a five-year period.) In each case the story centred on the resolution of a problem with the help of Kleenex tissues. This mini-soap approach has been much hyped and widely used in other advertising campaigns such as that for Nescafé Gold Blend coffee. These advertisements feature the continuing romance of a couple as it develops through a number of different episodes. In each case, the use of a common structure enables the advertisers to take short-cuts in the telling of a story which holds audience attention whilst at the same time making the product the fulcrum of each episode.

The willing audience

Analysing texts in this way without reference to actual audiences and readers can be misleading, especially if it relies on an implicit assumption that audiences are passively manipulated by advertisements. On the contrary, we have already seen how audiences are actively involved in making meaning by being implicated in the narrative process. Recent classroom research has also shown that analysis of advertisements texts may lead to understanding how they work but have little to do with their actual meaning and value for children (Buckingham 1990: 19–59). Such analysis is therefore not enough on its own. Rather than assuming that texts have meanings which rationalistic analysis can unlock and display for all to see, effective classroom work on persuasive communication needs to begin with the meanings which children bring to texts.

Understanding the complexity of responses to advertising (or, as the

Americans call it, 'commercial speech') should enable us to grasp why some advertisements work while others do not. Studies by psychologists of major campaigns like those against AIDS, drugs and drink-driving support the idea that effective advertising needs willing audiences. But research into these campaigns also shows that the wrong kind of advertising can fail badly with some members of intended audiences.

> Something that is condemned in campaigns or in the media takes on a certain attraction ... people weigh up the various advantages or disadvantages of engaging in certain behaviours. They know that the odds of becoming HIV positive are fairly low but they realise that they might get status from engaging in so-called risky behaviours and this is of greater benefit to them in their own particular social worlds or their social communities, and so ironically some of the advertisements may lead to more of exactly the same behaviour that you're trying to inhibit.
>
> (Roger Ingham)

The long-term effects of such campaigns has been poor. In many cases, they have failed to increase knowledge about the problem and have increased confusion. There is little evidence that they have led to any major changes of life-style either amongst specific sectors of the population or the population as a whole. Although awareness and understanding amongst the general population apparently increased, only 5 per cent of respondents claimed any change in their behaviour as a result of the AIDS campaigns in 1987 (Shaw and McCron 1988: 95).

> Advertising can't sell anything to anyone unless people want it to happen.
>
> (Rita Clifton)

So what is it that goes wrong? One problem is caused by a failure to use appropriate language which the audience will understand. For example, some newspaper advertisements on AIDS carried detailed pictures of viruses which were not understood by the sort of people who read them. Terminology was being used which was simply not grasped in a standard way by the different sectors of the population.

> One advertisement talked about the phrase 'intimate kissing', and when this was researched amongst a group of gynaecologists they came up with three completely different interpretations of what this meant. Or similarly the phrase 'you must get to know your partner.' What does it mean?
>
> (Roger Ingham)

But it was not simply a language problem: there were also some ambiguities over visual representations. For example, one of the models used to illustrate the long-term effects of heroin produced some unpredicted

Figure 5.7 Anti-heroin advertisement

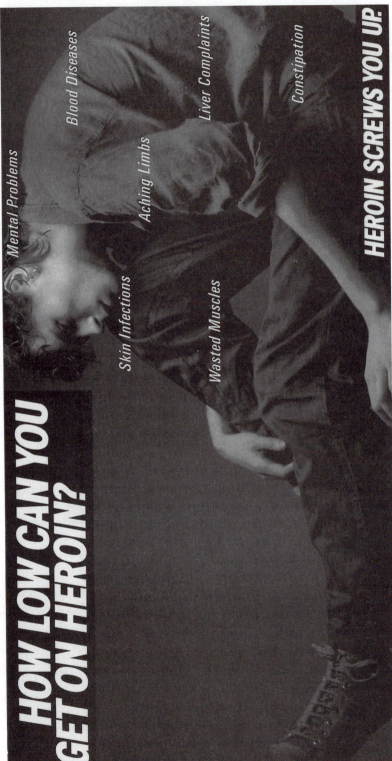

Source: Yellowhammer agency for the DHSS

responses. Some young people found the actor portraying the addict attractive and read the picture *oppositionally*, even to the point of sending off for copies of the poster to put on the wall. This was not true, of course for most readers.

> I wouldn't want to look like that. He looks stoned out. He reminds me of me. It makes me want to do something about it. It affects people in different ways, but it makes me feel worse. It makes me want to get off it.

(Regular heroin user, male, Wirral)

The mass media may be good at raising awareness but not necessarily at providing information or changing attitudes. Quite simply, they may not be able to reach the right groups with the right message. In some contexts, face-to-face contact may be the only effective means of persuasion.

> The starting-point is the target's own views and perceptions and misunderstandings and misconceptions. And in that way you can have a more tailored campaign. So, for example, in Amsterdam and New York there are street-workers now walking around looking for people involved in drug use, talking to them, getting to know them, getting them to be trusted. And these campaigns or interventions are thought to be much more successful than any one way mass campaign using the media.

(Roger Ingham)

But other campaigns have been spectacularly successful by using advertising techniques as part of a communication strategy, like the *Live Aid* concert for Ethiopia. It demonstrated both the power of the pop industry and the desire (particularly amongst young people) to be part of a world movement.

POP AND PROMOTION

Music power

Pop music, like advertising, is a massive industry. As well as being available in our homes at the touch of a switch, it seeps into our consciousness in the form of piped music as we work, shop and enjoy our leisure. It is a pervasive and powerful force in our lives. Yet as well as working on a massive scale, it is also a very personal phenomenon. It offers a space in which individuals are invited to become uniquely themselves.

> Music, by natural bent, is that which at once receives an adjective.

(Barthes 1977: 178)

Music is capable of generating a whole range of meanings through its resonance. It has the power of evoking memories, suggesting moods and triggering emotions. This power comes from a combination of sounds and silence which work at a very deep level of consciousness. Unlike words, musical sounds and rhythms alone have little meaning except through association and connotation. So, for example, cascading strings evoke romance and up-beat rhythms suggest excitement. But these effects vary with context and can only work in the most general way. In pop music, an extra dimension of meaning is created through the lyrics. The words of pop songs work like the captions of news photographs (see Chapter 3). Just as captions serve to inflect and anchor the meanings of photographs, so do verbal tracks define the particular meanings of songs and relate them to the cultural worlds of listeners.

The 'grain' is the body in the voice as it sings, the hand as it writes, the limb as it performs.

(Barthes 1977: 188)

Pop music's ability to particularise gives it great strength. Like advertisements, pop songs flourish by telling stories. They are always highly compressed, encompassing a range of crises, complications and resolutions. Their narratives are invariably framed in the first person so that the singer becomes the subject of the song. The singer becomes an actor who presents fictional experience in a transparent way. But the singer is also an actor in another sense. For the 'grain' of the singer's voice creates layers of meaning through its individual quality and timbre. So simple lyrics, like those in *Stand By Your Man*, can take on a much greater significance when sung by the song's writer, Tammy Wynette. She presents herself as the embodiment of a woman who has suffered in love yet won through, by dedication and faithfulness. This information is conveyed not only by the lyrics but by her performance. The sad voice with a catch in it seems to suggest a life of raw edges and hard experience. The whole message of *Stand By Your Man* is captured in the title which is used as a chorus line and supported by the song's most memorable melody. It would be easy to write off such a song as a mass-produced, ersatz experience full of reactionary views about the role of women. But its attraction, and that of pop generally, is that its words and music combine to provide a powerful emotional construction which taps into experiences common to many people. So the emotions presented by Tammy Wynette in the song can become particularised by listeners, as they add their own meanings and emphases to the words and music on offer. Indeed, although written to be sung by a woman, the song has been given new meaning by also having been performed by The Blues Brothers.

Life-styles and hair-styles

If adults consume songs like *Stand By Your Man* in their millions, then it is small wonder that most young people find the messages of pop music appealing as they begin to learn about the world and to try to understand their feelings. But the songs themselves are only half the story. Choosing the types of music they like also allows young people to define their own individuality and to make statements about gender, race, age-group, class and sexual identity. Pop both influences and echoes the clothes they buy and the way they do their hair. And interest in it starts early. Despite the falling numbers of 8–14-year-olds in the population as a whole, they increased their buying of singles by 4 per cent in 1988. Not surprisingly, the record industry sees them as an important market and is keen to encourage buying habits at an early age.

Promoting patterns of consumption to such young audiences is regarded with suspicion by many teachers. They argue that young people are being lulled into a state of passive consumption in the process of enjoying pop music. This has often resulted in a scepticism about the value of dealing with pop music in the classroom. Yet, as shown earlier when discussing advertising, audiences are not necessarily the victims of the values which are being promoted. A whole range of tastes, cultures and life-styles is represented by the pop industry and audiences bring their own experiences to bear on the material they consume. So studying the pop industry presents not only an opportunity to examine how people interact with a major aspect of popular culture but also offers the possibility of beginning to understand the mixture of social, economic, political and technological forces which underpin it. For these reasons a systematic study of pop demands a place in any Media Studies curriculum.

Post-war pop

The post-war years saw the growth of the modern pop industry. Developing technology in the form of long-playing records, portable record players, tape-recorders and pop stations such as Radio Luxembourg helped promote pop music to an increasingly affluent teenage audience. The 1960s saw the pop industry develop into top gear with the sophisticated promotion of pop through pirate radio, television and Radio 1, the nation's first legal, all-pop station. Alongside these developments a burgeoning fashion industry began to provide High Street versions of what the stars were wearing. The artists were not just seen as singers but also as symbols of teenage rebellion or objects of romantic desire. Their hair-styles and clothing were avidly copied and their views on life were sought out by an increasing number of magazines devoted to them. Many of the stars were from humble origins and their 'rags to riches' success stories appealed directly to working class youth. The chance of emulating the images of pop idols made them appear more accessible and added fuel to the notion that the pop industry offered a new democracy where there was room for anyone to side-step the normal impediments to youthful progress. For a few individuals this was true, but the industry's driving force was always turnover rather than revolution. Pop music was a means of promoting goods, ideas, images and life-styles.

So while pop seemed to be the voice of rebellious youth, it was mainly being produced by large corporations who appeared to be more interested in profits than music. This apparent contradiction caused some critics to argue that the music produced was really quite sterile and that any signs of rebellion were merely a publicist's illusion. Whilst there is some truth in this argument, it fails to address how pop music develops and regenerates itself and often provides a focus for minority interests. The answer,

Table 5.1 Share of total UK sales of recorded music, 1988

	LPs, Cassettes & CDs % Units	*Singles % Units*	*Overall % Value £ Sterling 1988*	*1977*
UK companies				
EMI Group	12.6	11.2		
Virgin	7.7	10.1		
PWL	1.7	4.7		
Mute	3.5	3.9		
Island	1.1	3.9		
Others	17.0	14.0		
Total	**43.6**	**47.8**	**44.1**	**41.9**
Companies based in continental Europe				
PolyGram Group	16.1	14.4		
BMG	7.0	7.5		
Others	0.4	0.1		
Total	**23.5**	**22.0**	**23.3**	**24.3**
Companies based in North America				
WEA	12.6	9.3		
MCA	1.5	4.7		
A&M	2.0	1.5		
Others	2.5	1.9		
Total	**18.7**	**17.4**	**18.6**	**31.7**
Companies in all other countries				
CBS	12.6	11.4		
Others	1.6	1.4		
Total	**14.2**	**12.8**	**14.0**	**2.1**

Source: Scaping 1989: 87

perhaps, lies in the many faces of pop and the uneasy relationship which exists between the mainstream and some of pop's alternative practitioners. For the corporations, selling singles has become a means of determining which artists might sell well on albums and CDs. They spend vast sums on the promotion of certain artists who, their market research tells them, are bankable properties. Once a record is past a break-even point, there is more profit in attracting further huge sales of the same disc than putting money into the promotion of other artists with uncertain futures.

> The ratio of just over seven percent of [recording industry] income (£45 million) being spent on advertising compares with figures of between three and four percent in the mid 1970s and the reluctance of record companies to increase spending at a faster rate whether on advertisements in television, radio or press, underlines their need to be specific and selective in targeting the audience and tailoring the campaign accordingly. Broad-based generic advertising and attempts to advertise labels or retail chains without specific reference to a particular artist or recording, have met with little success in the past.
>
> (Scaping 1989: 47)

So a star system has evolved which inevitably limits the range of music available in high street record stores. Pop music has become the starting-point for further promotion and commercial exploitation, not the final product. But audiences for pop are heterogeneous as well as homogeneous. Its highly specialised forms, like Acid House, Northern Soul, Cock Rock, Glam Rock and various ethnic musics, which help define urban sub-cultures, provide audiences with a vehicle for expressing different ways of life. Such alternative music is often part of anti-establishment movements. It can find a following through releases on small independent record labels, promotion by club DJs, word-of-mouth publicity and plays on pirate radio stations, in danger of being closed down at any moment. The lack of any mass promotion usually adds to devotees' enthusiasm, who see it as having more value and integrity than the commercialised mainstream.

The industrialisation of pop has meant that most people hear music which is part of the mainstream and run and ruled by established tastes. Hence there are allegations that the resulting material is bland and unadventurous. When super-groups receive their OBEs, commendations from royalty or plays on Radio 2, there can be little left in their work which is either subversive or threatening. But whilst their continued mass sales depend on such safe images, their music will still have borrowed from, and added to, the music of the streets like rap, reggae, ska, African music and the blues. Such constant movement means that popular music remains responsive to audience tastes and changing musical influences. This makes it very difficult for record companies to predict what will be a success.

Table 5.2 Sales by musical category (per cent units), 1986–8

	LP 1986	1987	1988	Cassette 1986	1987	1988	CD 1986	1987	1988
Pop/Disco	55	65	64	49	55	56	NA	57	55
Rock	14	12	8	9	7	6	NA	11	11
Jazz	1	*	1	1	1	*	NA	1	1
Country/Folk	3	2	2	4	4	5	NA	*	2
Classical	6	5	5	8	9	8	NA	15	14
Film soundtracks	1	1	2	2	1	2	NA	1	1
MOR	6	6	7	8	10	8	NA	5	7
Electronic	2	1	1	1	1	1	NA	1	1
Reggae	1	1	1	1	1	*	NA	1	*
Other	11	7	10	17	12	14	NA	9	7

Source: Scaping 1989: 88
Notes: NA = not available   * = less than 1 per cent

In the 1970s, 90 per cent of records released failed to cover their costs. In the late 1980s, 7,000 titles were released on the album formats (LP, CD, Cassette) but less than 200 made it to the Top 100 album chart in the year of release. Such uncertainty is partly due to the unpredictability of audience tastes, which in turn, will have been influenced by gatekeepers such as DJs, journalists and concert promoters. And spending large amounts of money in promoting certain acts does not guarantee success with audiences. Furthermore, attempts by the companies to invent groups and foist them on to an unsuspecting public have generally met with failure. Who now remembers, or even cares about, the 1980s group Kagagoogoo?

Image and perception

Image-making has always been part of the pop music industry and it works at both a personal and public level. Those who bought the records of Bob Dylan in the 1960s and Sting in the 1980s were buying an image of themselves as socially aware people as well as enjoying the performances of the musicians themselves. And teenagers who become fans of particular pop idols are expressing the adolescent need to conform with their peers as well as making a statement about themselves and their newly acquired tastes. So pop music provides its customers with the opportunity of expressing themselves by defining images and activities to aspire to.

> Pop music provides the possibility of living 'in exile' – for the mods a fashionable 'cool' removed from the dull prospects of everyday routines, for the motorbike boys ('Rockers') the mythological highway of masculine fulfilment. But exile also provides the opportunity to experiment with new cultural possibilities: social, sexual and stylistic.
>
> (Chambers 1987: 238)

In the public arena pop music can affect the way we perceive recent history and world issues. Both the *Live Aid* and *Nelson Mandela* concerts, with their vast television audiences, heightened public awareness of the issues of world poverty and apartheid. Furthermore, the plight of youthful American GIs and the conditions they endured in the Vietnam War were chronicled in Paul Hardcastle's album *19*. But, as with advertising, the messages are inevitably restricted to easy slogans such as 'Feed the World' or 'Free Nelson Mandela' which do not offer much scope for exploring contradictions. And pop may also glamorise past events as in *Dear America*, a television documentary on the Vietnam War, which made extensive use of pop music as a back-drop to the pictures.

> The rock and roll which genuinely accompanied the fighting can still, in retrospect, give documentary footage the callow excitement of rock videos. Watching an airborne attack on a Vietnamese hamlet to the sound of the Rolling Stones, it was impossible to ignore the malign glamour – as one writer put it, 'You know this is war – the hippest thing in the world.'
>
> (Suttcliffe 1990: 32)

And using pop inter-cut with news events from the 1950s and 1960s provided the basis for the popular television history series *The Rock'n Roll Years*. Each half-hour programme represented one year. Whilst not overtly attempting to glamorise the past, the series edited the events to the music. Complex recent history was fleetingly recreated through the diffusing lens of pop. The music set the agenda, and with the benefit of hindsight new meanings about the past were created. And on a more basic level, the music probably triggered individual memories of both public and private events in the minds of the audience.

> Thirty years of music from the crooning complacency of the hit parade in the early 1950s to the cosmopolitan college sounds of the 1980s, cross, and in turn are crossed by multiple histories – histories of the record industry, of radio and television, of youth, fashion, gender, class, race, sexuality, consumerism, marketing, entertainment, leisure, and politics. Music has consistently assisted in signifying a passing sense inside all of them.
>
> (Chambers 1987: 233)

Marketing music

Because pop can offer consumers instant identification with a trend, idea or style, it provides a useful promotional tool to those seeking specific audiences. As well as using modern music to add currency to messages, advertisers have been quick to spot the nostalgic power of certain songs. So an advert for jeans uses a hit tune from the past along with romanticised images of the era which is being evoked. This has the effect of widening the range of people who will be attracted to the advert. The music supplies pegs on which an older audience can hang fragments of personal history as well as introducing a younger audience to recycled fashion images. Music used in such a manner has often become a hit for a second time.

Radio stations also use pop music to create images which will attract certain audiences and in the case of commercial radio, attract advertisers. By strictly regulating the type of music they play, they are able to build up a specific image for the audiences they seek to attract. They compile play-lists of records which they think suit the image of their station. Radio 1 has a play-list committee where producers vote on records to be included. They argue that this diminishes the influence of pluggers who are employed by the industry to persuade producers and DJs to play certain records. Whilst such a committee may indeed have this effect, their primary motivation is to use music to target their desired audience. Many commercial stations have separated their allocated FM and AM frequencies in order to play different music for different audiences. This has seen the development of 'Gold' stations playing pop from the 1960s and 1970s to audiences who now have the affluence the advertisers are seeking.

Typically, a station has a play-list of about a thousand records. For the 35–50 age-group, there is a steady diet of Beatles, Beach Boys, The Everley Brothers, Cliff Richard and Motown. The two most popular songs recently have been *If You Leave Me Now* by Chicago and *Whiter Shade of Pale* by Procul Harum.

> Gold radio becomes merely an audio theme-park to indulge rose-tinted dreams, as DJs fondly remember and dismember them for us. Roland Barthes, who didn't know much about Clodagh Rogers, but who knew a thing or two about mythologies called it the privation of history. 'We marvel at this beautiful object without ever wondering where it came from.' ... Meanwhile, back on a certain East Midlands oldies station, Arthur Brown segues effortlessly into Brenda Lee. Later a man will scream at you to buy carpets from his warehouse. Another man will provide seamless continuity between the separate components. He will say 'time to squeeze in a couple more before the top of the hour' in such a way that the top-of-the-hour is far more important than the two he is trying to squeeze in. He will tell you each record brings back many memories, but never tell you what those memories are. Everything is equal under the auspices of the leisure industry. Meanwhile, from 1969 here's Jethro Tull. Whoever he is.

(Chapman 1990: 22–3)

Using pop music to target audiences or as a means of promotion usually means that the music being played has to be familiar. Such policies inevitably reduce the variety of music which is heard, adding further

Figure 5.8 Gold Radio advertisement

ADVERTISEMENT

Muriel Strikes Gold

The home of Hampshire housewife Muriel Flowers will be a richer place from now on.

It's all thanks to a chance discovery made earlier this week when she switched on her radio.

For years Muriel had been tuned in to a certain station on the medium waveband.

"I listened to it because it was there," she confessed. "But to my amazement, when I tuned in on Monday, it was gone."

"I've never been much of a knob-twiddler but somehow I managed it" Then all of a sudden she struck Gold.

One musical memory after another gushed from Muriel's trusty transistor. Clapping her hands with joy, Muriel rushed out to broadcast her news.

"I can't believe it even now," she said, clearly choked.

"It was there all the time and I didn't know it."

Experts predict a spate of similar discoveries in the very near future.

1170 kHz MW (257m) or 1557 kHz MW (193m)

MUSIC MEMORIES ON MEDIUM WAVE

Source: Southampton Advertiser, 30 August 1990

limitations to those already imposed by the restrictive polices of the recording industry conglomerates.

The promotional value of pop music means that even the record companies themselves may well be moving away from making money out of the sale of records and moving into exploiting the rights they hold in the music of their artists. One result of this may mean that radio stations will be charged more for the records they play. In the past, record companies saw radio as a useful means of promoting discs but the move to rights exploitation means that they will be less interested in volume sales. The growth in commercial radio in the late 1980s meant that more records were played. This resulted in a 52 per cent increase in rights income for the record industry.

> Record industry income from broadcasting and public performance has grown consistently over the past few years ... Revenue from PPL (Public Performing Licence) provides a growing percentage of record company profits and for many companies, especially the independent labels, these broadcasting fees are a vital part of their income. The fees provide funding for numerous projects throughout the industry which would otherwise not be feasible ...
>
> The second major source of income for record companies via PPL is performance from outlets which either rely on records for their business such as discos and clubs, or which use music as a background or to enhance an environment such as shops, pubs, restaurants and sports venues ... the most significant gain is in usage itself as recorded music becomes the norm in every possible type of setting.
>
> (Scaping 1989: 52)

As a result, the industry will probably look for multi-media tie-ups which combine records, advertisements, books, films, fashion and cable networks in gigantic deals. So a situation will arrive when best-selling records will only be made when a total package has been sold to television shows and advertisers. The effect could be to turn pop into an even greater promotional form than it has been hitherto. The music, as ever, is not the only focus of attention. A survey in 1987 showed that 7–19-year-olds spent a total of £797 millions on clothes whilst spending on records and tapes accounted for £334 millions (Ferrari and James 1989: 222). So it is easy to see why the selling of T-shirts commemorating an artist's tour has achieved a greater significance in the financing of such events. And those principles extend to other items such as posters, bed-linen, badges, puzzles, clocks, watches, sleeping bags and wall-hangings, to name but a few. One company specialising in the exploitation of such materials on behalf of a range of pop stars is capable of turning out 120,000 T-shirts a day.

A further encouragement for large corporations to look to rights exploitation is the development of sophisticated home-taping devices which mean audiences are buying fewer original discs or CDs. One of Britain's largest record producers, Thorn-EMI, along with its retail outlet

Figure 5.9   Real value of record industry output, 1978–88

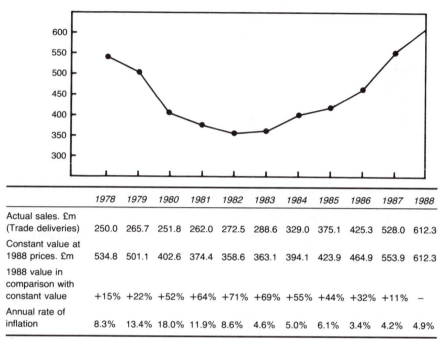

	1978	1979	1980	1981	1982	1983	1984	1985	1986	1987	1988
Actual sales. £m (Trade deliveries)	250.0	265.7	251.8	262.0	272.5	288.6	329.0	375.1	425.3	528.0	612.3
Constant value at 1988 prices. £m	534.8	501.1	402.6	374.4	358.6	363.1	394.1	423.9	464.9	553.9	612.3
1988 value in comparison with constant value	+15%	+22%	+52%	+64%	+71%	+69%	+55%	+44%	+32%	+11%	–
Annual rate of inflation	8.3%	13.4%	18.0%	11.9%	8.6%	4.6%	5.0%	6.1%	3.4%	4.2%	4.9%

Source: Scaping 1989: 11

HMV record stores, has announced that it will stop producing and selling vinyl records by 1995. This is partly due to the developing popularity of the CD and cassette market but it could also be seen as a step away from selling recordings as products. The effect of these trends will be to turn pop into an even greater promotional form than it has been hitherto. However, a paradox is at work here. The more rarified the pop products of the multinational leisure corporations become, the more they will leave room for small independent record labels to feature 'the sound of the streets' where most trends in pop begin.

Pop and the tabloids

Being notorious is more valuable than being anonymous in the music business. You may cringe at what they write, and the people around you may get hurt, but in the long run any publicity is better than no publicity.
  (Wham!'s manager Simon Napier-Bell, in Ferrari and James 1989: 279)

The tabloids have assumed a crucial role in providing information about the pop industry. They all have a specialist pop page as well as running news stories based on what is happening in the pop world. Increasingly, the tabloids compete to attract readers with the most titillating gossip. The stories usually concern the private lives of stars and often expand in the telling.

> You have to recognise that because tabloid newspapers want stories like that they are prepared to go along with them without investigating them. They want that to be a true story. It's a better story than 'Andrew Ridgeley's had plastic surgery.' I also think equally frequently, if not more frequently, the tabloid press make things up about the pop industry.
>
> (Lilie Ferrari)

News agencies and 'stringers' bombard the papers with tit-bits of information often labelled for the 'gossip-desk' and journalists promote contacts with key members of the industry. Information also comes from the friends of the stars themselves. Both sides acknowledge that they often fabricate material in order to maximise publicity and create entertaining reading.

ANDREW RIDGELEY'S NOSE

The story broke in the *Sun* newspaper with a very dramatic headline WHAM! STAR SCARRED BY BOTTLE IN CLUB. This was the story about how Andrew Ridgeley had been smashed on the nose by somebody in a nightclub ... The following day the story was that the person who had whacked Andrew was a singer called David Austin who was a friend of Andrew. And it just so happened that David Austin's record was about to be released. On the third day it was confessed that this entire story was a fabrication and that Andrew had in fact had plastic surgery on his nose. The story then appeared several months later when Andrew was seen wearing bandages covering his nose so this was another opportunity for Wham! to appear in the paper. And then when Andrew's new nose was released there was another reason for Andrew's face to appear in the paper ... When we interviewed one of Wham!'s staff it transpired that this was a story constructed by their manager Simon Napier-Bell who has been in the pop business for years ... He was pleased with getting his act onto the front of the tabloid newspapers for many days.

(Lilie Ferrari)

We made up a story which we leaked very slowly to the journalists (asking them not to tell anyone), that Andrew had been in a nightclub and had been hit on the nose with an ice-bucket by his friend David Austin. The papers fell for it. In twenty-five years of dealing with the press, I'd never known them fall for something so totally and absolutely. The next day David Austin got on to the front page of every tabloid paper as the man who has smashed England's major heart-throb with an ice bucket. I think we were in the papers every day for a week. Then on the fifth day we announced that Andrew had, in fact, had a nose job. Of course the papers looked totally stupid, but in fact, I think they had known the truth in the first place but they'd been happy to go along with the other story we fed them because it made good copy.

(Simon Napier-Bell, in Ferrari and James 1989: 282)

The tabloids' interest in pop stems from their need to build mass readerships in order to survive commercially. By presenting information about pop music in the way they do, they present the illusion that they are giving their readers special access to an important community. Gossip pages with names like 'The White Hot Club' suggest they are dispensing up-to-the-minute privileged information. What they are really selling is an imaginary community existing only in the pages of the newspapers but uniting the audience in the pursuit of information about pop. It provides something which people can imagine themselves as being part of. At best it can be seen as mildly amusing fiction but at worst it becomes a palliative, diverting attention from the real world.

The tabloids are in the business of building mass readerships, as many people as possible. Those readers will be divided in various ways in their actual lives, in their conditions in life, but they can be unified by certain appeals. One of the appeals is to the market – that they're all consumers, they're all equal in the face of the market, so they can all buy the same things. The other is this notion of the nation – that they're all equally members of the great British nation. And those two 'imaginary communities' are ways of appealing to a broad readership without having to bother about all the differences and divisions that fracture them and that's the whole art of mass appeal ... You have to find categories that people can subscribe to, people can imagine themselves as part of, that somehow don't mention all the things that divide them.

(Graham Murdock)

Teaching pop

Students know about pop and teachers know about institutions and somewhere along the line those two things have to merge in the classroom.

(Lilie Ferrari)

Teachers' unfamiliarity with the pop industry often makes them both sceptical and uncertain about dealing with pop in the classroom. However, many approaches used in other areas of Media Studies can equally be applied to the pop industry. A key concept like *Media Audiences* can underpin work on the way pop fans behave and what it means to be a fan. This could involve looking at how fans get their information, what they do with it and how they express their feelings. Exploring what it means to be a fan would reveal some interesting contrasts between male and female approaches. Do fans desert stars who change and develop their style? Is it the image or the product (or both) which is being sought?

> Teaching about pop does raise questions of sexuality and I think that teachers should be aware of that before they go into the classroom and be prepared to deal with it. I think being a female fan is a different thing from being a male fan. Boys, from our research, tend to collect data – 'what year did that record get released?' or 'what record label was that song on?', I think that's a very male form of knowledge. With girls it's a far more internalised business. They might collect cuttings but it's more about feelings. Teaching pop is very sensitive and talking to young people about their feelings in relation to people they admire is very difficult.
>
> (Lilie Ferrari)

If students feel that their own territory is being invaded then a sense of distance could be provided by looking at the activities of fans from former generations. Apart from giving an ideal opportunity to interview parents about the idols of their youth, this would also allow the possibility of drawing up some general principles of fan behaviour. Such information could then be used to investigate why some people are feted more than others. Is it to do with how heavily a personality is promoted? What role do fan magazines play in forming impressions of stars? The question as to whether fans are merely the unthinking recipients of a constant stream of merchandising could also be tackled. How do they affect the popularity of a star by refusing to buy what is offered? And in addition to economic power what part does personality play in the process of winning hearts and minds?

Examining the appeal of apparent failures like Eddie 'The Eagle' Edwards, who came last in everything at the Winter Olympics, might be a useful way of extending work on fans. He started out with no sponsors but as he became popular he began to attract public and commercial interest and a string of personal appearances. Although not part of the pop music world his case has many parallels with the way stories about stars are promoted and could lead to examining how the stories were circulated, in what form, how they were used and who they were aimed at. Investigating such a range of questions will not fully explain the fan phenomenon (no one has yet done so) but it will provide a framework which validates the experiences of young people and helps them understand the processes they are encountering.

> One of my clearest memories . . . is of a bus-ride from my housing estate in Birmingham into the city centre. An atmosphere like a cup final coach, but with all of us on the same side and with one even more radical difference – there were no boys. At every stop, even more girls got on, laughing, shouting, singing the songs we all knew by heart. We compared the outfits and banners we had spent hours making, swapped jokes and stories, and talked happily to complete strangers because we all had one interest in common: we were about to see the Bay City Rollers.
>
> (Ferrari and James 1989: 206)

Investigating *Media Audiences* could also involve examining how pop music is used to target audiences and segment markets. This might involve studying the schedules of various music stations and asking what audiences they are trying to attract. Additional information could be culled from the rate cards and sales literature which most stations produce in order to attract potential advertisers. How does the station sell itself, who is it claiming to reach and what evidence does it offer to back up such claims? Such work would naturally lead on to studying how pop music is used in advertising to attract specific audiences by creating the appropriate mood and pace. And students could carry out their own surveys amongst different age groups in order to consider the effects of recycling old hits in certain advertisements.

Starting to ask how pop stories get circulated leads inevitably on to the key concept of *Media Representation* and this in turn suggests work on the tabloid press. The tabloids have increasingly made pop and entertainment the major object of their attention and students may want to start by devising some guidelines which help audiences evaluate the information provided. This involves considering what news is and also what a newspaper is. Any conclusions reached could be on the basis of a careful monitoring of the tabloids using methods devised jointly by student and teacher.

> Readers do not believe most of what they read in the tabloid press. They accept that this is a kind of fiction. Saying that Michael Jackson has a monkey in his bedroom is not a fact. It's something that we all think we know but it's not a fact. Saying that Michael Jackson came to London in 1989 and did some sell-out concerts is a fact. So by making students think about Michael Jackson you can actually get them to discuss the sorts of knowledge that they have about pop and where it comes from.
>
> (Lilie Ferrari)

Another useful starting-point for work on pop is to examine it as an *institution*. This means that it could then be seen as being at the centre of an interaction between young people, the music industry, musicians and the state. Looking at pop in this way means asking questions about what influences the production of music and why certain types of music get promoted whilst other forms are ignored. It also means examining the social, political and economic practices which affect the consumption of pop music. In practical terms it means using student knowledge about what is happening or has happened in the pop industry and then relating it to the pop industry as an institution. This may mean studying the production history of bands which have been created by record companies to meet a perceived market trend and then not worked (e.g. Kagagoogoo). Or it might involve looking at the role television plays in promoting pop music. For instance the BBC classifies *Top of the Pops* as a light entertainment programme and not as a pop programme, claiming that it merely reflects the pop charts rather than influences them. According to some commentators this is so that it can avoid any accusations of acting in a promotional capacity for the industry. Examining why the industry views the matter differently would be a useful starting-point for looking at television's promotional role. Vast sums are spent by the record industry on pop videos which are supplied at a notional cost to programmes like *Top of the Pops*. Students might like to consider why this is done and why the practice may change if, as predicted, the industry moves away from selling records to selling the rights it holds in artists.

QUESTIONS ON POP AS INSTITUTION

What effect has the social and cultural use of music had on the shape of the music industry itself?

What effect have the new technologies (Walkmans, CDs) had on patterns of consumption?

What effect does the financial structure of the music business have on the range of music styles available on the market?

What values are embedded in the professional practices (e.g. poster design, marketing or the standard artist's contract) of the music industry?

What are the influences that have had an effect on the words, rhythm or rhyme of any particular song?

What social, cultural or economic factors have contributed to a particular band's success or demise?

How is the development of new media markets likely to affect the industry?

How does the state (through implicit or explicit censorship), control the records that we actually hear, and how do we, the audience, respond?

What historical pattern can be seen in the way that consumer demands have shaped the production process of music (e.g. what did punk rockers mean to the music business)?

What effects have other inter-related institutions (the music press, the power of mega-star as institution) had on the music industry?

This is neither an exhaustive list nor a range of ready-made essay
questions for students but hopefully indicates the scope of analytic and
critical work we feel necessary for good educational practice in the field
of music and Media Education.

(Ferrari and James 1989: 2)

Teaching about pop demands sensitivity. It should not be seen as simply an
opportunity for discussing individual musical tastes and preferences. Nor
should it be seen as a means of subjecting students' evaluations of pop
music to adult interrogation. Perhaps it is better to start with accepting that
being a fan is not the same as being a victim and that to be one does not
render an individual gullible or stupid. Nor are pop audiences necessarily
the victim of a mass-marketing machine. By positively using student
knowledge of the pop industry and combining it with the teacher's
knowledge of media institutions, some common ground can be established.
But whatever methods are used, there needs to be an acknowledgement of
the expertise and interests of students. Creating a climate which values
students' enthusiasms and knowledge is a sound basis from which to launch
further investigations.

In transforming pop music into a problematic area of study within the
context of students' own everyday knowledge, there emerges the
potential for that important tension between how the cultural experience of pop music is lived and how, through a critical exploration, it can
be made to speak with new accents.

(Chambers 1981: 35)

Like advertising, the appeal of pop music depends on identification with
images and life-styles. It is about belonging, about membership of
identifiable groups which express and echo the cultural practices and habits
of those groups. The boundaries of these categories are defined by details
of dress, language, gesture and style, but they are not fixed. Indeed, it is
the very possibility of change from one to another which makes the
definition of boundaries so necessary.

Like advertising, pop music also depends on creating difference. It
requires refined distinctions in taste and consumption.

Advertising is necessary ... to be able to build differences and to
express differences and to sell differences ... between different
products that actually in other ways might seem to be rather similar.

(Rita Clifton)

Both pop music and advertising demand serious attention as part of a Media curriculum. Not simply because they are the persuasive tools of commerce, but because they are such important components of our cultural identities and relate so closely to our sense of who we are. This sense is constantly created and sustained through our interactions with the media. When we understand the limits of persuasion as well as its power, we will know that we can shape our identities ourselves.

TEACHING IDEA 1: VOICE COLOURS IN ADVERTISING

Aim

To introduce students to simple ways of classifying voices used in advertising. They should be able to specify how different connotations are used to suggest cultural values and explain why these are used for particular products.

Time

One double lesson.

Materials

Sample voices on cassette, cassette player.

Method

- Briefly explain purpose of lesson to *whole class*.
- Ask *whole class* to list as many different kinds of voices as they can (using just one adjective).

- Write list of ten colours on blackboard.
- Play sample voices while *whole class* listens.
- Play sample voices again and ask class *individually* to colour-code each voice.

- Ask class to move into *groups (of 4/5)* to compare their codings.
- Give each group names of two different products or services (one easy, one hard, e.g. toilet soap and computer).
- Ask groups to decide amongst themselves what kind of voices they would choose for each product *and why* (this could be written up as a memo from an imaginary advertising agency to an imaginary production company).

- Groups report back as *whole class* to explain and discuss their choices.

Further work

See Dyer, G. (1982) *Advertising as Communication* London: Methuen: 139–57; Boyd-Barrett, O. (1989) *Study Guide to Block 6* and *Tea-folk Talk* (audio-cassette 3, band 10) Open University Course EH 207.

TEACHING IDEA 2: ANIMALS IN ADVERTISING

Aim

To examine some ways in which animals are used in advertising. Students should be able to identify the particular aspects of animals which are invoked by advertisements. They should also be able to explain how and why these aspects of animals are expected to enhance the appeal of particular products or services. This exercise explores (like the previous teaching idea) how different visual and linguistic signs are linked by advertisers and audiences with cultural values.

Time

One double lesson.

Materials

Sample advertisements on video or from magazines.

Method

- Briefly explain purpose of lesson to *whole class*. What initial ideas do they have about why animals are used in advertising?
- Ask *whole class* to list as many different advertisements as they can which use animals to present their message.
- List ten of these on blackboard or OHP.
- Select one or two well-known examples from this list and briefly discuss with class why they think these adverts use these animals.

- Ask class *individually* to list three animals used in particular adverts and the kind of product being advertised.
- Ask class *individually* to write a brief explanation of the links between the animals and the products.
- Ask class to move into *groups (of 4/5)* to compare their findings so far.

- Groups report back as *whole class* to explain and discuss their ideas. Are there any adverts where animals are used for no apparent reason (e.g.. Guinness's dolphin) or where the connections are more complex than normally (e.g. Sony's use of a tiger to advertise a professional video camera)? What rules are there for choosing appropriate animals?

Further work

If time permits, the general rules of animal selection could be developed through setting up a team quiz based on sets of correspondences between animals and products. For example, one team lists five possible products which might feature a particular animal (or vice versa). To be correct, another team's answer should match one product from the list.

TEACHING IDEA 3: BEING A FAN

Aim

To explore the musical tastes of the class and to find out the extent to which they consider themselves fans.

Time

One double lesson.

Materials

Notebooks and drawing materials.

Method

- Ask the class to work in small groups (4/5) to design a questionnaire to be used with other groups in the class. Questions might include:

  How would students classify their pop tastes?
  Who are their favourite artistes?
  What have been their previous musical crazes?
  For how long?
  How much time do they spend listening?
  In what circumstances?
  What contact do they have with other fans?
  How do they obtain information about stars they admire?
  What information do they believe about their star(s)?
  What information don't they believe?
  How do they decide what to believe?
  What is the most/least interesting information they have about their star(s)?

- Groups exchange and complete questionnaires.
- Ask the students to devise ways of presenting the information to the rest of the class in an easily understandable form, e.g. charts, graphs, etc.
- Students could also put similar questions to their parents. This would provide an opportunity to compare the activities of fans from other generations with those of today.

Further work

See *Wham! Wrapping* (Ferrari and James 1989).

TEACHING IDEA 4: PROMOTING PERSONALITIES

Aim

To develop an understanding of some of the processes of the promotion industry.

Time

Several double lessons – probably the culmination of some preparatory work on the promotion industry.

Materials

Newspaper cuttings about the character being promoted.

Method

- Ask the class to imagine they are in charge of marketing a personality like Eddie 'The Eagle' Edwards. Discuss ways of promoting this character. What would be the purpose of the promotion?
- Students should work in pairs and first of all decide the qualities of the personality they are promoting. Is he or she funny, quick-witted, cuddly, strong or have pin-up potential? How could these qualities best be exploited?
- Having decided on specific qualities, each pair should then work out a strategy for promotion. Will it include getting the name of the person-ality on merchandise like T-shirts or will it involve setting up personal appearances either on radio or television or at sports or commercial events?
- A number of written projects can then emerge from this kind of preparatory work. Students could be asked to:

  - Write a press release of not more than 100 words promoting their personality. Decide who the press release is aimed at (e.g. local or national radio and TV, local or national newspapers) and what the purpose of the release should be. What activity is it promoting? How has the activity been arrived at or devised?
  - List the kinds of objects that their personality would look good on then write a letter to the manufacturers of such objects persuading them that their 'property' would be an asset to the manufacturer's marketing strategy.

– Imagine they are members of the production team for a chat-show such as *Wogan*. Write out a list of questions for the host to ask the chosen personality. Remember it has to make interesting live viewing for at least 6 minutes. If there is time, they might act out the interview for the rest of the class.

Further work

See Mills and Stringer (1990): 8–11 for suggestions on further discussion and examples of media reactions to Eddie Edwards.

Chapter 6

Looking to the future

Throughout this book, we have explored practical ways of teaching about the media in relation to the actual experience of teachers. We have also tried to relate our approaches to relevant theory. In the final chapter, we shall re-examine the role of teaching about the media in the light of new developments in media technology, forms and structures. We shall also review key concepts through the eyes of some of the people who have contributed most to its development in Britain over the last decade. We shall be raising a number of practical questions which have immediate policy implications for the future of Media Education and Media Studies:

- How are media structures changing and adapting to meet new demands?
- How can innovation in Media Education and Media Studies be encouraged and supported in secondary schools and colleges?
- What kind of policies for development and consolidation do we need?
- How can a coherent curriculum for understanding media be developed?
- What is the role of specialist media teachers?
- What is the likely future of Media Education?

CHANGING MEDIA STRUCTURES

The last few years have seen great steps forward . . . in a general climate of low professional morale and dwindling resources . . . by the dedication and enthusiasm of . . . media teachers . . . Given the increasing sophistication of information and news management techniques and marketing strategies, as well as the general proliferation of PR, Media Education represents one of the best hopes we have of challenging the growing inequalities of knowledge and power which exist between those who control the media and information systems and those who consume media innocently as news or entertainment.

(Masterman 1986: 100)

In order to be able to challenge inequalities in power and knowledge, we need to understand not only the languages and processes of the media, but also how they are developing and adapting to economic and social change. Much of what is currently happening can be followed in the press, in specialist journals and magazines, or on radio and television. Many of the discussions and analyses of institutional change within the media are very informative and may even provide material for work in the classroom. But there is a large amount of such information and it needs careful sifting before it can be made accessible to students. As teachers, we need both to monitor this information and to identify its implications for the media and their audiences in the future. To illustrate how key issues can be identified, we can focus here on the familiar topic of changes in television broadcasting in the context of the Broadcasting Act of 1990.

The Broadcasting Act, 1990

The new legislation on broadcasting sharpens some old issues and raises some new ones. It covers both television and radio, but its effects are most marked on ITV. Current ITV output will be known as Channel 3, but there will be an additional national channel from 1993 known as Channel 5. The new channel will be based outside London and reach about 70 per cent of UK households. It will provide similar programmes to Channel 3 and compete with the rest of ITV for advertising revenue. Channel 4's remit for a range of specialised programming remains, but it is also in direct competition for advertising.

Some programming requirements continue to be laid down, but bidding for franchises is more crudely commercial than in the past. The IBA, which had powers to preview programmes, vet schedules and ensure that statutory requirements were fulfilled, is replaced by a new regulatory body, the Independent Television Commission, which operates with a 'lighter touch'. The BBC continues to be financed by the licence fee, but in the long term may depend on a subscription system.

The net effect of these changes, when considered alongside competition from satellite and cable channels, is likely to be a reduction in the range and quality of television programming. Expensive, difficult or controversial programmes are less likely to be made because the financial risks will be too great. Take, for example, regional television programmes. This may seem an unimportant area, since many viewers have no idea which programmes are made by their regional stations and which are made elsewhere. But viewers do show powerful allegiances to their programmes, especially local news and weather. So ITV companies are now developing new forms of regional programming, especially in the news area.

The ITV companies

There is also competition for advertising revenue amongst the ITV companies, especially around the boundaries of the current ITV regions. Their annual reports to shareholders increasingly focus on the superior 'demographics' of their regions. This inter-regional rivalry has been held in check until now by the offices of the Independent Television Association and the IBA. But it is likely to hot up in the wake of the Broadcasting Act and the proliferation of television advertising space. So there are going to be attempts to create stronger corporate images for the different companies and greater loyalty amongst viewers.

> It's been presented as offering a greater degree of choice for consumers. In fact it's much more a charter for advertisers. It heralds an explosion of commercial media and, in a fairly obvious way, an undercutting of the basis and the financial future of public service broadcasting.

(Len Masterman)

Attracting viewers who can be delivered as potential consumers to advertisers is only one reason for regional programmes. There is also a strong populist argument. Viewers actually like local programmes because they can more easily identify with the known and familiar. Popular serials like *Coronation Street*, *EastEnders* and *Neighbours* all capitalise on their strong sense of specific and familiar communities.

On a more general level, there is a pluralist argument in favour of regional programmes. Television is a British rather than English institution (although many would complain that it is insufficiently so). In spite of strong centralist tendencies within national television, there has been a clear commitment from the very early days of broadcasting to the preservation and promotion of regional identity and cultural diversity. As early as 1935 the BBC's Director of Regional Relations asserted the principle that 'the differential pace and tone of life and feeling in the provinces . . . require adequate expression.' And the Board of Governors concluded that regional programmes were needed to 'meet the legitimate demand for programmes suited to local taste and humour'. The regional structure which the BBC has built up reflects this concern but is already under financial pressure from the centre as a result of financial restrictions.

> If people merely wanted to see themselves, television would have died out to be replaced by the family video. People want to see themselves in the context of an audience big enough to give them importance and small enough to give them a chance.

(Howell 1989: 6)

The ITV network

The relationships between the fifteen ITV companies are complex. The 1954 Television Act (following the regional policy of the BBC) required the IBA to ensure adequate competition between the different companies who supplied the programmes and a 'suitable proportion of matter calculated to appeal specially to the tastes and outlook of persons served by the station or stations'. The IBA recognised that the high costs of production needed to be equitably distributed. It therefore created a distinction between the larger network companies and the smaller regional ones. The network companies would be responsible for most of the network output in the more expensive areas of current affairs, drama and light entertainment.

All of the ITV companies are currently obliged under the terms of their franchise with the new ITC to produce and transmit programmes of local interest. As with BBC output, the most obvious example of this is local news and weather forecasts. On average, local news and weather make up about 10 per cent of the ITV companies' total transmission. Local news magazines like *Northern Life*, *About Anglia* and *Coast to Coast* are amongst the most popular programmes on ITV. In a typical week, early evening local news reaches an aggregate audience similar to that of *News at Ten* (nearly 8 millions). This is over 40 per cent of the available audience and enough to put local news half-way up the top fifty television programmes on any channel. The local audiences are clearly loyal, since these figures hardly fluctuate from day to day. They also comprise a demographic cross-section which makes them particularly attractive to advertisers. As a result, some regional news magazines also return a similar amount of advertising revenue per minute as *News at Ten*.

Although this sort of information is easily available to the public, collating and making sense of it requires some persistence from teachers. But it is just the kind of information which media personnel are often happy to share when they are invited to talk to teachers' groups. It is clearly an important part of keeping up-to-date with developments in the media in order to encourage students to ask the necessary critical questions. These particular developments raise a number of issues which are central to understanding broadcasting as a changing institution rather than an indestructible monolith. The Broadcasting Act may seem to encourage regional provision in the form of ITV 3 but it has clearly not devised the means by which it can be maintained. It might be seen as more concerned with the break-up of the 'comfortable duopoly' of broadcasting rather than a commitment to the regions. Is ITV's regional provision likely to suffer as a result of smaller stations being taken over by larger ones, so as to become mere appendages of big stations? Might there be an all-out advertising war between the different ITV companies which will drive

Figure 6.1 BIFF cartoon, 'Quality' advertising?

some of them into the arms of predators or even bankruptcy? Will the BBC, under new commercial pressures, be able to maintain its commitment to regional programmes? The new multi-channel future may actually be more destructive of cultural diversity that our present arrangements.

Access and accountability

But this kind of structural change is not confined to television. It is not just public service broadcasting but public information systems in general which are undergoing change.

> Public service information systems in general – and by that I mean not simply broadcasting but research institutions such as universities, library systems, museums, art galleries, art centres and media centres and so on – all of those areas are now very much under threat and the argument needs to be made for the social value of information systems. We need to move away from regarding information as simply an extension of private property. And I think teachers as such have a *de facto* commitment to defend public information systems since they work within the state education system which is a public information system.
>
> (Len Masterman)

This is not just a question of access, but also one of diversity and accountability. We need to know where information is coming from before we can evaluate and respond appropriately to it. As we showed in earlier chapters, marketing techniques and public relations agencies often work in covert ways.

> Most information that we receive is tainted information and access to information is really beside the point if the information that we have access to is in itself contaminated. It's rather like having access to a poisoned well. One of the features of the media of the future ... is that there is a greater convergence of advertising and non-advertising material in the media. The vast majority of material that we see which is presented to us as news or feature material has its origins in the promotional industries and this has got enormously important implications for our work in Media Education in the future. My own view is that we need to be moving towards an understanding of marketing rather than advertising ... we've got to take on board public relations, advertorials, the implications of sponsorship. The challenge for us as media teachers is to try and hold on to critical response to these phenomena.
>
> (Len Masterman)

Schools are also part of our public information systems and are similarly open to the commercial pressures of the enterprise culture, especially when money is tight. Some courses in schools may encourage students to use their media skills in running campaigns to raise sponsorship. Teachers have used freely available and attractive materials which carry the sponsor's message for many years. In some Hampshire schools, students may be under the impression that *Roget's Thesaurus* was produced by a well-known construction company. Bright yellow hardback copies have been provided which feature not only the company's name but also its claimed characteristics as a series of synonyms on the cover.

> There are ... moves to have advertisements within schools and hoardings along school corridors. Now I've heard some teachers and, to their shame I think, some Heads encouraging this kind of development. But I think a much more important problem is the rather glossy, well-produced, ostensibly helpful materials which are produced by commercial organisations ... These kind of glossy materials are now finding their ways into schools in very large numbers. They're enormously attractive to teachers and pupils alike, given the fact that proper textbooks are now much more difficult for schools to afford than they've been in the past. So there is an enormous reliance on this kind of material. That's not necessarily a bad thing if teachers are treating this kind of glossy material critically ... if they're encouraging students to read it in terms of the interests of those who've produced the material. But when such material is used to replace textbooks then we're really entering into a very dangerous situation.
>
> (Len Masterman)

INNOVATION IN MEDIA EDUCATION

> Fifteen years after the Bullock Report, language across the curriculum is a dead letter. I hope that Media Studies across the curriculum isn't going to go the same way.
>
> (Len Masterman)

Teachers may use commercial material in an entirely instrumental and uncritical way as a 'window on the world' through which students are encouraged to look for information. But they may also use the opportunity to raise the basic questions 'Who is communicating with whom and why; how has the text been produced and transmitted; how does it convey its meaning?' emphasised in the Cox Report (DES 1989: 7.23). It may even extend the study of media across the curriculum.

> What's increasingly happened in History teaching is that people have been raising questions and encouraging kids to raise questions about the status of evidence. So it's not simply ... about handing down a body of facts which are seen to be objectively true. On the contrary, it's about

> looking at a range of different accounts of what has taken place in history, looking at the sources of those accounts, looking at the interests of the people who produce those accounts, and beginning to raise questions about the status of this material as evidence ... those kinds of questions are exactly the kinds of questions which people are raising in Media Education.
>
> (David Buckingham)

This is not just a question of using 'Media Education concepts' in another subject area, as Cox suggests for English (DES 1989: 9.9), but of permeating the barriers between subjects and allowing a much more productive interaction between them which can make them all more comprehensible to students.

> I'm not against subjects, of course. But where those subjects in fact are so rigidly defined that you can't think in any other than the way of the subject which is predetermined, that is extremely unhelpful. What we've got to look for are the various ways ... the kind of discourses which are available to us as teachers and to students to use in order to make sense of different subjects and to see the inter-relationship.
>
> (Bob Ferguson)

So how do the discourses of media study contribute to developing this inter-relationship? And what kind of working partnerships need to be created between teachers in different subject areas?

> this overall way of approaching education is critical, is concerned with the discursive (the way in which people tell you about their own subject), is concerned with concepts like *representation*, is concerned with *ideology*. Those issues are all extraordinarily important and are there for the Media Studies teacher. But for it to be successful the Media Studies teacher should be working with the English teacher, the Science teacher, the History teacher, and they should all recognise those shared concerns wherever it is possible. Where it is not possible then they clearly from time to time have got to be working in individual subject areas. But they must all share a recognition of their inter-relationship, because the whole world is being mediated daily to people who are studying *all* subjects.
>
> (Bob Ferguson)

POLICIES FOR DEVELOPMENT

The need for Media Education has been well established for some time. Len Masterman's work over the last decade has been very influential (Masterman 1980, 1985, 1986, 1988). In spite of a few detractors, he remains the most incisive and reliable guide for teachers. There remains the large question of how real development can happen. How can we devise a curriculum which is broad enough in coverage, which includes practical learning experiences, which is based on consistent concepts and principles, which relates learning to students' developmental levels and which links media study with the rest of the curriculum?

> Some practical work may call for the use of sophisticated equipment, but even here most media teachers are now more concerned to encourage students to experiment with alternatives, and to break or play around with dominant codes and conventions, than to slavishly reproduce dominant media forms.
>
> (Bob Ferguson)

Media Education is not about uncritical imitation of existing media forms, still less about celebrating them.

> Cultural reproduction ... is a poor aim for Media Education. It is uncritical. It enslaves rather than liberates. It freezes the impulses towards action and change. It naturalises current conventions, and thus encourages conformity and deference. Media Education, on the other hand, in raising questions about how media texts are constructed (and might be constructed differently) and in its insistence upon the nature of media texts as the products of specific human choices, aims to encourage not only practical criticism but a genuinely critical practice.
>
> (Masterman 1988: 21)

Although some progress has been made in this direction, much of the debate has been out of touch with the needs of classroom teachers (Buckingham 1990: 3–9). The contrast between Scotland's *Media Education Journal* and *Screen/Screen Education* is a stark one. Only recently has this begun to change, with the growth of the BFI's interest in media other than film and its publication of guidelines for primary and secondary work.

The place to start is with a realisation of what kinds of knowledge the subject offers to students and what possibilities it can generate within a traditional school curriculum.

> The subject material of Media Education is around us, it's in the world out there. Media Education consists in a critical examination and analysis of media products. What's liberating about that I think is that it puts students and teachers on the inside of the process of constructing knowledge. Knowledge is something that is liberating, that we create ourselves in a critical interaction with our world. That lies at the heart of media study. It ought to lie at the heart of the study of most academic subjects, sadly it doesn't.
>
> (Len Masterman)

Unfortunately, the fact that the media are so generally familiar causes confusion and problems in teaching about them. It often means that the agenda for studying the media are set outside the classroom and derive from 'common sense' views within popular debates about the role of the media.

> The trouble about the media ... [is that] everybody's experienced [them] so everybody thinks they know how it should be done and should be dealt with. And there's a public agenda for the discussion of the media which centres on sex and violence and on bias and misinformation, and people tend to think 'Well, that's what Media Education would deal with.' There's also a public agenda about the media which says that a great deal of what is on television or on radio or in the press is trash and not worth discussing and certainly not worthy of study in school.

> (Cary Bazalgette)

So we need to recognise the inadequacies of these 'common sense' views and ask what Media Education should really be aiming at. It is not simply a defensive process, nor is it merely a critical one. It is an enabling one which seeks to enhance capacities as well as knowledge, competence as well as confidence.

> It's not a defence against the media, it's not a way of teaching people to resist what the media do to them. It's a way of teaching them to understand what the media are capable of and to expect them to deliver that and to be able to produce it themselves. So [it's] not just educating children or people generally as audiences but also opening up some possibilities of what they themselves can do with media like video or photography, and also in their own access to media forms like local radio or even national television.

> (Cary Bazalgette)

DEVELOPING A COHERENT CURRICULUM

> It's not enough within Media Education for the student to regurgitate the ideas of the teacher. It's not enough at the end of term for the student simply to reproduce what he or she has learned during the course of the year. The objective ... is ... for us to encourage students to stand on their own two critical feet as quickly as possible, to know which aspects of media evidence to trust and to know which aspects of media evidence to distrust.

> (Len Masterman)

Provided that we have actually thought through an adequate educational rationale for studying the media, children can begin to understand and do things with media at a very early age, as the BFI's curriculum statement for primary schools demonstrates so clearly (Bazalgette 1989). The questions they ask 'naturally' about media language, conventions and ownership are a good basis from which to start.

> As soon as children start to talk they're asking questions or making observations or formulating theories about how they did that, is that really true? When the people on the television say 'we'll see you next week' will they really see us next week? Children are already thinking really about questions of ownership and control at 7, about
>> Who made that programme?
>> Could I get on the television?
>> How did they make such-and-such happen?
> When they use the word 'they' there's a sense that this has been made and people have made decisions about it. Those are questions that start off Media Education and I think when parents answer those questions, which they do usually very intelligently and productively, that's Media Education that's going on there.

(Cary Bazalgette)

But learning about the media 'naturally' has its limitations. Studying the media needs a more systematic approach. With this in mind, the BFI and DES formed a working party on Media Education at primary level which began to meet in 1986. It was made up of teachers, advisers and trainers. They began by identifying what worked in the classroom and exploring the principles behind accounts of practice. They then developed a set of key concepts (or 'signpost questions') which can provide a framework for the development of Media Education at primary level.

> We had to identify the *conceptual* elements of Media Education – what we thought children ought to know about and understand. From that framework, the skills and the study objects and the classroom practice would follow.

(Bazalgette 1990: 24)

The published report (Bazalgette 1989) is more of a discussion document than a definitive statement of their work. Yet it has been extremely influential, especially on the recommendations of the Cox Committee on English 5–16 (DES 1989). The more recent statement on secondary media work (Bowker 1991) builds on the same foundations and takes the process further.

Signposts

Let us take one of these key concepts and explore its implications. What is meant by *media agencies*, for example? The BFI primary curriculum statement offers a limited sketch of proposed attainment targets at levels 3 and 5 within the National Curriculum (Tables 6.1 and 6.2) and the secondary statement suggests how the signposts might relate to the key concepts in the Non-statutory Guidance (DES 1990b).

Figure 6.2   Summary of the areas of knowledge and understanding in Media
Education

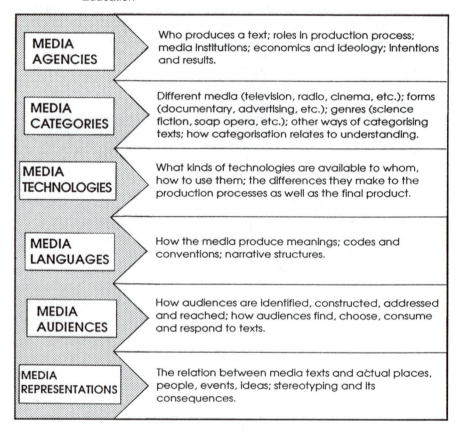

MEDIA AGENCIES	Who produces a text; roles in production process; media institutions; economics and ideology; intentions and results.
MEDIA CATEGORIES	Different media (television, radio, cinema, etc.); forms (documentary, advertising, etc.); genres (science fiction, soap opera, etc.); other ways of categorising texts; how categorisation relates to understanding.
MEDIA TECHNOLOGIES	What kinds of technologies are available to whom, how to use them; the differences they make to the production processes as well as the final product.
MEDIA LANGUAGES	How the media produce meanings; codes and conventions; narrative structures.
MEDIA AUDIENCES	How audiences are identified, constructed, addressed and reached; how audiences find, choose, consume and respond to texts.
MEDIA REPRESENTATIONS	The relation between media texts and actual places, people, events, ideas; stereotyping and its consequences.

Source: Bazalgette 1989: 20

If somebody listening to [a] programme were to spin their radio dial and hear other stations and perhaps switch to another station with another kind of broadcast going on, they would almost certainly be able to make a judgement in the first few minutes about whether, for instance, it was another BBC channel, whether it was perhaps an independent or perhaps a pirate music station. And they know enough about radio to be able to make that sort of judgement about that from the evidence that they're hearing. That would be an example of making a judgement about media agencies.

(Cary Bazalgette)

Table 6.1 Proposed Attainment Targets for Media Education: media agencies

Level 3		Level 5	
Performance	*Knowledge & understanding*	*Performance*	*Knowledge & understanding*
Know ways of finding out source(s)/authorship of text (e.g. credits, title pages, labelling). Be able to offer description of basic production roles (e.g. writer, director, camera operator etc.). Co-operate in a group, under adult direction, to produce a media text (e.g. sound tape, tape-slide, video, cartoon strip etc), re-drafting where appropriate. Produce their own media text individually (e.g. photograph, poster, optical toy) and make decision about intended audience.	Know that media texts are produced by people: some by individuals, some by groups. Know that media production may involve many different roles, working co-operatively. Know that there are different ways in which a text can reach numbers of people	Be able to identify and describe the main roles listed in film, TV and video credits, title pages, packaging. Be able to offer description of less 'visible' production roles e.g. producer, publisher. Be able to identify major media institutions (e.g. BBC, ITV companies, local radio stations, national and local newspaper publishers, book publishers etc.) Co-operate in a group without close adult supervision to produce a media text (e.g. sound tape, video, tape-slide), re-drafting where appropriate.	Know that many media texts are produced by media institutions, involving many stages of production and complex decision-making processes. Begin to understand the processes by which texts reach large numbers of people (e.g. an understanding of what broadcasting is, without knowing technical detail).
Make decisions about how to circulate a text to a number of people (e.g. noticeboard, photocopier, photograph, sound tape etc.)		Make decisions about how to circulate a text to an audience not known to them personally (e.g. printing/local sale, local newspaper, radio). Make editorial decisions (e.g. shortening or extending a text as necessary; including or excluding material on grounds of taste, tact, clarity etc), and be able to argue for and against such decisions. Make predictions about the results of producing a particular text (e.g. profit, publicity, opinion-changing etc.) Be able to speculate about producers' intentions.	Begin to understand the differences in cost and status between simple production (e.g. pen and paper, photographs), complex production (e.g. video, printing) and industrial production (e.g. broadcasting, mass publication). Know how to address and reach media producers (e.g. how to write a letter to a newspaper or to the Advertising Standards Authority; how to telephone a television company).

Source: Bazalgette 1989: 22

Table 6.2 Proposed Attainment Targets for Media Education: media languages

Level 3		Level 5	
Performance	Knowledge & understanding	Performance	Knowledge & understanding
Be able to observe, identify and discuss features of audio/visual texts, such as: – different camera angles and distances* – arrangement of people and objects within the frame* – different sounds and levels of amplification* – colour, black and white, variations in colour tone, light and dark, sharp and soft focus – different transitions from shot to shot (e.g. fade, dissolve, *cut*, *wipe*) – camera movements (e.g. *pan*, *tilt*, *dolly* and *zoom*) – variations in writing, print size and typeface* – variations in size and quality of paper* * Be able to deploy these purposefully in their own texts. Recognise *as conventions* certain features of media forms and genres (e.g. who speaks direct to camera and who does not; how invisible 'effects' such as speed, impact etc are shown in comic strips). Follow and comprehend a simple narrative structure. Be able to identify and discuss structuring features such as music, special effects, location, interior/exterior settings, actors, presenters, commentators. Be able to distinguish between presenting (e.g. reading the news, announcing a programme) and acting (e.g. playing a role in a drama or an advertisement).	Understand that all parts of a media text have meaning and were put there on purpose (i.e. that texts are constructed). Begin to understand the concept of *convention*. Begin to understand that objects may be used symbolically or indicatively (e.g. a Rolls Royce may symbolise wealth).	Be able to identify and discuss how conventions are used in media texts (e.g. speech bubbles and frames in comics; headlines, photographs and captions in newspapers; zooms, cuts, wipes and dissolve in film and television). Be able to follow and discuss editing procedures in film and television and to identify and discuss how space and time can be altered to tell a story. Be able to plan, draft and story-board an audio-visual text. Be able to imagine and experiment with modifying and breaking conventions. Recognise and describe some historical changes in media conventions. Be able to deploy purposefully most of the features listed in column 1 (according to available technology). Be able to explain or hypothesise plausibly why particular features of a text were selected, e.g. music, locations, setting, actors, *voice-over*, typeface, layout, sound effects, etc. Speculate on consequences of choosing different features. Identify and describe symbolic use of objects. Begin to express aesthetic judgements of media texts.	Understand the concept of convention. Understand that each media form has to some extent its own specific language, that has developed over time, and will continue to develop, and that we learn these languages. Understand the basic principles of editing: that the meaning of a text can be altered by: – deleting parts – adding parts – altering the sequence of parts.

Source: Bazalgette 1989: 25

We can be similarly specific about *media languages*.

> Every medium has its own particular way of communicating, and calling
> that a language is perhaps a way of drawing attention to that fact. And
> the way that you might tackle that in the classroom could be, for
> instance,to take something as simple as a printed photograph and to
> look at it very carefully, simply first of all by asking the question 'What
> actually can we see here?' . . . you'll find that people will make different
> assumptions about what it is that they can see there. Then a lot of
> judgements come in about the meaning of the photograph, which are
> based on the actual evidence in the photograph, the way that it's
> framed, perhaps the colour of the photograph, the angle that it's taken
> at and so on. All of those contribute to what it means. It's not just
> what's in the photograph but the way that it's taken.

(Cary Bazalgette)

Is there any inherent logic within these areas of knowledge which would
enable us to prioritise some of them? Is one starting-point more appropriate
than another? Perhaps we could begin at the production end with *agencies*
and relate this to *technologies*? Or we might start at the reception end and
consider *language* and *audiences*. Is it possible to put them all into some sort
of order for a curriculum which would develop in complexity over time?

On the other hand, since some of these concepts are more difficult to
grasp than others, perhaps we should be approaching them in terms of
their appropriateness to the developmental stages of our students? This
might mean starting with practical work through *technologies*, with the
process of making things. Analytical work on, say, *representations* would
then be delayed until students became old enough to cope with it.

In practice, all of the key concepts are interdependent, each one
overlapping with the others, so it is not possible to separate, say,
agencies from language. Nor is it desirable. Questions about *representation*
constantly arise in classrooms in the process of work on language. The
areas cannot and should not be neatly compartmentalised. As we showed
in Chapter 1, practical and analytical work need to be integrated and
mutually reinforcing.

What are the implications for teaching of these organic relations? If the
areas of knowledge cannot be taught separately, how can they be taught all
at once? The National Curriculum insists on linear development through a
hierarchy of levels across a range of profile components. This may offer
some convenience for assessment purposes, but not a model for how
students learn. At any age, they need to be working in all of these areas
and exploring the relations between them. The way they learn involves a
blurring and blending of emphases and activities.

> As teachers get used to, and comfortable with, thinking about Media
> Education concepts, they're going to have them in the back of their

minds, and when comments come up in the classroom like 'Oh that photograph doesn't look like me, I've got another one that's much better', teachers can signal to themselves 'that's a representation question really, that's a judgement about what I really look like and how do I know and what I look like in this photograph', and in the end you can never separate out concepts into . . . hierarchies. You always find that you're really tackling them all at once. But all of those concepts would operate at any level in the school system. You would simply be undertaking them, perhaps, in a more sophisticated way with 15-year-olds than you would with 7-year-olds, but the conceptual framework is still there at any level.

(Cary Bazalgette)

Figure 6.3   A curriculum framework

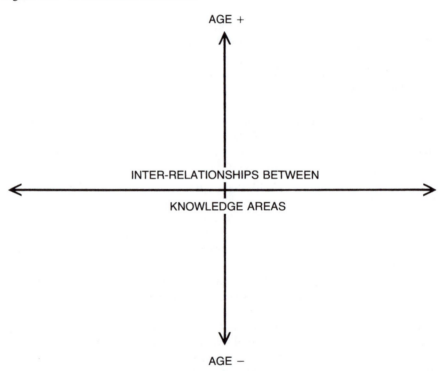

In summary, an effective media curriculum needs:

- To be internally *coherent*, with due weight given to how its parts make up a whole.
- To integrate *analytical and practical* approaches.
- To *permeate* the rest of the curriculum.
- To be related to students' experience and *developmental* levels.

How can this be done? Where will the teachers be found who can put such a curriculum into practice? How will they be trained? What forms of organisation will need to be devised within schools to make it possible? Permeation does not happen by magic. Unless we can resolve these problems, Media Education may go the same way as 'language across the curriculum'.

> It seems to me that it's a fond hope to assume that Media Education across the curriculum can take place and will take place without their being a strong specialist base within the school.
>
> (Len Masterman)

The very rigidity of the National Curriculum means that much more careful planning and monitoring is now a statutory requirement on schools and this may, ironically, work to the advantage of Media Education work.

> I think it's going to be very different within a National Curriculum context, where we're going to have a much more rigorous examination of what we're doing and what we're covering. The difficult question, I think – and it's really an institutional, an administrative question for secondary teachers – is how that work is going to be made consistent and coherent across the curriculum, and that doesn't just apply to Media Education, it applies to other cross curricular themes like economic and industrial awareness or health education. It's going to be a difficult problem to tackle but really I think it has to be tackled.
>
> (Cary Bazalgette)

So permeating the curriculum means more than expecting a number of subject specialists with no Media Education training to include some work on media in their teaching. It may mean abolishing subjects as we know them, throwing all the Attainment Targets into a heap, as a recent NCC document suggests (NCC 1990: 1) and rethinking the whole curriculum in terms of the best means of achieving the Targets. This could be partly achieved through modular courses. Yet there would remain huge problems of coherence. There would also need to be a concentration of administrative energy to create and co-ordinate the necessary cross-curricular organisation.

The BFI's statement on secondary media work (Bowker 1991) has a very useful chapter on Media Education across the curriculum, with a section describing its relations with other subjects. It also contains case-studies of media work in different areas of the curriculum. Most important, its chapter on Curriculum Management suggests four different models for different school structures.

> The danger inherent in this mass of connections and possibilities is that Media Education may simply vanish into the curriculum like water into sand. The full potential of Media Education across the curriculum is only likely to be realised where schools can create a whole-school policy and the INSET relating to it.
>
> (Bazalgette 1991)

Media Education is an area which everyone has some basic experience of and therefore all teachers can contribute to. Although it may sometimes appear forbidding, with its range of engagement and its use of semiological jargon, it is something which can be begun, at least, in a fairly simple way.

> There has to be a real commitment. At the same time, one's also got to recognise that there are ways into Media Studies where you can start teaching because of the knowledge you have of the media by having grown up in our society, plus having read one or two useful texts and possibly going to the British Film Institute or getting hold of some of their teaching packs . . . So it is possible to start. What I stress, however, is that that's the start.
>
> (Bob Ferguson)

The recent BFI/NFER survey (Twitchin and Bazalgette 1988) showed that over 35 per cent of secondary schools were doing some form of media work and this figure is now likely to be over 50 per cent on recent trends. In Hampshire, numbers on GCSE courses have been doubling for the past two years. This nlearly calls for many more teachers to take on Media Education than have been trained to do it and many have risen to the challenge in spite of the other pressures currently upon them.

THE MEDIA STUDIES SPECIALIST

> I think it needs a new confident kind of teacher who's happy with change, who recognises that the world is changing fast and the media world is changing faster than most other aspects of the world, and who is interested in developing alongside his or her students, a commensurate expansion in his or her own critical consciousness.
>
> (Len Masterman)

Recent GCSE and new A-level courses have often thrown teachers in at the deep end and necessitated crash courses in Media Studies. The fact that the NEA GCSE syllabus includes a glossary of technical terms for teachers must be unprecedented. Yet the net result of these courses has probably been a big increase in confidence amongst teachers and of coherence in their teaching, especially where specialist work was already happening.

> It gave people who are already teaching about media in 'O'-level and CSE an opportunity to really rethink their practice and to formulate it,

and when you look at the GCSE syllabuses you see quite a consistency of approach and a consensus about what the key concepts are.

(Cary Bazalgette)

I think the big step forward over the past three or four years has been the development of national GCSE courses in Media Studies now offered by five Boards and taken by something like 20,000 students each year.

(Len Masterman)

Yet a willingness to 'have a go' is not enough. Just as every student now has an entitlement to Media Education under the National Curriculum, so too every teacher should have entitlement to training for teaching it.

I do think there's a basic minimum, that everyone who is trained as a teacher should have had some engagement with media representations and teaching about the media. But then I cannot divorce that from also an engagement with issues like race, racism, sexism and the issue of class. Just as teachers should have to engage with those so they should engage with the major mediator of those issues which is the mass media. So I think that there is a very great need for that constant provision. But I'm arguing that in the context of being a strong believer in in-service education as being something totally necessary to keep teachers alive, intellectually and, if you like, psychologically too.

(Bob Ferguson)

There is clearly an urgent need for staff development and training, both for Media Studies specialists and for staff in other subjects who could contribute to the development of Media Education across the curriculum. (For practical advice and information on this, see the Appendix to this book, the BFI secondary statement and the BFI INSET advisory pack)

It's only if we have specialist Media Studies teachers in schools – certainly in secondary schools – it's only if we have those specialists that we can really begin to talk about Media Education across the curriculum in any meaningful way. Otherwise I think Media Education becomes one of those things which are in the end just about good intentions.

(David Buckingham)

The Media Studies specialists are clearly vital, for without their expertise and organisation of resources there will be no direction or back-up for willing colleagues.

In the past, where Media Education across the curriculum has taken place, it's taken place in those schools where the subject has had strong specialist roots. My own experience, for instance, in working in schools was that I was quite determined to have my own Media Studies room, to have my own Media Studies Department, and the work that I was doing created quite a lot of interest from amongst, say, one member of

> the History Department, one member of the Art Department, a Geographer and so on, and I was able to show materials and provide material support to members of other departments who wished to experiment and who wished to take on some media work.
>
> (Len Masterman)

This point is strongly supported in the conclusions of a study of Media Education across the curriculum (Robson *et al*. 1990: 171–93) which sees Media Studies as 'the essential prerequisite'.

THE FUTURE OF MEDIA EDUCATION

We have discussed the aims and methods of Media Studies and Media Education throughout this book. But in order to consider the future of Media Education, we need to remind ourselves of our long-term goals. What do we expect students to know, understand and be able to do as a result of Media Education? What does the 'critical autonomy' we want them to develop consist of? We can put this in the form we used in Chapter 1 and simply ask: 'What would a Media Educated Person be like?'

> He or she would have training in the basic decoding of media products and media texts. He or she would have a strong motivation to want to think about and learn about and talk about and discuss the mass media. This is an interest that hopefully ought to be lifelong. Media Education is a lifelong process. A Media Educated Person ought to be a model democratic citizen.
>
> (Len Masterman)

In spite of low morale, poor conditions, lack of resources, low pay and an apparent loss of independence, there is still a genuine possibility that we can reach this goal.

> The possibilities for teaching are still there if teachers ... are determined to make the maximum, open, liberal and inquiring use of every possibility they've got within the curriculum as it is now being stipulated. In other words, teachers must not abdicate the right to think or the right of their children to think.
>
> (Bob Ferguson)

The development of Media Education, is not, in any case, a matter of narrow national concern. It is already a European and increasingly a global process.

> Things are happening in different ways all over the world. It's worth bearing in mind that the European Ministers of Education ... resolved that there should be Media Education throughout compulsory schooling in all European countries, and it's worth remembering that UNESCO

have taken it on as a five–year plan to develop Media Education throughout the world.

(Cary Bazalgette)

In the twenty-first century, the problems which Media Studies and Media Education have experienced in defining and establishing themselves may seem strange and small.

> I think in the long term Media Education will quite obviously be an established part of the curriculum. If you asked a teacher eighty years ago 'What's the future of English within the curriculum in schools?' they might have been very tentative and uncertain about the answer because it was really a serious question then as to whether that was a subject that was worth studying, although obviously language [and] literature were an essential part of everybody's culture. Education tends to lag behind cultural change by anything up to fifty years and I think there's no question that there will be Media Education as an established part of schooling in twenty years' time.
>
> (Cary Bazalgette)

Yet this process is not an inevitable one. Some of the forces which operate in and through the media would find it very inconvenient if students became responsible for their own learning and exercised their rights as democratic citizens. There is clearly a major challenge for teachers to take up, if they can.

> Any education is only as good as the people who teach it, so when people make extravagant claims for Media Education, saying that it will transform society and change your life or make your hair grow or whatever, I think these are always very dubious ways of doing Media Education. Conceptual structures for Media Education can be offered to teachers, they can be given materials and things to work with in the classroom, but basically it's dependent on how teachers, together with their pupils, develop Media Education and they are the people who are going to work with it and take it ahead in ways that we maybe haven't thought.
>
> (Cary Bazalgette)

It will not be an easy process. Realising that the media are not all-powerful and that audiences are not helpless will necessitate changing the way that the media actually are. It will mean making important connections between the outer public worlds which the media have traditionally inhabited and the inner private worlds of imagination and reflection. As Brecht pointed out to actors and audiences in his poem *The Curtains*:

> ... this is not magic, but
> Work, my friends.

Appendix 1

Getting help

- What initial and post-experience training opportunities are there for teachers?
- What material resources are available?
- What existing support services and networks can teachers call upon?
- What can teachers' self-help groups, sharing of resources and ideas, and links with media professionals contribute?

TRAINING FOR MEDIA TEACHERS

Very few teachers have any degree-level experience of Media Studies. Almost none have had any formal training in the area. For most teachers, occasional INSET courses are all that are on offer, and in future it seems likely that even INSET will be happening on a do-it-yourself basis. But fortunately we have not yet reached the level of depending on a *Teach Yourself Media Studies* booklet. There are several places (e.g. London, Nottingham and Southampton Universities) where initial training through the one-year PGCE offers Media Studies as an essential part of main subject work. There are also MA courses which offer specialised work in Media Studies for experienced teachers. Yet these opportunities are clearly limited. So what can be done within existing constraints?

Whilst many Sixth Form College media teachers are supported by working in teams, teachers in schools are very often isolated. Local and regional Media Education Groups have been set up which include teachers, advisers, parents and HMI to develop educational strategies for work on the media. At the same time, the British Film Institute, the Regional Arts Associations, the Scottish Council for Educational Technology, the Educational Television Association and UNESCO have done a great deal to encourage and develop Media Education. Occasional regional conferences have helped a little in the process of providing systematic support for media teachers. Many LEAs have Advisory Teachers for Media Education and there is an association for Advisers and Teacher Educators. What we now need is a National Association for Media Education.

RESOURCES

The cost of published materials is often prohibitive. Most are currently aimed at teachers and are often weak in suggesting how they might be used in the classroom. Local needs are so variable and some materials date so quickly that many teachers are driven to developing their own. This clearly involves a major commitment of time and effort without any necessary spin-off in usage by other teachers. But organisations like Film Education, with its range of free materials on film, and the BFI, with its network of Regional Resource Banks, are obviously valuable.

Unfortunately, recent attempts to create an archive of materials to which teachers would contribute and from which they would borrow have yet to prove their value, since they are only used by a small number of teachers and have not managed to develop as comprehensive a range of materials as might have been hoped.

The exchange of materials needs to take place at a local level and we need to use the expertise of other teachers as a resource. That depends on a network of strong and active local Media Education Groups along the lines encouraged by SEFT before its demise.

'Top Ten' Media Education resources

During 1990, the Southern Region Media Education Group (created in response to the DES's *Popular Television and Schoolchildren* initiative in 1983) undertook a small qualitative survey of published resources for Media Education in the hope of providing some guidance for teachers. All members of the Group, most of whom are involved in Teacher Education and have specific responsibility for Media Education in different counties in the South, were asked to nominate their ten most favoured resources. Many of those most frequently mentioned have been around for some time and there is a clear bias towards items produced by members of the group. This could be because they are very popular, but is more likely to be the result of a 'demand effect'.

Title	Author/s	Publisher	Date
Eye-Openers	Bethell, A.	Cambridge	1981
Picture Stories	Davies, Y.	BFI	1986
Reading Pictures	BFI	BFI	1981
Talking Television	Bowker, J.	TVS	1989
Teaching Television	Hart, A.	Cambridge	1988
The Cinema Pack	SMEG	SMEG	1989
The Media File	Wall, I. & Kruger, S.	Mary Glasgow	1988
The Media Pack	Kruger, S. & Wall, I.	Macmillan	1988
The Media Resource Pack	SMEG	SMEG	1988
Understanding the Media	Cooper, G. & Hart, A.	BBC Radio 4	1990

NETWORKS

What can a Media Education group offer? The Southampton group is based in the School of Education at the University and has been active since 1986. It offers a range of teaching materials (including a Regional Resource Bank), audio and video recording and editing facilities, space for meetings and a means of exchanging information about what is happening in Media Education by means of an extensive database. Above all, it is a forum within which teachers can help themselves and support each other. They can share their ignorance as well as their expertise. And they can find opportunities for the careful evaluation and development of teaching ideas.

But the Southampton group did not happen by accident. Nor did it happen by design. Its growth was organic in the sense that it began from local INSET work and has continued because teachers have needs which it seems able to satisfy. It provides a voice for them as well as a space and a resource. As a result, the group has been able to work closely alongside local cultural developments. For example, it mounts a substantial film-based Media Studies programme each year as part of the Southampton Film Festival, it has raised support from local media operators like Television South, produced a range of its own free teaching materials and carried out original research and development work (Hart 1988; Bisson and Hart 1989).

Sustaining a correspondent membership of over 200 teachers demands a large amount of organisation. The group's success depends on holding regular (fortnightly) and well-publicised meetings, arranging for appropriate visiting speakers from the media professions and other sectors of education. It also depends on briefing them carefully as to the kind of approach necessary for working with groups of teachers who are giving up their own time to attend. More intensive short courses under INSET provision are generated by the group's meetings. At the same time, we are able to draw on expertise within the core elements of Media Studies work in the PGCE and MA(Ed.) courses at the University's School of Education.

Sample programme of meetings: Southampton Media Education Group, Summer 1990

Wednesdays 7.30 p.m. to 9.30 p.m.

2 May   GCSE Media and English
John Teasey and Pip Beck, Robert May's School, Odiham

16 May   Teaching About Newspapers
Tony Bisson, Alderman Quilley School, Eastleigh

30 May   Half-term Break

6 June   Teaching the Media
Andrew Hart, School of Education, Southampton University, and Gordon Cooper, Bournemouth Polytechnic

20 June   Media, Technology and Information in the National Curriculum
Brent Robinson, Dept. of Education, Cambridge University

4 July   Members' Meeting

18 July   Teaching Pop Music
Lilie Ferrari and Christine James of the BFI

MEDIA PERSONNEL AS RESOURCES

Opportunities to meet and debate with media professionals seem to be extremely attractive to teachers. But such meetings can sometimes be less than helpful if the media guests are not really aware of why they are there or are inadequately briefed by the organisers. Unless they have a clear idea of why teachers are interested in the media, they may slip into their 'meet the public' presentation mode and glamourise their work. Alternatively, teachers may exploit the occasion as a moral offensive against the guests and it can degenerate into a slanging match which does more harm than good.

Making the best of visits from media professionals means very careful planning of the session's aims and organisation. The sample below is an unusually complex one, based on several hours of discussion and planning between the organisers and Jenny Cuffe. Clearly such sessions can only be occasional ones, but these details demonstrate how much thought needs to go into ensuring that visitors' and teachers' time is used to best effect.

Sample meeting outline/publicity: 'The Journalistic Process'

How do journalists decide what is relevant and important when covering a current affairs story and how does 'house-style' affect the way an item is constructed?

Are such insights of value in teaching about media? If so, how can we go about exploring and utilising them most effectively?

Jenny Cuffe, free-lance journalist, will lead this practical session. She will look in some detail at the *Woman's Hour* interview she conducted with Dr Marietta Higgs after the findings of the inquiry into the Cleveland Child Abuse Case were made public.

The evening will take the form of a simulation designed to enhance understanding of the journalistic process and to provide some ready-made teaching material suitable for classroom use.

THE JOURNALISTIC PROCESS

Introduction   **Est. time**

Structure of session: A CONTEXT   C COMPARISON
                          B BUILD-UP   D EVALUATION   5'
Time limitations mean that informal questions and discussion will have to
be after the meeting.

A Context

1 Explain context: * personal   * institutional
2 Explain task: (issues, angles, questions)
3 Briefing (Jenny Cuffe interviewed by Gordon Cooper)
   What background information available before contact?
   What knowledge of situation and issues brought by journalist?
   What sources of info. available?
4 Issue background documents
   Details of information available at time of interview and context of
   Woman's Hour interview   15'

B Build-up

1 Read briefing, decide and write down main issues.   20'
   (individual, then shared in pairs)
2 Decide and write down agreed news-angles   10'
   (Groups of 4/5)
3 Decide and write down agreed questions for interview   10'
   (same groups)

C Comparison (during coffee-break)

1 Groups report back and discuss variations   20'
2 Play back original interview on tape   20'
3 Comments and discussion   10'

D Evaluation

1 What learning has occurred?
2 How could it be assessed?
3 How can journalists best be utilised?   10'

TEACHERS AS RESOURCES

Teachers themselves have a large role to play in presenting and developing their own ideas at some sessions and it is vital to have more experienced members to encourage those who are new to media work. Defining policy for development and reporting back to the membership have also been important factors in the group's growth.

So if there is no Media Education Group near you, perhaps it is time to start one? The role of such professional groups is crucial for the development of Media Studies and Media Education. Firstly, they show that teachers mean business. They show that teachers are serious about Media Studies and are an index of their commitment to its growth. Secondly, they provide a launch-pad, a place where teachers from different disciplines can test out new teaching ideas and develop the confidence they need to take off into media work which is new to them. Thirdly, such groups provide a forum in which teachers can keep in touch, through visits by media personnel, with structural changes in the media. Fourthly, they offer continuity. They are places to which teachers can return in the knowledge that they will be supported and sustained, where they can develop their material resources and refresh their personal ones. Finally, they present a challenge, an opportunity to argue and debate with others who may not share the same views or are at different stages of development in their Media Studies work.

Questions for group discussion and individual study

By using the key questions listed for each chapter, readers can assess and develop their own understanding of the media. These questions may also act as a basis for teachers to run staff development sessions for themselves in their own schools and colleges.

It will be helpful at the outset to remember the basic aims of this book. Each chapter has tried to:

- increase understanding of media processes and practices
- provide concrete examples of current practices in media education
- look at ways in which the study of the media is being established
- examine the developing theoretical bases for media teaching
- suggest lesson ideas which teachers can try out or develop for themselves.

How to use the notes

Under each chapter heading below you will find a brief summary of content and a set of questions. These questions should provide a basis for individuals or groups to:

- clarify and focus what has been said in the chapter
- help relate the issues to individual teaching experiences
- identify areas to follow up in more depth.

Special note for discussion group leaders

Here is a workable way of using the materials:

1 **Read the chapter in the book.**
2 **Discuss what answers the chapter provides for the questions listed.**
3 **Discuss what you would add from your own personal experience.**
4 **Using the insights from the chapters and your own experience, try to formulate ways in which you can develop your confidence and expertise.**
5 **Examine the suggested teaching ideas and discuss their potential with particular classes and courses.**

6 If time permits, construct your own lesson outlines and/or teaching materials.
7 Try out the ideas in the classroom.
8 Evaluate what you have done.

CHAPTER ONE: *GETTING STARTED*

This chapter focuses on starting points for teachers new to Media Education. It examines some of the everyday problems of teaching the media such as how practical work can be encouraged, how it relates to theory and how to assess what students have learned.

Key questions from the chapter

1 What should students be learning when they study the media?
2 What sort of problems do teachers have in teaching about the media?
3 How can teachers begin to overcome those problems?
4 Where does Media Studies belong in the curriculum?
5 To what extent do teachers need to develop their own theoretical knowledge of the subject?
6 How does teaching Media Studies affect classroom methods and management?
7 What is the role of practical work?
8 How can work in Media Studies be assessed?
9 How can teachers get started?
10 What resources are available to develop teachers' expertise?

CHAPTER TWO: *AUDIENCES*

This chapter explores the study of audiences by drawing on students' own experiences as well as looking at current theories and recent studies of audience behaviour. It suggests ways of looking at audiences without relying at one extreme on personal anecdotes or, at the other, on masses of indigestible figures.

Key questions from the chapter

1 What is an audience?
2 How can audiences be categorised?
3 How do people listen to radio or watch television?
4 How do audiences make meaning?
5 How consistent are audiences in their media habits?
6 How restricted are some audiences (like young people) in their media habits?

7 How are audience loyalties created and developed by the media?
8 How predictable are audience reactions?
9 What do the media know about their audiences?
10 How do the media find out about audiences?
11 What different information is provided by qualitative and quantitative audience research methods?
12 What value has audience research for: students, teachers, researchers, broadcasters and policy makers?

CHAPTER THREE: *THE FORMATION OF FACTS*

Facts are the raw material of information, but where do they come from and how do they get circulated? This chapter looks at the way facts are filtered by the media. It features public relations consultants, editors, broadcasters and media researchers. It also features the work of some sixth-form students as they examine how news is edited.

Key questions from the chapter

1 What is a fact?
2 How do the media decide what to report?
3 What role do public relations consultants play in the dissemination of information?
4 Why does the Glasgow Media Group criticise the way news is reported?
5 Do you agree with their critique?
6 What effect do the professional practices of journalists have on how information is processed?
7 How does ownership affect media messages?
8 What influence do governments have on the way news is reported?
9 What general criteria of newsworthiness are there?
10 What are the consequences of these patterns of selection?
11 How do audiences affect news media?
12 What problems arise from the attempt to simplify and package information?

CHAPTER FOUR: *SOME FORMS OF FICTION*

This chapter looks at fiction in television, comics and literature. It considers how children and young people respond to different forms of fiction and examines the pleasures and dangers which fiction offers them.

Key questions from the chapter

1 Why are children drawn to fiction?
2 What is the appeal of television soap operas?
3 In what sense is watching a soap opera 'active viewing'?
4 What problems are there in the way soaps represent the world?
5 Should children be protected from every kind of disturbing fiction?
6 Why do children like comics?
7 How can an understanding of how readings vary affect the way we look at comics?
8 How can we find out about responses to fiction?
9 What practical problems are there in trying to track these responses?
10 What value does a 'reader-response' approach have for media educators?

CHAPTER FIVE: *PROMOTION AND PERSUASION*

This chapter examines the role of promotion and persuasion both on media products and on individual perceptions. It concentrates on the advertising and pop music industries. Traditional approaches to teaching about them concentrate on the process of manipulation but this chapter suggests some alternatives to the 'hidden persuaders' approach.

Key questions from the chapter

1 What effects is the deregulation of broadcasting likely to have on the independence of programme makers?
2 Advertisers claim that advertising only holds up a mirror to society. Do you agree with this?
3 What effects does advertising have on audiences?
4 How do advertisers involve their audiences (e.g. use of voices, drama and life-style appeal)?
5 Can advertising be successfully used to achieve socially desirable ends (e.g. famine relief, environmental awareness)?
7 What problems are encountered when advertising sets out to persuade people to change their habits (e.g. anti-drugs campaigns)?
8 Is advertising more successful when audiences are conscious of the persuasion, or does it work subliminally?
9 Is the pop music industry worth studying?
10 How is pop reported in the press?
11 How important is it to recognise the different ways in which males and females approach information about pop?
12 Suggest some practical ideas for the classroom which avoid the 'hidden persuaders' approach to promotion and persuasion.

CHAPTER 6: *LOOKING TO THE FUTURE*

Modern technological and economic developments have made the study of the media of critical importance. The final chapter of the book focuses on the aims of Media Education and the powerful role it can play throughout the curriculum. It shows how understanding the media begins naturally at an early age and suggests how it can be developed at school in a systematic way. Media Education is seen as a continuous process of examining our daily experience of media messages in the light of key concepts like *audience*, *language* and *representation*.

Key questions from the chapter

1 What changes in the media are likely to matter for media educators?
2 What arguments would you put forward for studying the media in school?
3 What forms of media study are there in your own institution?
4 What are the strengths and weaknesses of your current provision?
5 What opportunities or barriers are there in your own institution for the development of media study?
6 What mechanisms are there in your own institution for developing the study of media throughout the curriculum?
7 What role should specialists in Media Studies play in developing media work throughout the curriculum?
8 How do you see specialist Media Studies courses developing in your own institution?
9 What do you think are the most important concepts for a systematic approach to studying the media?
10 Examine any one of these concepts and illustrate how it might be taught in practice.
11 How do the the concepts relate to each other and how they might feature in a media curriculum?
12 What skills, knowledge and understanding would you expect a Media-Educated Person to acquire?
13 What can we do as teachers to develop our abilities in teaching about the media?

References

Alvarado, M, Gutch, J. and Wollen, T. (1987) *Learning the Media*, London: Macmillan.

AMES Survey Group (1986) 'Figures and grounds' *Media Education Journal* 4: 4–17.

Baker, K. (1988) *Sunday Times*, 22 February.

Barker, M. (1984a) *The Video Nasties*, London: Pluto.

—— (1984b) *A Haunt of Fears*, London: Pluto.

—— (1989) *Comics: Ideology, Power and the Critics*, Manchester: Manchester University Press.

Barlow, G. and Hill, A. (eds) (1985) *Video Violence and Children*, London: Hodder and Stoughton.

Barnett, S. *et al.* (1989) *The Listener Speaks: the Radio Audience and the Future of Radio*, London: John Libbey.

Barthes, R. (1973) *Mythologies*, London: Granada.

—— (1977) 'The grain of the voice' in *Image-Music-Text*, London: Fontana: 179–89.

—— (ed.) (1989) *Primary Media Education: A Curriculum Statement*, London: BFI.

Bazalgette, C. (1990) 'New developments in Media Education' in F. Potter (ed.) *Reading, Learning and Media Education*, Oxford: Blackwell.

—— (1991) *Teaching the National Curriculum: Media Education*, London: Hodder & Stoughton.

BBC (1989) *Annual Review of Broadcasting Research*, 15, London: John Libbey.

BBC Broadcasting Research Department (1984) *Daily Life in the 1980s*, London: BBC.

—— (1987) *Listening and Viewing in UK Schools*, London: BBC.

Benton, M. *et al.* (1988) *Young Readers Responding to Poems*, London: Routledge.

Bethell, A. (1981) *Eye-Openers*, Cambridge: Cambridge University Press.

Bisson, A. and Hart, A. (1989) *The Cinema Pack*, Southampton: Southampton Media Education Group.

Blanchard, S. and Morley, D. (1982) *What's this Channel Fo(u)r?*, London: Comedia.

Bogart, L.(1989) *Press and Public*, Hillsdale, N.J.: Lawrence Erlbaum Associates.

Bowker, J. (1989) *Talking Television*, Southampton: TVS.

Bowker, J. (ed.) (1991) Secondary Media Education: A Curriculum Statement, London: BFI.

Boyd-Barrett, O. (1989) *Study Guide to Block 6* and *Tea-folk Talk* (audio-cassette 3, band 10), Open University Course EH 207, Milton Keynes: Open University.

British Film Institute (1981) *Reading Pictures*, London: BFI.

Buckingham, D. (1983) '*Viewpoint 2*: a study of audience responses to schools television', *Journal of Educational Television* 9/3: 161–9.

—— (1987a) *Media Education*, Course EH 207, Unit 27, Milton Keynes: Open University.

—— (1987b) *Public Secrets: EastEnders and its Audience*, London: BFI.

—— (1987c) 'The construction of subjectivity in educational television', *Journal of Educational Television* 13, 2: 137–45; 13, 3: 187–200.

—— (1990) *Watching Media Learning*, London: Falmer.

Buckingham, D., Fraser, P. and Mayman, N. (1990) 'Beginning classroom research in Media Education' in *Watching Media Learning*, London: Falmer: 19–59.

Central Statistical Office (1985, 1989, 1990) *Social Trends 1985, Social Trends 1989, Social Trends 1990*, London: HMSO.

Chambers I. (1981) 'Pop music: a teaching perspective' in *Screen Education* 39 (Summer), 35–46.

—— (1987) 'British pop: some tracks from the other side of the record' in J. Lull (ed.) *Popular Music and Communication*, London: Sage.

Chapman, R. (1990) 'Still reigning – still dreaming' in *Radio* (June), 22–3.

Clarke, M. (1987) *Teaching Popular Television*, London: Heinemann.

Cooper, G. and Hart, A. (1990) *Understanding the Media*, London: BBC Radio 4.

Crisell, A. (1986) *Understanding Radio*, London: Methuen.

Cullingford, C. (1984) *Children and Television*, London: Gower.

Cumberbatch, G. *et al.* (1987) *The Portrayal of Violence on British Television*, London: BBC.

Cumberbatch, G. (1984) 'Sorting out little white lies from nasty pieces of research', *The Guardian*, 25 April.

Cumberbatch, G. and Howitt, D. (1989) *A Measure of Uncertainty: The Effects of the Mass Media*, London: John Libbey.

Curran, J. and Seaton, J. (1985) *Power Without Responsibility*, London: Methuen.

Davies, Y. (1986) *Picture Stories*, London: BFI.

Day-Lewis, S. (ed.) (1989) *One Day in the Life of Television*, London: Grafton.

DES (1983) *Popular Television and Schoolchildren*, London: HMSO.

—— (1989) *English for Ages 5 to 16* (the Cox Report) (June) London: HMSO.

—— (1990a) *Technology in the National Curriculum* (March) London: HMSO.

—— (1990b) *English in the National Curriculum No. 2* (March) London: HMSO.

—— (1990c) *English in the National Curriculum: Non-statutory Guidance*, London: HMSO.

Durkin, K. (1985) *Television, Sex Roles and Children*, Milton Keynes: Open University.

Dyer, G. (1982) *Advertising as Communication*, London: Methuen.

Dyer, R. *et al.* (1981) *Coronation Street*, Monograph 13, London: BFI.

Evans, H. (1978) *Pictures on a Page: Photo-journalism, Graphics and Picture Editing*, London: Heinemann.

Evans, R.B. (1988) *Production and Creativity in Advertising*, London: Pitman.

Ferguson, B. (1977) 'Liberal Education, Media Studies and the Concept of Action' *Screen Education* 22 (Spring), 56–62.

Ferrari, L. and James, C. (1989) *Wham! Wrapping*, London: BFI.

Fiske, J. (1990) *Introduction to Communication Studies*, 2nd edn, London: Routledge.

Fletcher, W. (1988) *Guardian*, 7 November 1988.

Geraghty, C. (1981) 'The continuous serial – a definition' in R. Dyer *et al.* *Coronation Street*, Monograph 13, London: BFI, 9–26.

Glasgow University Media Group (1976) *Bad News*, London: Routledge.

Goodwin, A. (1988) *Media Studies for Adults*, London: BFI.

Grahame, J. (1985) 'Media Education across the curriculum', *The English Magazine* 15.

—— (1990) '*Playtime*: Learning about media institutions through practical work' in D. Buckingham (ed.) *Watching Media Learning*, London: Falmer: 101–23.

Grahame, J. and Mayman, N. (1987) *Criminal Records, Teaching TV Crime Series*, London: BFI.

Gunter, B. (1987) *Poor Reception: Misunderstanding and Forgetting Broadcast News*, Hillsdale, N.J.: Lawrence Erlbaum Associates.

Hall, S. (1981) 'The determinations of news photographs' in S. Cohen and J. Young (eds) *The Manufacture of News*, London: Sage Constable.

Hargreaves, I. (1989) *Impartiality*, London: BBC.

Harris, R. (1983) *Gotcha! The Media, the Government and the Falklands Crisis*, London: Faber & Faber.

Hart, A. (1986a) 'Television and children: research perspectives' in *Media in Education and Development* 19/1 (March), 20–5.

—— (1986b) 'Children and television: audience and influence' in *Media in Education and Development* 19/2 (June), 80–5.

—— (1987) 'Making sense of television science' in *Media Education Journal* (Autumn), 48–51.

—— (1988a) *The Media Resource Pack*, Southampton: Southampton Media Education Group.

—— (1988b) *Making 'The Real World'*, Cambridge: Cambridge University Press.

—— (1988c) *Teaching Television: 'The Real World'*, Cambridge: Cambridge University Press.

—— (1988d) *Teaching Television: 'The Real World – Dead as the Dodo?'*: a Case-study, Cambridge/Southampton: Cambridge University Press/TVS.

Hartley, J. (1982) *Understanding News*, London: Methuen.

Hemming, J. and Leggett, J. (1984) *Comics and Magazines*, London: ILEA.

Hind, J. and Mosco, S. (1985) *Rebel Radio*, London: Pluto.

Hodge, B. and Tripp, D. (1986) *Children and Television*, Cambridge: Polity.

Holroyd, M. (1982) 'Seeing in the dark', *Sunday Times*, 10 January.

Horsfield, P.G. (1986) *Taming Television*, London: Lion.

Howell, L. (1989) 'Blowing the local tune', *Airwaves* (Autumn), 5–6.

Independent Broadcasting Authority (1986) *Attitudes to Broadcasting in 1985*, London: IBA.

'The Independent' Information Pack (1988), London: *The Independent*.

Jefkins, F. (1985) *Advertising*, 4th edn, London: Heinemann.

Jones, N. (1989) *The Thatcher Years*, London: BBC Radio 4.

Kruger, S. and Wall, I. (1988) *The Media Pack*, London: Macmillan.

Labov, W. and Waletzky, J. (1966) 'Narrative analysis' in J. Helm, *Essays on the Visual and Verbal Arts*, American Ethnological Society Press.

Lewis, J. (1986) 'Decoding television news' in P. Drummond and R. Paterson (eds) *Television in Transition*, London: BFI: 205–34.

Lusted, D. and Drummond, P. (1985) *Television and Schooling*, London: BFI.

Masterman, L. (1980) *Teaching about Television*, London: Macmillan.

—— (1984) 'The battle for Orgreave' in L. Masterman (ed.) *Television Mythologies*, London: Comedia, 99–109.

—— (1985) *Teaching the Media*, London: Comedia.

—— (1986) 'A reply to David Buckingham' in *Screen/Screen Education* 27, 5: 96–100.

—— (1988) *The Development of Media Education in Europe in the 1980s*, Strasbourg: Council of Europe.

McLuhan, M. (1973) *Understanding Media*, London: Abacus.

McQuail, D. (1987) *Mass Communication Theory*, 2nd edn, London: Sage.

Messenger Davies, M. (1989) *Television is Good for Your Kids*, London: Hilary Shipman.

Miller, J. (1971) *McLuhan*, London: Fontana.

Mills, J. and Stringer, L. (1990) *Media Choices*, Oxford: Oxford University Press.

Morley, D. (1980) *The Nationwide Audience*, BFI Television Monograph 11, London: BFI.

—— (1986) *Family Television*, London: Comedia.

Morrison, D. *et al.* (1988) *Keeping Faith? Channel Four and its Audience*, London: John Libbey.

Moss, G. (1989) *Un/popular Fictions*, London: Virago.

Murdock, G. and Phelps, G. (1973) *Mass Media and the Secondary School*, London: Macmillan.

Naidoo, B. (1985) *Journey to Jo'burg*, London: Longman.

—— (1987) 'The story behind *Journey to Jo'burg*', *School Library Journal* (May), 43.

—— (1989) *Chain of Fire*, London: Collins.

National Curriculum Council (1990) *Curriculum Guidance 3: The Whole Curriculum*, York: NCC.

Palmer, P. (1986) *The Lively Audience*, London: Allen & Unwin.

Paterson, R. and Stewart, J. (1981) 'Street life' in R. Dyer *et al.*, *Coronation Street*, Monograph 13, London: BFI: 81–98.

Poole, M. (1989) 'No News is Good News' in *The Listener* 2 Feb., 12–13.

Potts, C. (1987) '*Teaching the media: a cautionary tale*', unpublished MA (Ed.) seminar paper, Southampton University.

Redfern, M. (ed.) (1989) *Impartiality*, London: BBC.

Regester, M. (1987) *Crisis Management*, London: Hutchinson.

Robson, J. *et al.* (1990) 'Implementing a media education policy across the curriculum' in D. Buckingham (ed.) *Watching Media Learning*, London: Falmer: 101–23.

Root, J. (1986) *Open the Box*, London: Comedia/Channel 4.

Ryder, N. (1982) *Science, Television and the Adolescent*, London: IBA.

Saynor, J. (1990) 'The condemned sell', *Listener*, 12 April, 38.

Scaping, P. (ed.) (1989) *BPI Year Book 1989/90*, London: BPI.

Shaw, I. and McCron, R. (1988) 'Monitoring public attitudes towards AIDS' in *Annual Review of Broadcasting Research* 14, London: BBC.

Silverstone, R. (1985) *Framing Science*, London: BFI.

Smith, A. (1980) *The Geopolitics of Information*, London: Faber & Faber.

Suttcliffe, T. (1990) *The Independent* 14 April, 32.

Svennevig, M. (1984) *Research for 'Horizon: A New Green Revolution?'*, London: BBC Broadcasting Research Department.

Taylor, L. and Mullan, B.(1986) *Uninvited Guests*, London: Chatto & Windus.

Twitchin, R. and Bazalgette, C. (eds) (1988) *Media Education Survey Report*, London: BFI/NER.

Wall, I. and Kruger, S. (1988) *The Media File*, London: Mary Glasgow.

Whitaker, B. (1981) *News Limited*, London: Minority Press.

Williams, R. (1974; 2nd. ed., 1990) *Television: Technology and Cultural Form*, London: Routledge.

—— (ed.) (1981) 'Introduction' to *Contact: Human Communication and its History*, London: Thames & Hudson, 7–20.

Williamson, J. (1978) *Decoding Advertisements*, London: Marion Boyars.

—— (1982) 'How does Girl Number Twenty understand ideology? in *Screen Education* 40 (Winter 1981/2), 80–7.

Winn, M. (1977) *The Plug-in Drug*, New York: Viking Press.

Wober, J.M. (1986) *Children and How Much They View*, discussion paper, London: IBA.

Woolley, B. (1989) 'Small World' in *The Listener* 14 Dec., 20.

Index

ALSO AVAILABLE FROM ROUTLEDGE:

UNDERSTANDING THE MEDIA: THE RADIO SERIES

A Practical Guide in six half-hour programmes

These BBC Radio 4 programmes offer an accessible way of gaining confidence in teaching the media with GCSE and A-level students. Written and researched by Gordon Cooper and Andrew Hart, they are designed for use by individual listeners, INSET groups or in the classroom. They draw on the BFI and National Curriculum 'Key Concepts' and cover:

- **getting started on media education**

- **teaching about audiences**

- **interpreting facts and opinions**

- **responding to popular fiction in the classroom**

- **developing fresh approaches to teaching advertising, promotion and persuasion**

- **involving new strategies for Media Education within the National Curriculum**

By featuring lively documentary material and comment from classroom teachers, media practitioners and researchers the programmes aim to:

- **increase understanding of media processes and practices**

- **provide concrete examples of current work in Media Education**

The cassettes come complete with teachers' notes which make detailed suggestions for follow-up discussion and classroom activities.

ORDER FORM

Understanding the Media: The Radio Series cassette pack is available from all good booksellers. Alternatively, please use this form to order direct from **Customer Services Department, Routledge, FREEPOST, Cheriton House, North Way, Andover, Hants SP10 5BR**. If paying by credit card, please use our **Customer Hotlines: 0264 342811** or **0264 342939**. All pre-paid orders to Routledge are dispatched within a week of receipt, subject to availability.

Please send me ...... copies of

UNDERSTANDING THE MEDIA: THE RADIO SERIES
3 Cassettes in boxed set, plus teachers' notes
0–415–07223–9:   £14.99 (including VAT)

Pre-paid and credit card orders sent free in the UK.
Overseas, please add £5.00 per 3-cassette pack airmail, £2.00 per pack surface mail

☐ I enclose a cheque/International Money Order may payable to Routledge for £ _____

☐ Please invoice me: Purchase Order No. _____

☐ Please charge my Access (Eurocard)/Visa/Diners Club/American Express (delete as applicable)

Credit card expiry date _____   Signature _____   Date _____

NAME _____

ADDRESS _____

_____

TOWN _____   POSTCODE _____

COUNTRY _____